SOUL

AND

SWORD

Celebrating 35 Years of
Penguin Random House India

ADVANCE PRAISE FOR THE BOOK

'The book *Soul and Sword: The History of Political Hinduism* is a riveting, soul-searching narrative of India's journey towards self-discovery. Hindol Sengupta makes an exceptional contribution to countering colonial misconceptions of India through a masterful analysis of twentieth-century Indian thinkers—Vivekananda, Aurobindo and more. Hindol brings the necessary clarity to the subject of political Hinduism, which had been distorted through partisan speculation. Political Hinduism, also referred to as Hindutva, occupies contemporary political discussions that frequently devolve into name-calling using the word "Hindutva" as a pejorative. Dispelling misconceptions about Hindutva, Hindol demonstrates the cultural and social aspects of political Hinduism, which is not merely political in nature but deeply entrenched within the history of India. *Soul and Sword* is a refreshing new work on modern India, combining captivating narration with deep analysis. A must-read'—Lavanya Vemsani, distinguished university professor, Shawnee State University, Ohio, USA

'The terrain of political Hinduism is so vast that it requires a skilled researcher and writer like Hindol Sengupta to sift and produce a coherent narrative. Written in a very engaging style, the book teases out various strands and weaves them together, resulting in a compelling and readable book'—Bibek Debroy, chairman, Prime Minister's Economic Advisory Council, India, and bestselling author

'Hindol Sengupta has authored a long overdue book. By situating political Hinduism in its long intellectual history, he offers invaluable perspective and historical context. The book will be welcomed by even those who disagree with his narrative on a controversial topic. It highlights changes with deep roots, which cannot be dismissed as transient'—Gautam Sen, former lecturer, international political economy, London School of Economics and Political Science

'Given the inherently polarizing nature of this topic, *Soul and Sword* is a refreshingly even-handed account of a complex movement, made up of many ideological strands. Perhaps this book's most important contribution is its account of the widespread popularity of this movement in India today'—Jeffery D. Long, professor of religion, philosophy and Asian studies, Elizabethtown College, Pennsylvania, USA

SOUL AND SWORD

The History of Political Hinduism

HINDOL SENGUPTA

VINTAGE

An imprint of Penguin Random House

VINTAGE

USA | Canada | UK | Ireland | Australia
New Zealand | India | South Africa | China | Singapore

Vintage is part of the Penguin Random House group of companies
whose addresses can be found at global.penguinrandomhouse.com

Published by Penguin Random House India Pvt. Ltd
4th Floor, Capital Tower 1, MG Road,
Gurugram 122 002, Haryana, India

Penguin
Random House
India

First published in Vintage by Penguin Random House India 2023

10 9 8 7 6 5 4 3 2 1

ISBN 9780670093786

Typeset in Adobe Garamond Pro by Manipal Technologies Limited, Manipal
Printed at Manipal Technologies Limited, Manipal

www.penguin.co.in

Contents

Introduction

Hinduness

This book is not about Hinduism, one of the oldest religions in the world. Perhaps the thing to emphasize at the very beginning is that it is a history not of Hinduism, the faith, but of the politics of Hinduism.

This book is an attempt to tell the story of the intellectual history of political Hinduism, or the history of political Hinduism as an idea. Though, history is far from the only thing that is interesting about political Hinduism. I am interested in this topic because it is the defining force of India's present. The world's largest democracy is today ruled by a political party, the Bharatiya Janata Party (BJP), which believes in political Hinduism. India's incumbent, now two-time, and widely predicted to be third time in the next national polls in India in 2024, prime minister, Narendra Modi, is a lifelong disciple of the cause of political Hinduism. The BJP claims to be the world's largest political party, and its ideological parent, the Rashtriya Swayamsevak Sangh (RSS),[1] the fountainhead of the ideology of political Hinduism, says the RSS is the biggest volunteer body on the planet. While the exact numbers of members are fluid, there is no doubt that these organizations have millions of followers and supporters not only in India but around the world.

If the BJP wins in 2024, Modi will be set to almost equal the term of India's first, and to date, longest-serving prime minister, Jawaharlal Nehru.[2] Nehru was a key member of the Indian National Congress[3] (INC)—popularly 'Congress'—which had played the leading role in India's freedom from British rule. India was an impoverished country when Nehru became prime minister after Independence in 1947, and he remained in that chair for seventeen years. In 1950, Nehru and his team, with men like B.R. Ambedkar and Vallabhbhai Patel, led the creation of the Indian Constitution and the modern Indian republic. In 1947, the country emerged from nearly 200 years of British colonial rule. Nehru governed a country where barely 12 per cent of the people could have been called educated and was among the poorest 10 per cent of countries in the world. Modi, on the other hand, runs the world's fifth-largest economy, which is widely predicted to become the third largest within this decade (with the GDP forecast to rise to $7.5 trillion and an equity market cap of $10 trillion[4]). Where Nehru once hoped that India would be the first—status-wise— among post-colonial nations, Modi and his ministers proclaim an ambition to make the country *vishwa guru* or 'world teacher'.[5]

Modi governs a country of 1.4 billion, which is said to be gaining from global trends in 'demographics, digitalization, decarbonization and deglobalization',[6] which is growing at a faster pace than both the US and China—in fact, it is the fastest-growing major economy in the world. 'More importantly for investors,

MSCI India is among the top ten MSCI country indices in US dollar terms across all these timeframes—a position shared only by the US and Denmark.'[7]

If India made news two decades ago for offshoring or call centres taking up low-cost information technology jobs, today it is one of the world's biggest iPhone manufacturing hubs and makes some of the most cutting-edge military technology, including hypersonic missiles, anti-satellite weapons and aircraft carriers.

As India rises, so do its geostrategic conflicts. Consistently, as it has always had, not least with neighbour and arch-rival Pakistan, and more importantly, with the only competitor of its size and ambition, China. Political Hinduism has specific strategic thoughts and responses to these challenges, and it has a definitive vision of where India's place in the world should be, how to tackle competition and conflict and what India's agenda in the world ought to be.

Therefore, the ideological underpinnings of Modi and his political party matter. Understanding the ideological and narrative pitch that the BJP under Modi makes to voters is critical to comprehending India's present and future. And the key to deciphering this ideology is an understanding of political Hinduism.

It is important to address a prominent criticism of any ideological analysis of governance, namely that state policy is a product of a continuum rather than ideological leaps. This is true. Political Hinduism, no matter the rhetoric, has engaged with and manoeuvred around the framework of policymaking of the Indian state since independence in 1947—its real innovation is in infusing legitimacy to its cause by using the tools and frameworks within the governance system in India rather than seeking to supplant it. For instance, the strongest proponents, both Modi[8] and RSS chief Mohan Bhagwat, constantly reiterate their commitment to the Constitution created by the tallest leaders of India's freedom movement, including Nehru. This is perhaps best explained through an apocryphal story that is told about an RSS chief. He was once told by a follower that the RSS should have its own major newspaper like the *Times of India*,[9] which would ostensibly be more understanding of the political Hinduism cause than the country's Westernized press. The chief replied that the real success of political Hinduism would be to have people who understood political Hinduism be part of and run the *Times of India* rather than create a new organization.

Like political Christianity or political Islam, what political Hinduism really is and where it comes from or even what its timelines are vary depending on who you are asking.

Some researchers (Christophe Jaffrelot, David Ludden, Richard Eaton, Irfan Habib, et al.) trace the origins of political Hinduism to the nineteenth and twentieth centuries at a time alongside the political ferment against British colonial rule in India. Whereas others (such as Meenakshi Jain, Hans Bakker, Jadunath Sarkar, Ramesh Chandra Majumdar, Dilip Kumar Chakrabarti, etc.) point to a much older sense of 'Hindu resistance' to repeated Islamic invasions from around the eighth century onwards, followed by the battles between Hindu kingdoms and Muslim rulers in Delhi and elsewhere, including with the Mughal empire (sixteenth to nineteenth centuries) and the Deccan Sultanate (fifteenth to seventeenth centuries).

There is considerable debate about what part of this history of conflict for nearly 1500 years could be described in clear Hindu–Muslim terms, and what kind of accommodations were made by each side. For instance, two historical nuggets often offered are the pluralistic tendencies of the Mughal emperor Akbar and the Maratha warrior-king Shivaji.

Even though Akbar, under whose rule the Mughal empire reached its high noon, conquered numerous Hindu kingdoms, for his time, he was accommodative of his non-Muslim subjects, allowing them the right to worship, he married Hindu princesses who kept their faith, barred the slaughter of cows—an animal considered sacred by many Hindus—and even tried to create a new religion, Din-i-Ilahi, made up of, as it were, the best ideas from Islam and Hinduism.

To further complicate the story, Shivaji fought all his bitter battles against the rule of the great-grandson of Akbar, the sharia-enforcing, kafir[10]-taxing, Aurangzeb. Shivaji removed Persian—the court language of the Mughals—and replaced it with Sanskrit, the language of Hindu scriptures, in all the territories ruled by him, and declared an intention to create Hindavi Swarajya, which has been translated by some historians as 'self-rule for Hindu people'.[11] But Shivaji also hired Muslims in his army, and some of his trusted military commanders were Muslims. This has been used to argue that the battles of Shivaji were against the oppressive Mughal empire that he saw around him rather than against Islam. Like many things in this history, it is hard to conclusively demonstrate either argument and the truth was perhaps both. There were significant elements of counter-Islamic tenets in Shivaji's wars, for the repression he faced, including the tax on non-Muslims, was conducted by Aurangzeb in the name of religion. At the same time, as a product of a society that had both Hindus and Muslims living under his rule, Shivaji took the best talent he could find, especially for his armed forces.

This kind of duality exists later in the story too. For instance, the most interesting, and, in my opinion, the least deliberated, contradiction is that while its critics accuse the proponents of political Hinduism of religious chauvinism, the self-narration of political Hinduism has always been that it is secular (sometimes the word 'plural' is preferred because political Hinduism's advocates argue that 'secular' has a particular context in the Western Christian imagination that talks about the division between the Church and the State, but Hinduism has countless sects and subsects, and therefore, the formal separation of the state from one unified church is not relevant).

Be that as it may, the main point here is that political Hinduism has always sought to project itself as the 'true' secular or plural 'indigenous' ideology as opposed to a 'fake', 'westernized' secularism, which it criticizes as being partisan and 'against Hindu interests'. For instance, take Vinayak Damodar Savarkar.

Savarkar, a twentieth-century anti-colonial revolutionary, was both the man who made the word *Hindutva*, or Hinduness, mainstream[12] through his monograph 'Hindutva—Who Is a Hindu?' and was avowedly atheist. Of his time, Savarkar was one of the most fiercely anti-caste activists.[13] In his 1931 monograph, 'Seven Shackles of the Hindu Society', he wrote: 'One of the most important components of such injunctions of the past that we have blindly carried on and which deserves to be thrown in the dustbins of history is the rigid caste system.'[14] Savarkar even set up a special temple, called the Patit Pavan[15] temple, in his home district of Ratnagiri, which broke all traditional caste rules and allowed everyone in.

While seeing India as a civilization and land broken by repeated invasions of an Islamic nature, Savarkar, who, among other things, translated some of the writings of Italian nationalist Giuseppe Mazzini to Marathi, argued against religious discrimination and emphasized culture over religion. In his own argument, Hindutva was not a by-product of the religion Hinduism but a common cultural attribute, a shared heritage, if you will, bequeathed to anyone who was born in India—a 'sacred geography'—or had Indian roots. The most influential chief of the RSS, Sadashiv Golwalkar, called Mazzini 'the greatest interpreter of nationality (he used it synonymously with nationalism)'.[16]

In this book, there will be many such dichotomies about people and incidents where powerful arguments can be cited on both sides of the debates. It is not my intention to try and prove one against the other, a task that is ahistorical and futile. A more useful approach is perhaps to note that these exist and, more importantly, to emphasize that this book seeks not to take sides but to detail political Hinduism's 'narrative identity'. By narrative identity, we mean the stories political Hinduism tells about itself and the world, the arguments it poses and responds to, the histories it refers to and the future it envisages.

There is another reason why understanding political Hinduism is important—and this is one of the key interventions this book hopes to make. In the understanding of political ideology in India, the usual division made is between a 'secular mainstream' and 'sectarian political religion' (this could be political Hinduism or Islam or Sikhism). The reason this secular mainstream is considered mainstream is because in most parts of independent India's history, around sixty years, the country was governed by the Congress (often in alliance with a gaggle of regional political parties), led by Gandhi and Nehru and Nehru's family members, which propagated this version of 'mainstream secularism', or versions of it, at least. What defined this mainstream secularism? The most apt description is perhaps that it was a 'balancing act'. 'Historically, this balancing act has always been part of Congress' conception of its identity. After all, during the independence movement, it could make room within itself for both the Hindu right and the orthodox ulema, at the same time as it championed the cause of modern secularism.'[17]

This was a period when political Hinduism, because of its lack of electoral support, was considered 'fringe'. Until now, with two back-to-back full majority electoral victories for the BJP led by Modi, and buoyed by a prevailing mood of cultural nationalism, it has come to be considered mainstream with headlines such as 'How Hindu Nationalism Went Mainstream' (*Foreign Policy*)[18] and 'How Hindu Nationalism Went Mainstream in Modi's India' (the *Financial Times*)[19] and others[20] like these. This new mainstreaming of political Hinduism or Hindu nationalism has raised the question of how successful Congress's balancing act really was—and what kind of acceptance it really had, and why this acceptance, such as it was, changed.

For, as the trajectory of our story in this book shall show, far from being fringe, political Hinduism is a much older tradition in India, which existed long before Gandhi, Nehru or independent India came into being. Its resilience—which surprises many, especially Western, commentators—comes from its history and the references it taps, which are deeply embedded in Indian culture, history and religiosity. In part, it is the enduring popularity of the references of political Hinduism that gives it lasting appeal on the ground even when it does not have electoral backing, for the real agenda of political Hinduism is not, and has never been, political. It has always been social and cultural.

The idea is not to demonstrate which one is 'better' but to try and understand what happened, and what changed, during seventy-five years of Indian independence. Rather than seeking to validate or invalidate the theories of political Hinduism, this book is an attempt to chart its historical trajectory and detail the ideas and incidents that are important to its world view. This topic continues to be polarizing not only in India but around the world, and I do not intend to take any side. I am not trying to justify or negate the idea of political Hinduism, but attempting to talk about the themes, stories and anecdotes that have always driven it. Who does political Hinduism see as its heroes and who are its villains? What are the resonances and contradictions in the framing of this dramatis personae?

While it provides a historical mooring and trajectory to the story of political Hinduism as an idea, a large part of this book looks ahead and not behind. Like all political ideologies, political Hinduism is concerned with power and what to do with it, and a world view that it wishes to propagate and mainstream. Therefore, this book is concerned with trying to understand where political Hinduism is going and the future India that it is attempting to build.

If, as estimates suggest, India becomes the third-largest economy in the world within this decade, it shall do so—most probably—under the prime ministership of Narendra Modi. This would make Modi the most influential prime minister in India's history after Nehru, and arguably, since, as we have explained earlier, he governs a materially far more powerful India than under Nehru, even more influential than Nehru. This would give the ideology of political Hinduism power over India's destiny and its role in the world. Since the BJP proclaims its disdain for 'Nehruvian socialism', a sort of Left-leaning, Anglophile secularism combined with, what the BJP describes as, 'fake secularism',[21] two full majority victories[22] under Modi signify the wide uptake of the arguments of political Hinduism among the voting public. A third victory would cement in place the ideas of political Hinduism as the new mainstream of Indian societal and governmental imagination quite like Nehruvian socialism once dominated for most of the country's life as an independent nation.

An entire generation is now coming of age in India, who have seen nothing but the prime ministership of Narendra Modi and the dominance in the public sphere of the ideas of political Hinduism.

Adherents of political Hinduism consider it to be the foundational principle of nationhood in India, whereas its critics argue that it is an ideology with paramilitary roots that once drew revolutionary inspiration from people such as the Italian nationalist Giuseppe Mazzini, and accuse it of fostering divisiveness, especially between Hindus and Muslims and other minorities. Political Hinduism followers, in turn, argue that it is the 'fake secularism' that is practised by its opponents that creates conflicts by denying the same rights to all communities. One key thing that political Hinduism supporters point out is the absence, after seventy-five years of independent India, of a 'uniform civil code', which the Constitution-makers of India had envisaged as necessary. This means issues such as gender rights, personal laws on marriage, inheritance, etc., are different for different communities. The BJP consistently mentions this as one of the key goals it seeks to fulfil.

This is not to say that there isn't any political opposition to the BJP. A majority of Indian states are ruled by other political parties, including the Congress. But even there, many of the cultural ideas that were first promoted by the RSS and the BJP have become mainstream even among other political parties and their leaders. For instance, the protection of cows, an animal sacred to Hindus, was first championed by the BJP in electoral politics. It is now promoted by non-BJP political leaders too. Modi mainstreamed visits to Hindu temples and participated in widely publicized Hindu religious rituals as a sitting prime minister, and now it has become customary for many leaders, including Rahul Gandhi of the Congress, the great-grandson of Nehru, to take part in equally photographed temple runs. Before Modi, it was the iftar party or elaborate evening meals to break the day-long fast during Ramzan[23] often thrown by politicians during the Muslim holy month that would make news. Now, visits to Hindu shrines create headlines. Thus, I argue in this book that today, the ideas of political Hinduism and their application are not confined to the BJP and the RSS but are increasingly being used by other political (and social) forces.

Whether in movies or books, the rise of political Hinduism has brought with it a certain resurgence of cultural nationalism that now pervades and is becoming the mainstream of Indian social and cerebral life. Most of the practitioners or creators, producers or ideators, are not members of the BJP or the RSS. They are simply people tapping into a predominant cultural mood. Many of these people, part of 'Gen Z' or between the ages of fifteen and twenty-five, are inherently proud of their cultural roots and are turning more aggressively towards them.

There is also an underbelly of extremism in political Hinduism that involves a motley crew of rabble-rousers, ultra-conservative moral policing groups, social media bullies and conspiracy theorists of all hues. Many of these people are not connected to the mainstream of political Hinduism as represented by the BJP and the RSS, as well as non-politically affiliated scholars such as Kapil Kapoor, Arvind Sharma, Subhas Kak, Saradindu Mukherji, Walter Anderson and Sridhar Damle, Rajiv Malhotra, and others who have tackled specific important sub-themes in the broader universe of political Hinduism, such as S.N. Balagangadhara and Jacob de Roover (orientalism and colonialism) and Prakash Shah (caste and its origins), who have researched and written extensively from an 'insider' point of view about cultural nationalism, political Hinduism and revivalism among broader non-Abrahamic faiths.

The fringe groups, such as the Hindu Mahasabha, Sanatan Sanstha and others, are mostly affiliated with local politicians and political pressure groups. From time to time, some of these fringe elements have been involved in violent crimes. This, too, is not new. The assassin of Mahatma Gandhi was a member of the Hindu Mahasabha,[24] and in 2017, the murder of journalist Gauri Lankesh was carried out allegedly by members of the Sanatan Sanstha. Like every other political ideology, political Hinduism comes in all shapes, sizes and hues.

All of this has a history and context which we shall address in the course of the book, but for now, suffice it to say that political Hinduism is more than merely politics. Its real impact is cultural and the changes it seeks are deeply embedded in social behaviour. The RSS often says that it is no different from the broader Indian society and the day will come when 'Sangh[25] will become samaj'— that is, the ideas of the RSS will become indistinguishable from what the average Indian thinks, and that there will be no need for a separate Sangh. The two—Indian society and the Sangh—will merge into one whole.

It is important to understand this as the broad, long-term goal of political Hinduism.

I have been thinking about the ideas of political Hinduism for a decade now. As an editor for the Indian edition of *Fortune* magazine, and later as a senior fellow at the Observer Research Foundation, I wrote some of the earliest essays on the political economy of the RSS,[26] the economic mind of Narendra Modi[27] and the details of the history of economic thought within the RSS.[28]

I spent my time at Oxford thinking about the sources of nationalism in India's freedom movement and the common ground between what later became the BJP and Congress on issues of culture and civilizational values, including commonalities between Nehru and Savarkar. A paper I wrote while at Oxford was later published in India in the journal of the India Foundation, a New Delhi-based think-tank.[29] I have written papers on political Hinduism and its interaction with technology.[30] In all, trying to understand political Hinduism has taken me around a decade, and this book, in a sense, is a result of these efforts.

This book begins with interventions in trying to understand the narration of the ideas of political Hinduism both to audiences at home and in the larger world, the cues from history that it uses and its historical gaze. I spend more time trying to decipher where it is going, though, than where it comes from.

I delve into the intellectual interactions of political Hinduism with other faiths, most importantly, Islam, Christianity, Sikhism and Buddhism. While most researchers on political Hinduism consider its engagement with religions as the main prism through which it can be comprehended, I tend to believe that it is, in fact, political Hinduism's dialogue, even collision, with other ideologies (communism/socialism), and ideas, such as technological advancement, historical approach, strategic thinking, thoughts on familial and gender relations, and economic moorings that are far more important in understanding it. It is the 'political' that is more important in political Hinduism than the 'Hinduism', I believe.

Today, political Hinduism has an impact on everything, from the tenor of Indian economic and foreign policymaking to the narrative-building of India's rise, advertising campaigns and films that are made, to become multi-million dollar successes in the country's mega film industry.

The story of political Hinduism and its spread to the political and social pole position in India, I believe, is the single biggest transformation in the country since Independence. It has changed, and is changing the way many Indians think about their country, themselves in it and their place in the world. These Indians are not just the citizens of India, but diaspora communities that are some of the wealthiest and best educated in countries like the US (where it is consistently the best-educated and highest-earning minority), the UK, Canada and Australia.

Political Hinduism is often thought of, especially outside India, as synonymous with Modi, but as this book shall show, it has a far deeper and resilient history—and might have an equally ambitious future.

Finally, it is important to emphasize that it is not my intention in this book to pass judgement on the ideology of political Hinduism, to take a side, as it were. It is an ideology, like many others, which has fierce defenders and equally fanatical detractors. My only purpose in this book is to showcase the journey of the idea of political Hinduism, and its evolving contexts, and try and understand what its future could be.

1

The Age of Fire

The nineteenth century was a particularly turbulent and loquacious period in the history of India. It was a time when the Empire started talking back. Bengal in eastern India was the epicentre, in many ways, of this spirit of intellectual revolution. But it all began, not with words, but with war.

The defeat of the Nawab of Bengal, Siraj ud-Daulah in the Battle of Plassey in 1757, among mangroves not far from Calcutta[1], gave the British East India Company their biggest political prize, the ports of Calcutta and Dhaka, and control over some of the most lucrative trading hubs in the world. Siraj was replaced by a series of nawabs who were rulers only in name and were, in fact, puppets of the British administration of the Company. It was only in 1717 that the British had won trading rights in the Bengal region through a firman or grant by the emperor Farrukh Siyar, even as the once-great Mughal empire continued to shrink. Only four decades later, the British 'John Company', as the mercenary East India Company was popularly called, had defeated the ruler of Bengal to metamorphose from being traders to invaders.

It is easy to understand why the British, led by the buccaneering Robert Clive, a former clerk of the East India Company, wanted mastery over Bengal. Siraj ruled over India's wealthiest kingdom with vast treasuries and control over pivotal mercantile routes.

And the British were far from alone in their quest.

As the historian Sudipta Sen has explained:

'During the mid-eighteenth century, when the great French and English rival trading companies were vying for privilege and control in the coastal markets and inland manufactories of India, textiles, cotton and silk, metal, and porcelain . . . dominated the European markets and drained Europe of American silver. In eastern India, the Dutch, the French and the English followed the Portuguese in seeking out the coastal and provincial entrepôts of trade and commerce to establish factories for textiles, silk and saltpetre throughout the seventeenth and eighteenth centuries. Far-flung commercial circuits of greater Bengal connected the old Mughal city of Dacca and the rising provincial capital at Maqsudabad (later Murshidabad) developed by the astute Mughal deputy Murshid Kuli Khan, who had secured the administration of Bengal, Bihar and Orissa in the first decade of the eighteenth century, to the flourishing commercial cities of Patna and Banaras through the great waterways of the Gangetic plain. These centres of trade and administration were also linked directly to such maritime outlets as Hugli, Satgaon and the English settlement of Calcutta; further westward by river or over land they were connected to the imperial cities of Agra and Delhi. Other prominent land routes connected Patna to Agra, Banaras to Lucknow, Maldah in Bengal to the hinterlands of Patna and northern Bihar and Jaunpur in Awadh. This broad sweep of the alluvial lower Gangetic plains connected the revenue-rich territories of the Nawabs of Bengal and the Rajas of Banaras, nominally dependent on the ruling house of the Nawabs of Awadh.'[2]

It took only a hundred years from 1757 to 1857 for the East India Company and the British to become, amid the decay and chaos of the crumbling Mughal empire, the predominant political force in India. By 1857, it faced its greatest challenge in the shape of a mass mutiny, which would later be described as the 'first war of Indian independence' across northern India. Soldiers of the Company joined hands with local rajas and led a revolt against the rule of the East India Company, which had by then become the most powerful political force in the country, with an ability to bully and dictate terms to royal houses, often centuries-old, and demand supplication. The first shot of the revolution was fired at Barrackpore in Bengal on 29 March 1857, when the sepoy Mangal Pandey of the 34th Bengal Native Infantry regiments attacked officers. Soon the revolt spread to all ten Bengal Light Cavalry Regiments, most of the seventy-four regiments of the Bengal Native Infantry and other parts of northern India.

The revolution was defeated, not least because, apart from the Bengal armies of the British, other major divisions of the East India Company, such as the Bombay divisions and those in Madras, remained loyal and the mutineers were tried and executed.

But in that moment of defeat, a renaissance arose. In Bengal, which had been conquered first and then subjugated again after the rebellion, in the late eighteenth and the nineteenth centuries right up to the early parts of the twentieth century, there arose an age of intellectual rejuvenation and innovation that has never been repeated. The Bengal Renaissance was a moment of striking cerebral illumination as new ways of thinking and expressing sprung up as East confronted West, absorbing—even aping—the epistemological and pedagogical tools of the West but often refusing to accept intellectual suzerainty.

It was writers and thinkers who were part of this intellectual upheaval who first articulated a modern narrative of resistance to British rule, which moved from the East Indian Company to the British crown when the administrative control was taken over a year after the rebellion in 1858 when the British Parliament passed the Government of India Act. The Company was dissolved again through an act of Parliament in 1874—a direct result of revelation of the plunder it was facilitating and a recognition of the riches that could be extracted from India in a more institutional and less disruptive manner.

The historian Peter Watson has argued, using analysis by fellow historians such as Wolfgang Schivelbusch that, in the context of the French, 'The understanding of war as a "purifying and renewing force" is . . . the most important legacy granted to the defeated. And it is a short step from understanding defeat as an act of purification, humility and sacrifice . . . to laying claim to spiritual and moral leadership in world affairs.'[3] This, in a sense, is what happened in Bengal in the wake of the Renaissance. Using new tools brought by the West, whether it be mercenaries or missionaries, a new generation arose, not just to embrace the ideas of the West but also to use them to proclaim the superiority of the East.

This is not what Thomas Babington Macaulay, the colonial administrator and educationist, expected when he published his infamous 'Minute on Indian Education' (1835) with the intention of forming 'a class who may be interpreters between us and the millions whom we govern; a class of persons, Indian in blood and colour, but English in taste, in opinions, in morals, and in intellect. To that class we may leave it to refine the vernacular dialects of the country, to enrich those dialects with terms of science borrowed from the Western nomenclature, and to render them by degrees fit vehicles for conveying knowledge to the great mass of the population.'[4]

In order to achieve this goal, the British, led by missionaries, set up schools and colleges (some of the best-known were founded in Bengal), but some of the people to whom this learning was imparted broke rank.

The arrival of the printing press in Bengal in 1777 created a new genre of popular literature in the Bengali language by men who had been educated in British-founded institutions and trained to embrace ideas in English. The classic example was Bankim Chandra Chattopadhyay, now considered the father of modern Bengali literature. Chattopadhyay was among the earliest students at Presidency College and the University of Calcutta, both explicitly set up to impart English language education among the locals by the British.

Chattopadhyay went on to become a civil servant in the British administration, rising not only to the high rank of deputy magistrate but also receiving major honours such as the Companion of the Most Eminent Order of the Indian Empire (CMEOIE) in 1894 and the ultimate social prize of that time, the title of Rai Bahadur in 1891.

But it was Chattopadhyay who wrote the book that in a sense started what is now known as *agni yug* or the age of fire where the British consistently faced armed revolt and rebellion led usually by young men and women who had been trained in the best British institutions, many of them even in higher education in England. *Ananda Math*, which can be loosely translated as the 'shrine of happiness', was set against a real-life famine in Bengal caused by administrative malpractice and corruption under Company rule.

It told the story of a band of warrior monks fighting a guerrilla war from the forests of Bengal against the East India Company (and their puppet, the Muslim nawab) and its usurious taxes, and robbing the Company and the Nawab to feed the desperately hungry. *Ananda Math* had an anthem sung by the ascetics in praise of their motherland called 'Vande Mataram' (All Hail the Mother). It quickly became the war cry for the nationalistic stirrings that were emerging as the age of fire dawned. Revolutionaries cried 'Vande Mataram' as they bombed British vehicles and buildings while fighting pitched gun battles with the colonial police, and sang it loudly while marching up the gallows. It was a favourite of Mahatma Gandhi and was adopted as the national song of independent India.

Little commented upon or studied, though, is one major fact about *Ananda Math*. It is the earliest text to mention the word 'Hindutva'.[5] Tucked away somewhere in the middle of the story, there is a sentence in the third part of the book that, translated, reads, 'Because Hindu dharma was disappearing, many Hindus were eager to reestablish Hindutva.' There could be many reasons why this has not been commented upon earlier. First, even though Bankim is known to have increasingly worked on Hindu identity in his writing in this period, he never really returned to explore this word in detail, preferring instead to talk in terms of dharma, or the Hindu term for the moral law of the universe. His treatise on the subject published in 1888 is called *Dharmatattva*, which seeks to answer questions on the fundamentals of Hindu ethics. Second, one of the best-known translations of *Ananda Math*, by the Cambridge professor of Hinduism Julius Lipner, translates this sentence without using the word 'Hindutva', or for that matter 'Hindu dharma'. In Lipner's translation, it reads, 'Because the Hindu rule of life had disappeared, many Hindus were keen to establish a sense of Hindu identity.' Lipner prefers to give a rough translation of the phrase 'Hindu dharma', which is used by Chattopadhyay and translates Hindutva as 'Hindu identity', possibly to explain these terms lucidly to non-Indian audiences. Since the word 'Hindutva' is politically loaded, Lipner may have avoided its use too, preferring to offer an expanded translation.

Lipner, though, has written about the kind of vision Chattopadhyay offered in *Ananda Math*, and otherwise, about the Hindu world view and politics.

'This was not the traditional Hinduism that tends to be studied in scholarly introductions to Hinduism, nor indeed the kind of popular Hinduism practised by ordinary people in the towns and villages. It was rather a reinvented model, taking its cue from the thinking of the Hindu elite of the time who had been involved for a considerable period— outstandingly from the time of Rammohan Roy[6] in the first decades of the 19th century—in a kind of ideological dialectic with tendentious British reconstructions of Hindu religious culture. As Bankim formulated his model, he played an important role in imparting new dimensions and facets to the neo-Hinduism of the age. At the core of Bankim's thinking in this regard was the concept of the Eternal Code, or sanatana dharma. The idea was that there is an eternal Hindu dharma or way of righteous living which governs all aspects of existence—cultural, social, political, religious—in terms of which the Hindus would flourish in the modern age. This dharma is the fruit of the discipline of what he calls the inward knowledge: an introspective mode of awareness Hindu philosophers and savants, especially Vedantins[7], have distinctively and expertly developed from time immemorial. But this inward knowledge had been lost through neglect and the vagaries of time. As a result, Hindu civilization has suffered decline, and Hindus have been subjugated[8] by outsiders for a long period. The advent of the British—their mastery of the world of sense experience, which for Bankim was the fruit of the outward knowledge—provided Hindus with the opportunity to access anew the inward knowledge. For a judicious grasp of the former led to an understanding of the latter. After all, the inward knowledge was to establish the conditions externally on which a new Hindu civilization, adapted to modern times, was to be constructed.'[9]

It must be noted here that Bankim was not the only one concerned about this. 'Rajnarain Basu (Raj Narayan Bose) (1826–99) and Nabagopal Mitra (1840–94) were instrumental in promoting in Bengal some of the earliest ideas of nationalism based on Hindu superiority and exclusivity.'[10] In the years to come, Basu would devote himself to promoting a nationalism that had, as a key ingredient, a sense of revivalism of India's Hindu past and what he saw as its glorious achievements compared to Western civilization, while Mitra went on to create an annual event which was first called 'Jatiya Mela' and then came to be known as Hindu Mela to 'promote national feeling, patriotism, unity and self-help among Bengal's Hindus'.[11]

The decline of Hindu civilization and its uplift concerned another major figure in our story. He was also a pupil of Presidency College and Scottish Church College, promoted by the first overseas missionary of the Church of Scotland to India,

Alexander Duff, and his name was Narendranath Dutta. He went on to become the nationalist-minded ascetic (taking the monastic name) Swami Vivekananda.

Vivekananda appeared at the World Parliament of Religions in Chicago in 1893 and declared, to great applause:

> 'I am proud to belong to a nation which has sheltered the persecuted and the refugees of all religions and all nations of the earth. I am proud to tell you that we have gathered in our bosom the purest remnant of the Israelites, who came to southern India and took refuge with us in the very year in which their holy temple was shattered to pieces by Roman tyranny. I am proud to belong to the religion which has sheltered and is still fostering the remnant of the grand Zoroastrian nation. I will quote to you, brethren, a few lines from a hymn which I remember to have repeated from my earliest boyhood, which is every day repeated by millions of human beings: "As the different streams having their sources in different places all mingle their water in the sea, so, O Lord, the different paths which men take through different tendencies, various though they appear, crooked or straight, all lead to Thee".'[12]

Barely two decades after the British crown took control of India, a young Indian, trained in British ways, was proclaiming the greatness of his still-colonized country in another erstwhile British-colonized nation, America. This was astonishing confidence, ironically triggered in part (that Vivekananda spoke so fluently in English amazed many in the US) by the education provided by the British. Vivekananda is important in our story because he is often 'regarded as one of the architects of modern Hinduism, a pioneer of Hindu missionary activities in the West and a founder figure of modern yoga. His political importance resides in how he provided salient ideas on Hindu nationalism and its ideology of Hindutva'[13]. While he never used the word 'Hindutva' or spoke about 'Hindu politics', Vivekananda's message was profoundly political, even though it was rooted in spirituality.

Trained and schooled by missionaries, Vivekananda was acutely critical of the missionary project. In one of his speeches at the Parliament of Religions, he said:

> 'Christians must always be ready for good criticism, and I hardly think that you will mind if I make a little criticism. You Christians, who are so fond of sending out missionaries to save the soul of the heathen—why do you not try to save their bodies from starvation? In India, during the terrible famines, thousands died from hunger, yet you Christians did nothing. You erect churches all through India, but the crying evil in the East is not religion—they have religion enough—but it is bread that the suffering millions of burning India cry out for with parched throats. They ask us for bread, but we give them stones. It is an insult to a starving people to offer them religion; it is an insult to a starving man to teach him metaphysics. In India, a priest that preached for money would lose caste and be spat upon by the people. I came here to seek aid for my impoverished people, and I fully realized how difficult it was to get help for heathens from Christians in a Christian land.'

It is in this fertile landscape that political Hinduism took ideological and narrative shape. *Ananda Math* was published in 1882, in the same year Bankim Chandra Chattopadhyay wrote a rigorous repartee to the criticism thrown by Reverend William Hastie of General Assembly Institution, which later came to be called Scottish Church College, on Hindu rituals and customs. 'In 1882, Reverend Hastie of the General Assembly wrote a tract that was brutally critical of Hinduism. Bankim, who had always ridiculed Orientalist pretensions about scientific knowledge on India, prepared a long, careful and angry reply.'[14]

The argument happened in the pages of the venerable British-founded-and-run the *Statesman* newspaper, suggesting that Bankim's use of the English language by then was obviously evolved enough for the note to be accepted as a suitable riposte to a colonial official.

'Hastie had written in the most insufferably arrogant terms about a *sraddh* ceremony conducted on the occasion of the death of the grandmother of a Calcutta grandee, condemning the long list of English-educated Bengalis who had attended this ceremony. Since they had received English education, he declared, they couldn't have believed in the religious rationale of the sraddh; therefore they were either hypocrites or deluded. Bankim, who had not attended the ceremony, gave a robust answer under a nom-de-plume. We advert to this debate because in the course of it, Bankim reveals his understanding of image-worship in Hinduism. The issue is not whether this understanding was factual (whatever that may mean!); the issue is what Bankim's view happened to be. According to this view, image-worship in brief is the earthing, the embodiment of human ideals; or to put it differently, it is a human way of making the Divine accessible.'[15]

Ananda Math came the same year, and Chattopadhyay, the undisputed king of Bengali literature even in his lifetime, a product of oppressive colonialism and decaying, decadent and bitterly exploitative Muslim rule through the puppet nawabs, started to delve deeper into questions of identity and faith, such as 'What constitutes authentic Hinduism, what possibilities exist within Hinduism of the past and in the re-authenticated Hinduism of the future for nation-building, what precisely was the culpability of the Muslim in Indian history and how and why had Hindu power capitulated to it.'[16] The result of this exploration was the treatise *Dharmatattva*.

It is against this fertile backdrop that the word 'Hindutva' gained greater exposure, in Bengal in 1891–92, through the writings of a man who was quintessentially a product of the Renaissance.

Chandranath Basu was in the mould of Bankim and Vivekananda. He, too, was a product of Presidency College. He, too, had studied at a missionary-founded institution, Hedore School, before coming to Presidency. Not only was he a promising student, quite like Vivekananda and Bankim, but he even did a stint as a deputy magistrate (like Bankim). Chattopadhyay's journey as a man of letters also followed Bankim's pathway—he first started writing in English, and then entirely abandoned that language to return to Bengali. All his major works, as in the case of Bankim, are in Bengali.

It was Chandranath Basu who popularized the word 'Hindutva', through his 1892 publication *Hindutva: Hindur Prakita Itihas*[17] (Hindutva: The Real History of the Hindus), which has become synonymous with political Hinduism (even though many others use ideas from political Hinduism, they may not use the word 'Hindutva' to describe their ideology). In a volatile society, Chandranath Basu had hit a nerve.

Basu was conservative-minded and sought to understand and explain Hindu customs and culture beyond colonial critique. Amiya Sen has argued that Basu's importance lies in the fact that:

'At a time when the western educated Hindu intelligentsia was actively engaged in evaluating their own tradition in the light of "reason" and "utility", heuristic devices they had been repeatedly asked to imbibe and integrate with the emerging "modern" self, questioning positivist prescriptions for change did certainly amount to swimming against the tide. Such courage or conviction, as I argue in this paper, originated not in a blind rejection of the "modern" per se but in a deeper self-reflection than had been possible in the first flush of intellectual excitement of the early 19th century. The substance of Chandranath Basu's writings overturn the idea suggested earlier in time that the modern Hindu's hopes lay in suitably imitating the ways of the English . . . On the contrary he argued that meaningful change began with the self itself and not with the social or political environment in which it was historically located.'[18]

Perhaps the most important insight that Basu threw up, and which has since been embedded in the world view of political Hinduism is the contrast that he saw between the Hindu world view, and the European/Western world view, and his attempt to harmonize the two (rather than reject one for the other).

In Basu's 'comparative assessment of the two civilizations, the European, he alleged, was far too preoccupied with the world outside him, the Hindu with the inner self. Both these represented extremes that inhibited human progress. The Hindu, by blindly conforming to his inherited tradition and not creatively employing his personal judgement, only brought society to a standstill. The European, on the contrary, excessively exercised his individual judgement to the point of unleashing a state of perpetual revolution . . . The European was obsessed with the empirical habits of mind, ignoring the spontaneous outpourings of the soul. He viewed man in isolation, not in his larger relationship with the cosmos. For Chandranath, this explained the European's obsession with biographies. Whereas anything worth remembering about a man always remained as part of public memory, the egoistic celebration of human agency in modern biographies took away from both his social moorings and larger ties with the cosmos . . . What was required therefore was a synthesis, between the self and not self, between social conformity and personal judgement . . .'[19]

This idea of bringing together the East and the West, to learn from one another, appears again and again in the work of Vivekananda too, and in the writings of Bankim. The work of all three men envisaged, in a sense, a more equitable future, a balance and conversation between the ideas of the East and the West (rather than the supremacy of the West which was the prevalent thought process around them). Lipner noted that:

'The Bengal which Bankim created for the purposes of this novel gave him a chance to revisit history. The very fluidity of the situation, as it appears in the novel, allowed him to create the circumstances for a future whose trajectory was different from that predicted by the historians of the time. This predictable future envisioned, of course, the paramountcy of British rule. But the future which Bankim envisioned through the novel was different: a subversive version of the predictable future, in which the contingency of history could be used in such a way that Indians would be politically paramount in their own land. We see the template for this future outlined in the final chapter of the novel. Though it requires further analysis, my argument is that this chapter is integral to the narrative, not an 'add-on' or sop to vigilant British scrutiny as some commentators have maintained. The chapter contains an instruction which not only legitimates British rule in India for a temporary period but which also reconciles the bitter present experienced under colonial rule with the promise of a new future in which Indians would be free to rule themselves.'[20]

On his part, Vivekananda 'saw the Western way as the missing counterpart of Vedanta. He admired the Western spirit—its penchant for heading into the future with courage and tenacity; its impatience, not to wait for things to happen but to make them happen; and its readiness to take responsibility upon itself, taking risks, making mistakes, and forging ahead propelled by nothing but itself . . . The high voltage of pluck and the thrust of the Western spirit fascinated Vivekananda. He passionately believed that the wisdom of the soul would never be a social reality without the support of the Western spirit, and that the Western way—its speed and thrust—unless guided toward the wisdom of the soul, would be the surest way to doom and destruction.'[21]

Hindutva, as an idea, emerged from this boiling cauldron of revolutionary ambition and theological innovation. These men and their formulations were a simultaneous mix of reformist and revisionist ideals—they wanted the propagation of what they saw as the fundamental or the core of Hindu religion but their canvas of intended change was much larger than just religion. They sought national rejuvenation, where the quest for political freedom always simmered right below the surface of their arguments and, not least, the propagation of what they saw as the best of Hindu cultural and social ideals. All three men sought the reinvigoration of Hindu ideals, seeing them as universalist and a move away from blind ritualism and superstitions, though stridently defending Hinduism's relevance as essential to the growth and upliftment of Indian society, and to the respect they believed was due to India around the world.

In the case of Vivekananda, this propagation went far beyond Indian borders as, after his successful appearance at the Parliament of Religions, he extensively toured America, England and parts of Europe. Vivekananda also founded, in 1894, the first Hindu organization to be established in the West, which embraced non-Indian devotees. The Vedanta centres he started in America and England, which then spread to other parts of the Western world, showed a transcendental and all-inclusive face of Hinduism that was entirely at ease with modern science. In fact, Vivekananda argued, and showed, that the teachings of the Vedanta were far more egalitarian than most theological instruction the West had to offer. Vivekananda also showed the path to what I call the 'confidence of the colonized'—even though he was from a colonized country, Vivekananda showed the confidence of talking about what India had to offer that was superior, in his opinion, to what its colonizers could bring to the table.

The seminal years of political Hinduism were not without controversy, though. In the early years after publication, 'Vande Mataram' was sung by both Hindus and Muslims as they protested British injustice. In 1905, Lord Curzon, the British viceroy of India, implemented a plan to partition Bengal into Hindu-majority and Muslim-majority provinces causing ferocious protests across the region. Hindus and Muslims sang 'Vande Mataram', and carried Vande Mataram flags side-by-side in many of these protests. The regional meeting of the main nationalist party of the time, the Congress, was presided over in 1906 by a Muslim barrister Abdul Rasul, who, in the tradition of the men mentioned earlier in this chapter, was the first non-European to read at St John's College, Oxford[22]. It was held at a place in Bengal called Barisal against a backdrop of both Hindus and Muslims being brutally attacked by the colonial police force for singing 'Vande Mataram' at protests. Early versions of the Indian flag[23] all carried the words 'Vande Mataram' on them, including in 1907, the flag that Bhikaji Cama unfurled at Stuttgart in Germany, which became an early prototype of the final tricolour of independent India[24].

But this bonhomie would not last, for others had a different opinion. In 1909, the Congress's main rival, the All-India Muslim League, held a session at Amritsar in Punjab. At this session, League president Syed Ali Imam lamented:

> 'I cannot say what you think, but when I find the most advanced province of India put forward the sectarian cry of Bande Mataram[25] as the national cry and the sectarian rakhi-bandhan as a national observance, my heart is filled with despair and disappointment; and the suspicion that, under the cloak of nationalism, is Hindu nationalism preached in India becomes a conviction.'[26]

By the 1930s, and especially after its less-than-expected results in the 1935 provincial elections, the League, and other like-minded Muslims, was claiming that 'Vande Mataram' was un-Islamic because it professed the worship of the country as the mother and that was blasphemy according to Islamic laws. The League and its leaders declared that, 'In no circumstances could the song be recognized by the Muslims as their national song since with the passage of time it has become linked with idolatry and anti-Muslim feelings.'

In 1937, at the Congress session in Wardha in Maharashtra, the Congress committee designed to study this, on which sat both Jawaharlal Nehru and Mahatma Gandhi, decided upon a middle path, suggesting that only the first two stanzas of the song, which were neutral in a religious sense, would be sung while leaving aside the rest of the more fervent Hindu portions. But the League would not agree, arguing that:

'The very name Vande Mataram was enough to hurt Muslim feelings, and therefore the suggestion that the song should be modified by omitting some of the objectionable lines could hardly meet the case, for over fifty years the book of Bankim has been read and resented by Muslims and the song itself became indelibly stamped in their minds with the bitter spirit of insult to Islam and Muslims which permeates in the *Anand Math*. However expurgated or standardized, Muslims can never reconcile themselves to a single line of that song. The Young Muslim Association of Surat passed a resolution on 1 August 1937, saying that India's so-called National Anthem, Vande Mataram, "has become obsolete, is in a provincial language, revolts against modern unitarian sentiments, and entirely lacks the touch of chivalry, the sine-qua-non in such songs". While the song itself was not liked by the Muslims, the alleged way of its imposition in the schools added fuel to the fire. In schools, Muslim pupils were rather forced to sing it, since they could not defy the wishes of their teachers. Criticizing the Congress policy in imposing the song, Jinnah[27] said: "What did the Congress do when it got powers? With all its pretentions, it straightaway started with Vande Mataram. It is admitted that Vande Mataram is not the National Song, yet it is sung as such and thrust upon others. It is sung not only in their own gatherings, but Muslim children in government and municipal schools are compelled to sing it.'"[28]

Jinnah wrote in March 1938 in a newspaper article in the *New Times of Lahore*, 'Muslims all over India have refused to accept Vande Mataram or any expurgated edition of the anti-Muslim song as a binding national anthem.'[29] To this, Gandhi responded in July 1939,

'It was an anti-imperialist cry. As a lad, when I knew nothing of *Anandamath* or even Bankim, its immortal author, Vande Mataram had gripped me, and when I first heard it sung it had enthralled me. I associated the purest national spirit with it. It never occurred to me that it was a Hindu song or meant only for Hindus . . . It stirs to its depth the patriotism of millions. Its chosen stanzas are Bengal's gift among many others to the whole nation.'[30]

As the controversy heated up, Congress leader G.B. Pant wrote to Nehru that other songs could perhaps replace 'Vande Mataram'[31], and that the Congress should avoid making this a controversy by sending out private instructions to make the changes.

The middle path solution was applied, making 'Vande Mataram' about its first two stanzas. Upon Independence, it was adopted as the national song of the country, though the controversy ensured that it could not become the national anthem. Many Muslim Congress leaders, including Maulana Azad and Rafi Ahmad Kidwai, both prominent ministers in the first cabinet of independent India under Nehru, made it a point to sing 'Vande Mataram' at various gatherings.

But as with many other things in political Hinduism, this controversy never died out. It remains alive even today. In 2006, the Islamic seminary Darul Uloom issued a fatwa[32] or theological injunction against Muslims singing 'Vande Mataram'. The senior Muslim politician Arif Muhammad Khan[33] wrote in response that:

> 'The opposition to Vande Mataram came from the Muslim League, which, under the leadership of Mohammad Ali Jinnah, had developed a different attitude from those of nationalists on the question of India's freedom from foreign rule. I have no doubt that opposition to 'Vande Mataram' is not rooted in religion but in divisive politics that led to Partition. Those who persist in their opposition are actually negating a constitutional ideal. After all, the Constitution is not merely an exercise in semantics but expression of the people's national faith.'[34]

In 2013, veteran Muslim politician Shafiqur Rahman of the Bahujan Samaj Party (BSP) in India's largest state, Uttar Pradesh, walked out of the state assembly because the song was being played as part of the usual proceedings. India's incumbent home minister from the BJP, Amit Shah, has repeatedly said that the Congress decision to truncate the song spiralled into more demands from the Muslim League and finally led to the partition of India.[35] He has also said that stopping the performance of 'Vande Mataram' anywhere in India is akin to treason.[36]

The singing of 'Vande Mataram' is so frequently debated—though the resistance is usually from small groups—that, as recently as November 2022, the Indian government told a Delhi court that citizens must give equal respect to the national anthem,

'Jana Gana Mana', and the national song, 'Vande Mataram'.[37] This assertion is not new. The first president of India said exactly the same thing when 'Vande Mataram' was adopted as the national song of India in 1950.[38] But the issue keeps raising its head every now and again.

We will see in the course of this book that many of the debates of political Hinduism are framed today as a contemporary tussle between the BJP and the Congress. They began life in many ways inside the Congress, and not outside, for they were fundamental to the process of nation-making before Independence and afterwards, and were never entirely resolved. Some analysts also frame these debates as an argument between a 'conservative' BJP and a 'liberal' Congress, but these too are inadequate. This is because many of the arguments on the 'conservative' side first came from within the Congress, and not from outside. For instance, Dr Rajendra Prasad had significant differences on issues related to political Hinduism with the founding prime minister of independent India, Jawaharlal Nehru. This will be detailed later in this book.

In fact, it is because ideas of political Hinduism always had support from within the Congress that they always had some political assistance, no matter how peripheral, even when the BJP or its predecessor, a political party called the Jana Sangh, was far from power. This is the reason why the BJP today reserves some of its deepest admiration for some of the tallest leaders in the Congress who came to power after Independence, including, most notably, the first deputy prime minister Sardar Vallabhbhai Patel. One of the biggest public works in terms of monument construction taken up by the Modi government has been a 182-metre (597-foot) statue of Sardar Patel called the Statue of Unity. We will delve into why Patel, a lifelong Congressman, has become such an icon for political Hinduism during the course of this book.

Another such figure is Babasaheb Bhimrao Ambedkar, the anti-caste champion who wrote India's Constitution. Even though political Hinduism is described as conservative, and certainly in his lifetime Ambedkar was fiercely against upper-caste Hinduism and its politics, ironically, today the BJP has widespread support among so-called backward castes[39] (of whom Modi himself is a part), Dalits, once considered 'untouchables', and people from Ambedkar's own caste, which has been a key factor in many of its election victories in some of India's most populated states, such as Uttar Pradesh and Bihar.

All of this is to suggest that the story of political Hinduism is far more complicated than what most people, especially outside India, usually comprehend. Straight Right/Left labelling in this topic is only nominally useful. The BJP and the RSS do not define themselves in these terms, and even though in the West they are termed right-wing, many of their ideas are in fact left-wing, especially on economics. This book is designed to fill these gaps and build a broader understanding of the place of political Hinduism in Indian society and its rising influence around the world.

The saga of 'Vande Mataram' and the early nationalists who provided the framework for thinking about political Hinduism is critical to understand because it shows not only how the world view of political Hinduism came into being but who its opponent forces were from the very beginning and its 'other', as it were. That the same debates continue seventy-five years after India's independence shows the longevity of both the issues and the ideas of political Hinduism. One of these key issues is the contestation of history.

2

The Victory-Seekers

At the end of *Ananda Math*, the nineteenth-century novel written by Bankim Chandra Chattopadhyay, which gave the revolutionary war cry 'Vande Mataram', one of the warrior sages, Satyananda, meets a mystic figure who is not given any name in the book but is only called the Healer. The Healer offers a very precise path to Satyananda on the establishment of 'Hindu rule' or a time when, according to the monk, justice and fairness will follow the path of the eternal code or dharma.

First, the Muslim rule with its puppet-nawabs had to end, and through that, the end of the rule of the East India Company would come about, and the British, meaning the British crown, would be forced to take up the task of directly ruling India. This, says the Healer, would be better than the rule of the Muslim vassals and would be the first step towards finally establishing the rule of dharma.

Considering that *Ananda Math* was published only eight years after the dissolution of the East India Company by British

government decree, there was considerable circumstantial impetus
for Chattopadhyay, an administrative officer of the British
government, to praise the rule of the British crown. As someone
born under the rule of the later nawabs of Bengal (controlled by
the East India Company) in 1838, no doubt there was an impact
on the social collective memory of that period.

But it is the final theme in *Ananda Math*, and later works
of Chattopadhyay, that has particular relevance for political
Hinduism—the idea of resistance, of the eventual triumph
of the superior philosophies offered in Hindu dharma and its
world view.

There is finally a victory.

This idea of 'eventual victory' is one of the most potent themes
in political Hinduism. In its world view, there is a lot of historical
emphasis on 'where India lost' but not enough on 'where India
won'. It is a particular concern of Vinayak Damodar Savarkar in
his 'Hindutva'. Savarkar wrote,

'The Mohammedans had crossed that stream even under Kasim,
but it was a wound only skin-deep, for the heart of our people
was not hurt and was not even aimed at. The contest began
in grim earnestness with Mohammad and ended, shall we say,
with Abdalli? From year to year, decade to decade, century to
century, the contest continued. Arabia ceased to be what Arabia
was; Iran annihilated; Egypt, Syria, Afghanistan, Baluchistan,
Tartary—from Granada to Gazni—nations and civilizations
fell in heaps before the sword of Islam of Peace!! But here for
the first time the sword succeeded in striking but not in killing.
It grew blunter each time it struck, each time it cut deep but as
it was lifted up to strike again the wound stood healed. Vitality
of the victim proved stronger than the vitality of the victor. The

contrast was not only grim but it was monstrously unequal. It was not a race, a nation or a people India had to struggle with. It was nearly all Asia, quickly to be followed by nearly all Europe. The Arabs had entered Sindh and single-handed they could do little else. They soon failed to defend their own independence in their homeland and as a people we hear nothing further about them. But here India alone had to face Arabs, Persians, Pathans, Baluchis, Tartars, Turks, Moguls—a veritable human Sahara whirling and columning up bodily in a furious world storm . . . Heaven and hell making a common cause—such were the forces, overwhelmingly furious, that took India by surprise the day Mohammad crossed the Indus and invaded her. Day after day, decade after decade, century after century, the ghastly conflict continued and India single-handed kept up the fight morally and militarily. The moral victory was won when Akbar came to the throne and Darashukoh was born. The frantic efforts of Aurangzeb to retrieve their fortunes lost in the moral field only hastened the loss of the military fortunes on the battlefield as well . . . The day of Panipat rose, the Hindus lost the battle, but won the war. Never again had an Afgan [sic] dared to penetrate to Delhi. While the triumphant Hindu banner that our Marathas had carried to Attock was taken up by our Sikhs and carried across the Indus to the banks of the Kabul.'[1]

The lines above are worth quoting and unpacking because they sum up the eternal concerns about Indian history in political Hinduism—and because these concerns are repeated even today by everyone from Prime Minister Modi to his second-in-command, Home Minister Amit Shah, and other key members of the incumbent government.

In one recent speech, Shah said, 'I hear many times that our history has been misrepresented . . . it has been distorted. There is a possibility that what has been written was right, but who can stop us now from rewriting our history with pride? We will have to amend this and put our history in front of the world with pride.'[2] He also asked historians to look at 'thirty Indian empires and 300 heroes associated with the freedom struggle'.[3]

On his part, Modi has said, 'Unfortunately, we were taught, even after independence, the same history which was written as a conspiracy during the period of slavery. After independence, it was needed to change the agenda of foreigners who made us slaves; however, that was not done.'[4]

But what are they talking about? What is the history that politicians want underlined, from Savarkar to Modi? To understand this, let's return to the lines from Savarkar's text.

The first reference there is to 'Kasim', i.e. Muhammad ibn al-Qasim (also spelt Kasim), the Arab warlord who led the first Islamic invasion of India between 708 and 712 CE, defeating the Hindu king of Sindh[5], Raja Dahir, and establishing Islamic rule in the region. Qasim is so prominent in Savarkar's imagination because that attack started a series of Islamic invasions of India, which led to the eventual establishment of the Mughal dynasty in the sixteenth century that spread to rule most of India by 1707. The Mughal empire then started to shrink until the ouster of Bahadur Shah Zafar after the rebellion in 1857.

Savarkar says the wound was only 'skin-deep'. But why does he say this? By all accounts, it was a devastating blow and ended a nearly 100-year-old dynasty of Hindu rulers, the last of which was Raja Dahir, who died on the battlefield against Qasim in the Battle of Aror. So why is Savarkar saying, 'the heart of our people was not hurt and was not even aimed at'?

The reason is what happened afterwards. From around the eighth century, which is when Qasim attacked Sindh, the next big Islamic invasion of India took place only in the tenth century with the attack of Mahmud of Ghazni in 1001 CE. What happened in the 300-odd years in between is critical to political Hinduism, not least because colonial historiography never really took this period into account. In fact, even modern history textbooks in Indian schools, for instance, when I was in school, say very little or nothing about this period. After Qasim's success, why didn't Arab invasions continue and sweep through the rest of northern India? Why did they stop for nearly 300 years?

In fact, they didn't.

Several Arab incursions happened during this time, which were stopped by Indian rulers of various kingdoms and principalities. For instance, the Gurjara-Pratihara kings, who ruled most of north and upper central India for most of the eighth to the eleventh centuries CE, pushed back against Arab attacks. The Pratihara king Nagabhata I repulsed an invasion from Sindh from those who were left behind to control the territory after the Qasim attack. Other rulers, including Bappa Rawal from the desert kingdom of Mewar[6] and Nagabhata's own descendent, Mihira Bhoja, and others across north and western India played their own roles in holding the fort against Arab advances.

Therefore, as Savarkar highlights, while Qasim got his victory, 'the heart of our people was not hurt and was not even aimed at'. The battle commenced in earnest again with the invasion of Mahmud of Ghazni. Ghazni invaded India seventeen times, every few years till his death in 1030 CE. Some of his infamous attacks included the repeated loot of the Somnath Temple in Gujarat, one of the richest in India, and laying to waste the important

Hindu pilgrimage town of Mathura and ravaging its grand, ancient temple dedicated to the deity Krishna.

But even with Ghazni, whose attacks started a wave of relentless Islamic and iconoclastic invasions of India from the north, political Hinduism emphasizes the forgotten history. While Ghazni was successful in many of his raids on India, he faced some significant defeats. For instance, Ghazni tried to invade Kashmir twice but was thwarted each time by the armies of the Kashmiri king Sangramaraja[7]. After the second defeat in 1021 CE, Mahmud of Ghazni never attempted to approach Kashmir. That Ghazni and his loot of Somnath is well-known, but his defeat at the hands of Sangramaraja is hardly mentioned—this is something that political Hinduism is seeking to correct. It has a point in this; in my own schooling and even in the public discourse, Mahmud of Ghazni's attacks are deeply ingrained and embedded, but there are hardly any mentions of his defeats in Kashmir. Certainly, my school texts said nothing about these defeats.

But seeking to correct this through popular culture today also gives political Hinduism curious contemporary bedfellows. In recent times, the Bollywood actor Kangana Ranaut, who often espouses nationalist causes, announced that she would make a film on the Kashmiri queen regent Didda and how she defeated Mahmud of Ghazni twice[8]. Now it is true that Didda (924–1003 CE) is a charismatic figure in Kashmiri history, though, again, little known. Crippled by a childhood disease, most probably polio, she still rose to queenhood and ruled with an iron fist through her sons, ruthlessly eliminating foes, expanding the boundaries of the kingdom and powerfully controlling her sons. She was from the same dynasty as Sangramaraja but by all historical accounts, she was dead long before Ghazni's forces were repulsed from Kashmir.

Didda did not fight Mahmud of Ghazni, but, as we will see in our story, enthusiastic misreading of history at the level of popular culture to highlight hitherto little-known facts is, in fact, a sub-theme in the political Hinduism saga. While it does play an important role in bringing to the forefront histories that have been underplayed or hidden by colonial historiography or cancelled by more recent motivations, including Islamic iconoclasm, sometimes, inadequate attention to detail causes glaring mistakes and misinformation.

However, several stories from Indian history would have remained less well-known had they not become of interest to political Hinduism. This is especially true of the history of India's north-eastern regions. They have gained from the attention they received by being highlighted through the lenses of political Hinduism[9] as part of what can perhaps be understood as the construction of a 'pantheon of resistance' to various invasions, including colonization.

For instance, Prithviraj Chauhan, the Rajput king of Ajmer[10], defeated Muhammad Ghori, who also led repeated attacks on India from his base in Ghor in modern-day Afghanistan, in the First Battle of Tarain in 1191 CE. But, as underlined in bardic lore (such as *Prithviraj Raso*[11]) and political Hinduism storytelling, the Indian ruler allowed Muhammad Ghori to return alive after the defeat. A year later, Ghori returned with a greater army and not only defeated Chauhan's forces but beheaded the Rajput king. In the world view of political Hinduism, this incident of unrequited generosity repeats itself again and again in the history of India, and while Ghori's victory in the Second Battle of Tarain is often repeated, that of Prithviraj in the first battle is mostly forgotten.

The story of Prithviraj Chauhan was made into a major Bollywood film called *Samrat Prithviraj* (Emperor Prithviraj) early in 2022 starring one of the biggest stars of the Hindi film industry, Akshay Kumar, as the valorous raja. Mohan Bhagwat, the incumbent *sarsanghachalak* or chief leader of the RSS, watched the film and said, 'We have read about Prithviraj Chauhan and Muhammad Ghori. But that was written by others. This is the first time we are getting to see this from the Indian perspective. We are now looking at history from the Indian point of view.'[12] Political Hinduism, thus, permeates from popular culture to politics and vice versa.

Other notable figures in this story of resistance include the Rajput king Mularaja II of the Chalukya (Solanki) dynasty who led a combined force of desert chieftains to crush Muhammad Ghori's army near Mount Abu in modern-day Rajasthan in western India in the Battle of Kasahrada in 1178. Muhammad of Ghori is said to have barely escaped with his life and did not attack India for more than a decade before his face-offs with Prithviraj Chauhan.

The other major 'resistance hero' from the Rajput stable is Maharana Pratap, the king of Mewar from the Sisodia clan, who locked horns with the Mughal emperor Akbar, whose vastly superior army could only win a pyrrhic victory against the Rajput ruler in the Battle of Haldighati in 1576. The Maharana escaped capture, and from the hillocks around his capital, Chittor, carried out years of ruthless guerilla attacks against Mughal forces. He managed to win back most of his lost territories in the years that followed. Pratap is also lauded because he was—in his time—the only notable Rajput king who refused an alliance with, and the patronage of, Akbar. The RSS has lauded Pratap not only for his bravery but also as a social reformer for the king's dismissal of caste-based discrimination under his rule[13].

A BJP chief minister of India's largest state, Uttar Pradesh, Yogi Adityanath (a practising Hindu monk apart from being a politician) has said about Pratap, 'It is important that Maharana Pratap fought for several years in the hills of Aravalli with his self-respect and ultimately won back his forts.'[14]

But the story of Maharana Pratap also shows why political Hinduism is not just about religion. The army that Pratap fought, and lost to, at Haldighati was led by a Hindu, a fellow Rajput king, Man Singh I of Amer[15], the most trusted general of Emperor Akbar.

Akbar's story is also complicated by the fact that, while as emperor he unleashed the most deadly and bloody punishment upon kingdoms who refused to accept his overlordship, at the same time, he brought in a range of measures that show him to be more than the average iconoclastic sultan. Akbar not only had several significant Hindu compatriots, including generals and counsellors, but he also treated Hindu kingdoms that accepted ruling under his banner with courtesy, marrying Hindu women, removing the *jiziya*, the Islamic tax against 'non-believers', and in many cases, acceding to the request of some of his Jain and Hindu subjects to ban cow slaughter, especially on days considered sacred by those faiths. Akbar also attempted to bridge the differences between various faiths in his empire—one of the largest the subcontinent had ever seen—by creating his own faith, Din-i-Ilahi, a sort of amalgamation of Islamic, Hindu and other faiths.

With the massacre of thousands of Hindus in some of Akbar's campaigns, including his siege of Chittor (1567–68), where an estimated 30,000 Rajputs, including women and children, were slaughtered, Akbar is no favourite in the world of political Hinduism. And while it would be incorrect to project modern ideas like 'liberal' and 'secular' upon him, considered holistically, he was a more thoughtful Mughal ruler than many others, one who tried to make peaceful middle paths with his non-Muslim subjects.

The real vitriol of political Hinduism is, in fact, saved for the zealot Mughal emperor Aurangzeb, the man who re-enforced the jiziya, and a severe form of *sharia*. He led a crusade against 'infidels', destroying major Hindu shrines, including the ancient Kashi Vishwanath temple, and ordered the building of a mosque over it in 1669, which still stands as the Gyan Vapi mosque. Interestingly, the older Hindu shrine to Shiva had been constructed by Todar Mal, a famed Hindu courtier in the court of Akbar. Todar Mal had rebuilt this temple, which had been destroyed a few times during Islamic invasions, but each time it had been reconstructed. A Hindu queen, Ahilya Bai of the kingdom of the Holkar dynasty in current-day Madhya Pradesh, rebuilt the temple after Aurangzeb's destruction.

In fact, resisting Aurangzeb's attempts to capture the old Ahom kingdom, which existed for around 600 years from the thirteenth to the nineteenth century in India's north-east, has given political Hinduism another of its heroes who was, until recently, barely known outside of the state of Assam—Lachit Borphukan. Borphukan was an Ahom commander whose claim to fame was to have stopped Mughal expansion across the Indian north-east and into south-east Asia via Myanmar.

In what is now considered an iconic battle, Borphukan led the Ahom military force and a flotilla of war boats into conflict on the waters of the mighty River Brahmaputra, against the warships of the Mughal navy led by a Rajput king, and Mughal general, Ram Singh I. The Battle of Saraighat in 1671 led to Borphukan halting the Mughal advance and protecting the Ahom kingdom and, in a sense, preventing the further sweep of Mughal power north-eastwards.

The other Mughal king who is particularly detested by political Hinduism is the founder of the Mughal dynasty, Babur.[16] The destruction of a mosque built by Babur at a sacred Hindu site forms a critical part of the history of political Hinduism. For now, it is important to note that the rebuilding of sacred sites and shrines after Islamic iconoclastic destruction forms an important part of the ideological impetus of political Hinduism.

Most of the examples cited above are from north India, which faced the brunt of centuries of Islamic invasions, but there are several 'resistance heroes' from the southern side as well, though the context might be different.

For instance, Marthanda Varma is largely known, even today, only in the region where his kingdom used to be, in modern-day Kerala. But the story of this courageous king of Travancore who prevented the imperialistic expansion of the Dutch East India Company in India is increasingly held up as a forgotten but vital example of India fighting back and winning in the colonial era.

In 1741, forces of the Dutch East India Company were vanquished in the Battle of Colachel by the forces of Marthanda Varma. This is one of the earliest examples of an Asiatic principality landing a decisive military victory upon European colonialists. Varma had been squeezing the Dutch out of the spice trade from the Malabar coast, refusing to honour any trade treaty he thought unfair, and the European trading power, desperate to maintain its arc of influence on the lucrative spice trade, was ready to fight to keep its position.

The historian of Kerala A.P. Ibrahim Kunju noted that the Dutch sent their influential Governor of Ceylon (now Sri Lanka) Gustaaf Willem van Imhoff to negotiate with Varma, who proceeded to tell his Indian interlocutor that a failure to come to a conclusion would mean that the Dutch would declare war. In response, Marthanda Varma is said to have told the Dutchman that he did not really care about any attack from the Dutch, and in fact, he had been planning to attack Europe himself to spread his territory!

The challenge of an ostensibly small Asian principality to one of the most powerful, state-backed Western military-trader establishments, and its strategic deployment of military might to force a surrender, has never had adequate Occidental analysis. In fact, as in the case of many such victories, the incident is downplayed in Western history writing as a sort of fluke, a mere accidental win.

However, the battle had a significant psychological impact on Dutch designs in India. Dutch Commander Eustachius de Lannoy, who surrendered before Varma, went on to join the maharaja's army and rose to become its commander, leading to subsequent victories. Within barely a decade, the Dutch signed the Treaty of Mavelikkara with Travancore where they agreed to not be a hindrance to the maharaja's expansion and even supply arms and ammunition to him. Varma has been championed by the main English-language publication of the RSS, *Organiser*[17,] and in 2013, the death of Varma's namesake descendant attracted a strong condolence message from Narendra Modi[18], at that time chief minister of Gujarat, and the BJP's prime ministerial candidate. The other such character championed by the RSS and its affiliates as the 'lion of Kerala'[19] is an even more illustrious resistance hero. His story involves the defeat of no less a Western general than Arthur Wellesley, the Duke of Wellington (who would later defeat Napoleon at Waterloo). Between 1793 and 1806, the Kottayam (in present-day Kerala) prince Pazhassi Raja fought the British East India Company in a series of guerrilla wars, which was the longest armed resistance to British colonialism in India. Collectively called the Cotiote War or Kottayathu War, it pitched the resources and guile of Pazhassi Raja against the forces of the East India Company.

For several years at the turn of the century, the Company forces were led by Arthur Wellesley who, unsuccessful, is said to have confessed that the war could not be won as long as Pazhassi Raja lived. And so it was only after the death of the raja at the end of 1805, that the British could take over Kottayam.

Part of the story of victories that political Hinduism champions is the tale of the 1500-year reign of the Cholas, India's greatest maritime power. In the recent hit Indian film *Ponniyin Selvan*, the young prince Arulmozhi Varman sets off from the capital of his father's lavish kingdom, Tanjore or Thanjavur (in present-day Tamil Nadu), with a band of devoted generals to conquer Lanka (present-day Sri Lanka). The subsequent battle and rousing victory underline both the ambition and the power of the dynasty that Varman belongs to. Their routing of the Sinhalese (Lankan) army on the white sand beaches is cinematically reminiscent of the depiction of Achilles and his Myrmidons taking the beach of Troy for the Greek army.

Ponniyin Selvan is a fictional story based on the real-life Chola dynasty, one of India's most illustrious ancient kingdoms sprawling over 1500 years, one of the longest-ruling dynasties in history.

The Cholas were a maritime power devoted to spreading their influence through military and cultural expeditions across the Indian Ocean and planting the flag of their Hindu religious beliefs around South-east Asia.

From modern-day Malaysia and Cambodia to Indonesia and Vietnam, and Myanmar to Bali, Chola power and influence spread through numerous voyages by sea led by their intrepid kings and generals. The earliest diplomatic interaction between India and China was most probably a retinue from the court of Chola king Raja Raja I around 1014 CE to the court of the Song emperor, and it was during the time of the Cholas that adventurous merchants from their kingdom set up guilds in Indonesia and Myanmar.

This history has repeatedly been underlined by the BJP and the RSS. It has seeped into the foreign policy world view of Prime Minister Modi. The Indian Ocean has always been a cornerstone of his world view and he has emphasized[20] on many occasions that, 'India has had a long maritime tradition . . . The seas forged links of commerce, culture and religion with our extended neighbourhood across several millenniums . . . India has been shaped in more ways by the seas around us . . . So, the Indian Ocean Region is at the top of our policy priorities.' He has highlighted[21] that the Cholas are key to understanding India's long history with the Indian Ocean and its 'maritime legacy'.

In 2014, the year the Modi government first came to power, the RSS pointedly celebrated[22] the 1000th anniversary of the coronation of Rajendra Chola I (1014-44 CE), the Chola king who expanded the reach of the kingdom's might across South-east Asia.

We will see how the story of the Cholas feeds into India's current policy on the Indian Ocean, and how it is used in its rivalry with the Chinese in a chapter on the use of ancient Indian history in contemporary politics, which, too, is one of the great enthusiasms of political Hinduism. But for now, in this chapter, our story would not be complete without two other characters: an iconic kingdom and a warrior-king, adept especially in guerrilla warfare from the picturesque mountains of western India in what is today part of Maharashtra.

The kingdom is called Vijayanagara, or the City of Victory.

Vijayanagara is important because of its status as the last great Hindu kingdom of the early mediaeval period in India. The splendid ruins of the capital of the Vijayanagara kingdom called Hampi, 'one of the outstanding archaeological sites of Hindu

Asia[23], today lie only an overnight train ride away from Bengaluru, India's technology capital in Karnataka. For about 150 years between the fourteenth and sixteenth centuries, Vijayanagara was one of the richest kingdoms in the world. Its very founding legend has an embedded tale of unlikely resistance.

The story starts around 1336 when two young Hindu chieftains, the brothers Harihara and Bukka, laid the foundations of the Vijayanagara kingdom. They have a unique origin story.

While the exact details are slightly blurred, the story goes that Harihara and Bukka had been fighting the expansionary forces of the mad Muslim king Muhammad bin Tughlaq, who sat on the throne in Delhi and had sent his conquering legions southwards. The brothers had been captured in battle and taken to Delhi, and supposedly for their bravado, they had been set free and put at the head of the sultan's forces to lead his conquest. But the moment the brothers reached their own territory, they revolted and broke away. Either before this act of rebellion or simultaneously, they met Sri Vidyaranya, the high priest of the great Sringeri temple nearby. They told the ascetic, or so goes the legend, that they had seen an intriguing sight in the forest. A hound had been chasing a hare which was fleeing for its life, until, suddenly, the hare turned around and fiercely attacked the hound, and soon it was the hound that was fleeing from the hare.

The sage is supposed to have told them that this was a sign of the role the brothers could play by building an empire that protected the south from Islamic expansion.

Now, the Sringeri temple is no ordinary shrine. It was the first of the four great temples established by one of the greatest sages of Hinduism—Adi Shankaracharya, sometimes called 'Hinduism's greatest thinker'[24]—about 1200 years ago. So, the brothers took his advice seriously and founded Vijayanagara. It was at Vijayanagara, at Hampi, where the phrase '*Hinduraya Suratrana*' was first carved at a temple in the great capital. Hinduraya Suratrana has been translated to 'sultan among the Hindu kings'. It is one of the earliest assertions of Hindu kingship using the term as such.

So, the kingdom Harihara and Bukka founded was started, literally, with a blessing from a Hindu sage. Its theological importance lies not only in that blessing but also in the location the princes chose, in a sense sacred geography, dedicated to the local goddess Pampa and located on the banks of the Tungabhadra River. The Vijayanagara kings were builders of magnificent temples. The deity of their clan was Virupaksha, a manifestation of Shiva, the Destroyer in the Hindu trinity. Pampa, according to local tradition, is said to be the consort of Virupaksha. The Vijayanagara rulers built grand temples to various Hindu gods— Shiva, Vishnu and Ganesha—in their multitudinous forms. The soil around the kingdom was considered sacred, '. . . worshipped and understood to be literally the body of the Goddess; the features of the landscape—the mountains and forests, the caves and crevices and outcrops of rock, the mighty rivers—are all understood to be her physical features'.[25] There is reason for such worship. The land has a connection in legend even with the Ramayana, the great Hindu epic—it is said to be Kishkindha, the kingdom of Sugriva, the wise ape king and ally of the avatar Ram, the hero of the Ramayana.

The giant carved stone statues still stand amidst the ruins of temple-and-palace complexes, eerily in verdant forests and a river cutting through the ruins. Underdeveloped, and still underrated, Hampi retains a certain phantom limb syndrome[26] for many war-ravaged ruins. There is an overwhelming sense of interruption here, that this is not a civilization that grew stale and unenterprising and decayed away, but that it was interrupted.

It used to be one of the greatest cities on earth. When Abdur Razzak Samarqandi, the Persian Timurid chronicler, arrived to build diplomatic ties between Vijayanagara and the Timurid Empire, he was startled and mesmerized by its wealth; he found a city that 'simply has no equal in the world'[27] and a king so wealthy that he had 300 ports and 1000 elephants, and bazaars full of diamonds and rubies and pearls and gems of all kinds, and the king sat on a throne made of gold and studded with endless gems and jewels.[28] 'It is probable that in all the kingdoms of the world, the art in inlaying precious stones is nowhere better understood than in this country,'[29] wrote Razzak.

Vijayanagara was where some of the greatest diamonds from the famed Golconda mines arrived, and its treasury had some of the finest diamonds in the world. The sixteenth-century Portuguese traveller Garcia da Orta is said to have noted diamonds as large as a hen's egg in Vijayanagara and even jotted down the size of three other massive ones as 150 carats, 175 carats and 312.5 carats[30].

By the sixteenth century, Vijayanagara had become one of the richest kingdoms in the world. Domingo Paes, the Portuguese traveller who arrived at Vijayanagara around 1520, exclaimed: 'This is one of the best-provided cities in the world, and it is stocked with provisions . . . the streets and markets are full of laden oxen without count.'[31]

The Vijayanagara kings held sway surrounded by the Muslim sultans of southern India in neighbouring kingdoms such as Bijapur, Bidar, Ahmadnagar and Gulbarga but also defended the region against the armies of the sultanate in Delhi.

There was undoubtedly great rivalry between the kingdoms and some cultural exchange. The Vijayanagara kings adopted some cultural practices from the Muslim influence, whether dress[32] or the adoption of armaments and firearms, and the import of horses from Arabia and Iran[33], while some of the neighbouring sultans, such as Ibrahim Adil Shah II, the ruler of Bijapur, expressed deep devotion to the Hindu goddess Saraswati.[34]

But from the buildings they built, the grand festivals they organized and the gods they prized, there is no ignoring the overwhelming, celebratory Hindu identity of the Vijayanagara kings. A field survey published in 2004 revealed ruins of around 350 extant temples and shrines[35]. The 'most important annual event at Vijayanagara'[36] was the nine-day Mahanavami festival dedicated to the goddess. This festival was also the ritualistic site of an interweave, so to speak, between the regal and the divine. 'Celebrated in this rite were the victories, powers and protection of the tutelary goddess of the kings, the apotheosis of perfect kingship as symbolized by the god Rama, and the puissance and protection of all of the gods and people "of the world" by the Vijayanagara kings who were the focus of the festival.'[37] Not only were the rulers of Vijayanagara fond of building grand Hindu temples but they were also concerned with intermeshing their identity and lineage with the ideas of Hindu divinity.

Not without reason did the Vijayanagara flag, an amateur reproduction seen below, have the image of Varaha, the boar, one of the ten avatars of Vishnu, the Protector in the Hindu pantheon.

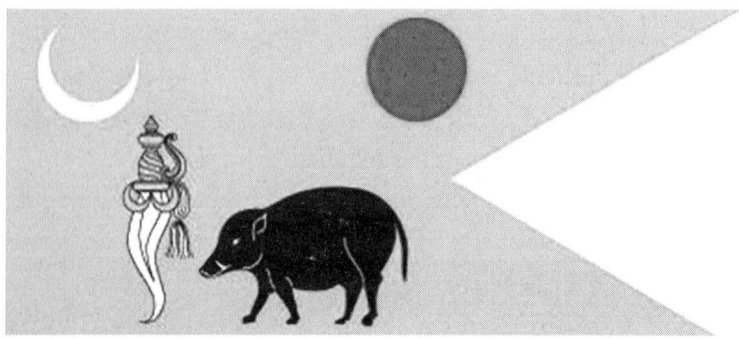

But in 1565, in the famous Battle of Talikota, a combined army of the Deccan sultanates defeated Vijayanagara, bringing an end to its glory years. The kingdom limped on for a little while longer, but irretrievable decay had set in.

The fall of Vijayanagara has been seen by many, and not just in the formal BJP and RSS universe, as the collapse of the edifice that stood as a bulwark against the marauding sultanate armies. For instance, this neglect and decay were given a worldwide voice when the Nobel laureate writer V.S. Naipaul opened the second of his India trilogy, *A Wounded Civilization*, with a description of the ruins of Vijayanagara. The book was first published in 1977.

Even at that time, Naipaul noticed 'there are university students in Bangalore, two hundred miles away, who haven't heard of it.' Visiting the Hampi ruins, Naipaul wrote that he 'wondered about the intellectual depletion that must have come to India with the invasions and conquests of the last thousand years. What happened in Vijayanagara happened in varying degrees, in other parts of the country.'[38]

The story of what was lost with the fall of Vijayanagara remains a crucial part of the narrative of political Hinduism. As recently as April 2022, the BJP chief visited Hampi and said that it represented, '. . . people's superior knowledge in science and architecture at the time and the administrative set-up that was in place during the time. Hampi is a manifestation of our glorious past.'[39]

What Vijayanagara represents remains debated. While writers like William Dalrymple highlight the 'hybridity'[40] and 'syncretism'[41] of Hampi, others, such as Vamsi Juluri, note the symbolism of the broken arm of the statue of Ugra Narasimha, the just under seven-metre figure of the part-man, part-lion avatar of Vishnu, the Preserver, whose image Juluri used on the cover of his book *Rearming Hinduism*.[42]

Certainly, attempts to gentrify the Vijayanagara story also tend to oversimplify it as scholars Mark T. Lycett and Kathleen D. Morrison pointed out in 2013, 'In spite of energetic scholarly challenges to the communal stereotype and demonstrations of the cosmopolitan nature of the city, the notion of the city's basic Hinduness has persisted, only slightly modified in response to suggest that its cosmopolitanism represented a sort of island of tolerance in a sea of (Muslim) bigotry and danger.'[43] In their paper, Lycett and Morrison even quoted one of the main archaeologists who worked on the excavations of the key areas in the Hampi ruins, B. Narasimaiah, to show how authoritative and fundamental these views are: 'The Muhammadan invaders were particular in looting the temples which were repositories not only of wealth but also of knowledge and culture. They mercilessly killed those who resisted and forcibly converted those who submitted to their fate.'[44]

There was no denying the interweave of cultures that Dalrymple pointed out, but to Juluri, the statue represented something else that was equally true. When Vijayanagara fell, one of the arms of the deity was broken and chopped off above the wrist. Vijayanagara and its ruins are significant in the history of politics in the name of Hinduism not only because of what was destroyed in an old war but the way the memory of what had been destroyed has been narrated and what it represented—a certain forceful resistance to iconoclasm, and not just in India. In December 2022, for instance, the veteran Sri Lankan diplomat Sirisena Amarasekara wrote, 'The Vijaya Nagar [sic] kingdom protected South India, including Sri Lanka, from Islamic Invasion. If not for the powerful Vijaya Nagar Kingdom in south India, Sri Lanka could have been subjected to Islamic invasion resulting in conversion to Islam. Intentionally or unintentionally, the Vijaya

Nagar kingdom has played a vital role in safeguarding the Sinhala-Buddhist identity in Sri Lanka.'[45]

Thus, the fall of the Vijayanagara empire is epoch-making in the story of political Hinduism, and the next most important event in its sense of self is the rise, nearly 100 years later, of a Maratha warrior-chieftain, Shivaji Bhonsle, who would go on to create an empire starting from areas which are today in Maharashtra, not far from the financial capital of India, Mumbai.[46]

Shivaji is critical to our story not only because of the support his story received to become part of India's nationalist movement against colonial rule but also because of his enduring appeal today. Not only does Shivaji have one major political party named after him, the Shiv Sena, which has been in government several times in Maharashtra and controls India's wealthiest municipal corporation in the country but its main rival in the state, the BJP, is planning to construct a 212-metre statue[47] of the seventeenth-century king in the middle of the Arabian Sea, which would be connected to the mainland through an undersea rail link. In fact, his name even today can trigger political controversy. When, recently, the Shiv Sena after a longstanding quarrel with the BJP—even though both parties adhere to the ideology of political Hinduism—split into two, the breakaway faction was compared to Shivaji's escape from house arrest in Agra by the Mughal emperor Aurangzeb in 1666.[48]

Shivaji's early years are, again, less simplistic than his legend as a Hindu warrior suggests. His grandfather and father were generals in the forces of the Deccan sultanates and had received lands and titles for their loyal service. But by the mid-seventeenth century, as Shivaji was coming of age, the Deccan sultanates were in disarray. The Mughal empire, which Shivaji's father Shahaji had rebelled against, with the backing of one of the Deccan sultanates, was also showing signs of overreach with Aurangzeb's ever-widening campaigns and tyrannical, iconoclastic rules aimed at non-Muslims.

Shivaji's story soon throws up elements that showcase why he has become the most important mediaeval historical figure in the political Hinduism pantheon. In an early struggle against the Bijapur sultanate, to which his father had been loyal, Shivaji crossed swords with a formidable sultanate general, Afzal Khan.

What strengthens the story from a political Hinduism perspective right from the beginning is that en route to his tryst with Shivaji, and to corner the Maratha warrior, Afzal Khan and his forces destroyed the Tulja Bhavani temple, which was the place of worship for Shivaji's clan, and desecrated the Vithoba temple, another major Hindu pilgrimage site nearby at Pandharpur. When he finally met Shivaji, the Maratha chieftain killed him. The story goes that after a long siege where neither army could defeat the other, Shivaji and Afzal Khan agreed to meet with just one sword—or no weapons, depending on the version. But Shivaji had gone prepared with chainmail armour under his clothes because he was expecting to be betrayed. When attacked with a knife, the armour protected him. In turn, Shivaji, who had been carrying hidden metallic tiger claws, used them to tear open Khan. The following battle resulted in the rout of the Bijapur forces.

The theme of this story is repeated throughout what can be called 'the legend of Shivaji'. Throughout his lifetime, Shivaji was constantly in battle, first with the Deccan sultanates, and then, on a more elaborate scale, with the Mughal forces of Aurangzeb.

Shivaji's battles with Aurangzeb continued for more than two decades during which the Maratha chieftain transformed himself, through the acquisition of territory, displays of battlefield daredevilry and uniting various Maratha clans under his banner, into Chhatrapati, upon whom the ceremonial umbrella of emperorship is bestowed. He became the undisputed ruler of the Marathas and constructed the foundation of the Maratha empire, which was the predominant power in India for around 150 years between the late seventeenth and early nineteenth centuries. Usually in Indian history-telling, the story cuts from the Mughals to the British. One of the things that political Hinduism is keen to emphasize, and which is one of the reasons why Shivaji is so emblematic in this tale, is that Mughal power, in fact, gave way first to the rise of the Marathas. The Maratha era actually came to an end only in 1818 with the defeat of Peshwa Baji Rao II against the British East India Company in the Third Anglo-Maratha War.

As usual, any neat Hindu-Muslim story is complicated by Shivaji's early allegiances with parts of the Deccan sultanates, and also by the fact that not only did Muslims not face any discrimination under Shivaji's or any other Maratha ruler's reign and in their territories, but several were also inducted at high positions in the Maratha administration. Shivaji, for instance, employed several Muslim commanders, while the name of Ibrahim Khan Gardi is well-known as one of the most loyal generals in Maratha history, who fought bravely to the end at the side of Maratha general Sadashivrao Bhau against the combined Afghan-Pashtun Rohilla-Mughal forces led by Ahmad Shah Abdali and Shuja ud-Daula.

But it was undeniably Shivaji who not only described his rule as 'Hindavi Swarajya'[49] or self-rule for the Hindus but also took the title 'Haindava Dharmodhhaarak' (defender or upholder of dharma).[50] He replaced the use of the Persian language and customs, favoured by the Mughals, with the use of Sanskrit and

Hindu customs.[51] Shivaji's banning of cow slaughter, considered anathema by most Hindus, and adoption of detailed Hindu rites and rituals led by Brahmins for his coronation as Chhatrapati also establishes the Hindu nature of his kingship, something Maratha rulers after him maintained.

Shivaji is a vital link in our story because his reinvention in service of the broader freedom movement of India from colonial rule was led by a somewhat broad consensus. Bal Gangadhar Tilak, the most prominent and vociferous leader of the Congress before the arrival of Mahatma Gandhi on to the scene,[52] organized public gatherings and festivals dedicated to Shivaji as part of the campaign for India's freedom and efforts for the country to know its heroes better. In 1895, only around forty years after the first war of independence in 1857, Tilak started the Shri Shivaji Fund Committee for celebrations of Shiv Jayanti, a festival on the birth anniversary of Shivaji, and for facilitating the rebuilding of the commemoration site for the Maratha ruler at Raigad, a city built by Shivaji with perhaps the most impenetrable fortress in Maharashtra, which had been destroyed by the British in 1818. Tilak is the man who said, 'Swaraj (self-rule) is my birthright and I shall have it!' Notably, he did not say how swaraj was to be had. In projecting India's martial Hindu tradition of fighting oppression, which is how he saw Shivaji, Tilak differed from Gandhi's promotion of non-violence.

Tilak was not the only one embracing Shivaji for the cause of Indian nationalism. Swami Vivekananda saw Shivaji in the same light.

One of his followers, a doctor, M.C. Nanjunda Rao, a well-known disciple of Vivekananda, recorded the following exchange with Swami Vivekananda on Shivaji. It was published in *Vedanta Kesari*, one of the publications of the Ramakrishna Math

and Mission which Vivekananda had started. Rao had heard
Vivekananda singing the following song:

> Like the effect of fire on the trees of the forest,
> Like the effect of the panther on a flock of deer,
> Like the effect of a tiger on a herd of elephants,
> Like the effect of sun on the darkness of the night,
> Like the effect of Krishna on Kamsa,[53]
> Such was the effect of Shivaji on the Mlechcha[54] gangs.

The doctor responded to this by telling Vivekananda that he had
only been taught in school that Shivaji was 'a cunning unprincipled
freebooter . . . a marauder . . . a mere child of fortune'. To this,
Vivekananda:

> '. . . immediately gave up his singing and saw me full in the
> face, his face being lit up with the fire of indignation and said,
> "Shame on you, Doctor . . . that is all you know of the greatest
> king that India had produced within the last three hundred
> years; one who was the very incarnation of Siva, about whom
> prophecies were made long before he was born; and his
> advent was eagerly expected by all the great souls and saints of
> Maharashtra as the deliverer of the Hindus from the hands of
> the Mlechchas and one who succeeded in the establishment
> of the Dharma which had been trampled underfoot by the
> depredations of the devastating hordes of the Moghals.[55]
> This is what comes of your reading Indian history written by
> foreigners who could have no sympathy with you, nor could
> they have any respect for your culture, traditions, manners,
> and customs which they could not understand. Is there a
> greater hero, a greater saint, a greater bhakta[56] and a greater

king than Sivaji?[57] Sivaji was the very embodiment of a born
ruler of men as typified in your great epics . . . It is a pity that
in our schools, the history of India written by foreigners alone
is taught to our boys. The foreign writers of the Mahratta[58]
history can never shake off their bias nor understand the real
character and greatness and the inner motive of the actions
of Sivaji."'[59]

Vivekananda goes on to tell the doctor that Shivaji was
misrepresented because colonial historians took their cue from
Mughal chroniclers who saw Shivaji as the enemy, instead of
referencing the stories told by Maratha bards and independent
Persian records.[60]

This idea that chronicles of history written by foreigners,
especially colonial sources, deliberately (or otherwise)
misrepresented Indian history, and especially Hindu history,
echoes across the timeline of political Hinduism, including in
November 2022, when Prime Minister Modi noted, 'The history
of India is not just about slavery. The history of India is about
emerging victorious, it is about the valour of countless greats.
Unfortunately, we were taught, even after Independence, the
same history which was written as a conspiracy during the period
of slavery. After Independence, it was needed to change the
agenda of foreigners who made us slaves; however, that was not
done.' The prime minister who idolizes Vivekananda, and in his
youth thought of joining Vivekananda's Ramakrishna order as a
monk,[61] could have been paraphrasing the monk.

In the late nineteenth and early twentieth century, the idea
that Shivaji was a resistance icon for Indian nationalism echoed
in every sphere. Rabindranath Tagore, who would become the
first Asian to win the Nobel Prize in literature in 1913, wrote two

poems about Shivaji.[62] One of them, *Shivaji Utsav* or The Festival of Shivaji, had these lines,

A few distant centuries ago, on a nondescript day
I can barely imagine
Upon what craggy hilltop, within a dense sunless forest
O sovereign Shivaji
Lightning-like, across your forehead, there flashed
The thought from above—
'With a singular religious thread, this torn up, fragmented
Bharata, I shall bind in One.'
Where were you then, O contemplative One, Hero of Maratha
Where was your valiant name!
Your saffron insignia, scattered in the dust, crushed
Into nothingness by decree of fate.
The mocking annals of the invaders brand you as bandit
As they break into raucous laughter—
All your noble efforts nothing more than a robber's failed work
What all have since known.

Ye false tale-spinners, cease your garrulous speeches
O ignominious Muse of Lies
Know that the true verdict of Destiny shall overwrite
The falsehood today, and Truth declare victory.
That which is deathless, how can it ever be smothered
By your words of scorn?
The sadhana[63] steeped in truth, nothing shall stand in its way
This I know for sure.

O Royal Savant, those soaring, unifying thoughts of yours
In the store-house of Fate are preserved

Forever, could the hands of Time, ever purloin
The minutest speck of it?
That sacrifice of yours at the shrine of your Motherland
That resolute sadhana for the Truth
Who would have known—these became from thence
Till the end of time, Bharata's inheritance!

Tagore's lines, too, echo the same ideas—Shivaji as a hero,
a 'unifier' of India, fighting enemies of the motherland, and
his legacy, though sullied by lies, was soon to be rescued and
revered.

Tagore was a pacifist, Vivekananda was a spiritualist and Tilak
had revolutionary ideals. But they all agreed on the importance
of Shivaji. So did Aurobindo (1872–1950), the Cambridge-
educated revolutionary-turned-ascetic. Trained at the best British
institutions to be a diligent loyalist of the Raj, in fact, to join the
British civil service governing India, Aurobindo instead became
one of the most prominent revolutionaries, running one of the
foremost secret revolutionary societies, Anusilan Samiti,[64] with
his brother Barindra Ghosh. Aurobindo was arrested for his
role in a series of bombings but released for lack of evidence.
He then moved to Pondicherry[65] to become an ascetic and set
up an ashram there. Aurobindo remained connected to Indian
nationalism even as an ascetic and wrote extensively about Indian
history, its manifest destiny and its role in the world.

In one of his texts, Aurobindo imagines a conversation
between Jai Singh, a Rajput king and commander of the Mughal
forces of Aurangzeb, with Shivaji, in which Jai Singh laments
that Shivaji broke the rules of war. The exchange, as imagined by
Aurobindo, goes like this:

Jai Singh: Your political ideal was great but your standard of means was abhorrent to our morality. Ruse, treachery, pillage, assassination, these were not excluded from your action!

Shivaji: Not for myself I fought and ruled, but for God and the Maharashtra dharma, the religion of Hindu Nationality, which Ramdas[66] enunciated. I offered my head to Bhavāni[67] and She bade me keep it to scheme and plot for the welfare of the nation. I gave my kingdom to Ramdas and he made me take it back as a gift from God and the Marhattas. Both commands I obeyed. I slew when God commanded, I plundered because He pointed out that as the means He had given me. Treacherous I was not, but I helped my weakness in resource and numbers by ruse and stratagem, conquered physical force by keenness of wit and brain-force. The world has accepted ruse in war and politics and the chivalrous openness of the Rajput is not owned either by the European or the Asiatic nations.

Jai Singh: I held the dharma as supreme and even the voice of God could not persuade me to abandon it.

Shivaji: I gave up all to Him and did not keep even the dharma. His will was my religion; for He was my Captain and I his soldier. That was my loyalty, not to Aurangzebe[68], not to a code of morals, but to God who sent me.

Jai Singh: He sends us all, but for different purposes and according to the purpose he moulds the ideal and the character. I am not grieved that the Mogul[69] has fallen. Had he deserved to retain sovereignty he could not have lost it, but even when he ceased to deserve, I kept my faith, my service, my loyalty. It was not for me to dispute the will of my emperor. God who appointed him might judge him; it was not my office.

Shivaji: God also appoints the man, who rebels and refuses to prolong unjust authority by acquiescence. He is not always on the side of power; sometimes He manifests as the deliverer.

Jai Singh: Let Him come down Himself then as He promised. Then alone would rebellion be justified.

Shivaji: But whence will He come down, when He is here already, in our hearts? Because I saw Him there, therefore was I strong enough to carry out my mission.

Jai Singh: Where is the seal upon your work, the pledge of His authority?

Shivaji: I undermined an empire and it has not been rebuilt. I created a nation and it has not yet perished.[70]

As evident from the portion above, Shivaji was being considered in a new light by these men dreaming of a free India. The positioning of Shivaji was backed by serious scholars who added to this understanding. Jadunath Sarkar, the most famous living historian of that time, yet another graduate of Presidency College, and a man knighted for his contribution to education and history-writing, wrote a definitive volume on Shivaji based on a wealth of new material. In *Shivaji and His Times*, first published in 1919, Sarkar argued that while Shivaji did not start out thinking of himself in Hindu terms—he was more concerned with fighting what he saw as oppressive regimes, both of Deccan sultanates and the Mughal administration—he evolved to become

'the last great constructive genius and nation-builder that the Hindu race has produced . . . He has proved by his example that the Hindu race can build a nation, found a state, defeat enemies; they can conduct their own defence; they can protect and promote literature and art, commerce and industry; they can maintain navies and ocean-trading fleets of their own, and conduct naval battles on equal terms with foreigners. He taught the modern Hindus to rise to the full stature of their growth.'[71]

Not only was Sarkar, the knighted historian[72], agreeing with revolutionaries and monks on the importance of Shivaji, but so was the *Imperial Gazetteer*, which noted that 'Sivaji [sic] not only founded a kingdom, he also created a nation.'[73]

Shivaji was considered a reformer by the pre-eminent anti-caste activist and freedom fighter Jyotirao Phule (1827–90) for his non-Brahminical origins and his non-discriminatory reign. Jawaharlal Nehru, the political antithesis of Savarkar, also had admiring things to say about the Maratha warrior: 'Shivaji was the symbol of a resurgent Hindu nationalism, drawing inspiration from the old classics, courageous, and possessing high qualities of leadership. He built up the Marathas as a strong unified fighting group, gave them a nationalist background, and made them a formidable power which broke up the Mughal Empire. He died in 1680, but the Maratha power continued to grow till it dominated India.'[74]

But one of the most important devotees of Shivaji was Savarkar, who popularized Hindutva and wrote a poem on Shivaji too, declaring that the 'Hindu nation bows to you . . . Ye who fulfilled our unspoken yearnings.'[75] It was Savarkar's poem that spoke of the despair under colonial rule and the need for a Shivaji-like resurgence in the nationalist movement:

> Every fort and coastal stronghold, wrecked!
> Every capital city, wilderness unchecked!
> Enslaved fortune in foreign coil, necked!
>
> Living in these ignominious times, oh shame! . . .
> Acclaimed by Ramdas: purity of heart yours . . .
> Your strategy that so many villains razed
> Your strength that vanquished a tyrant crazed . . .
>
> May that purity of purpose sustain!
> May our simple souls that intellect obtain!
> May such strength in our blood reign . . .[76]

It is this martial spirit that ignited the early years of political Hinduism, which objected to the pacifist non-violent path advocated increasingly by the Congress leadership after Gandhi appeared as its leader.

3

Freedom, with Hindu Characteristics

Men such as Bal Gangadhar Tilak, Aurobindo Ghosh (later Sri Aurobindo, after he became an ascetic) and Vinayak Damodar Savarkar had seen the worst excesses of the British Raj. Tilak, who was famous as an educationist before he turned to activism, had been charged with sedition thrice, spent eighteen months in prison in one sentence, was deported to Mandalay in Myanmar[1] in another, and acquitted in the third. Aurobindo had been trained in the best English schools and colleges to join the colonial civil service, but he had instead rebelled against the Raj and had been arrested and served prison time in a bombing case. Savarkar had started life as a revolutionary in Maharashtra running secret societies dedicated to opposing British rule in the manner of similar societies that people such as Aurobindo and others were part of in Bengal. Savarkar's brother Ganesh was the founder of one such famed society called Abhinav Bharat. The notoriety of the brothers among the colonial administration came to be known early—in 1910 a proposal to deport revolutionaries had Ganesh

Savarkar's name in it.[2] Ganesh Savarkar would go on to become one of the five founding members of the RSS.

Vinayak Savarkar studied in England, like Aurobindo, Gandhi and Nehru, and others like Vallabhbhai Patel and Muhammad Ali Jinnah, whom we will meet soon in our story. He even studied law, like Nehru, Gandhi, Patel and Jinnah. It was Savarkar who first described the revolt of 1857 as the 'first war of Indian independence' in a book he wrote by the same name. The book was promptly banned by the British Raj. In England, he continued his revolutionary activities and was arrested in 1910. He was being deported to India when he jumped ship and fled to France. Rearrested, he was sentenced to fifty years in prison. Widely considered the most dangerous enemy of the Raj in his time, Savarkar was given the harshest punishment of all—he was sent to the infamous Kala Pani or Cellular Jail in the Andaman Islands in the Bay of Bengal for more than a decade where for hours each day he was yoked to an oil mill and made to press oil physically like cattle.

All these men had much in common, including the fact that they turned against the British Raj; yet, they were destined to be history's antagonists, not allies.

All of them, barring Savarkar, were also once part of the Congress Party. But in time, the differences between them would be stark. While Tilak, Aurobindo and Savarkar are integral to the building blocks of political Hinduism, Gandhi, Nehru and others took the path of non-violent resistance. But the views of Tilak, Savarkar and Aurobindo, and others like them, never went away. In fact, they manifested themselves in pivotal debates before and after India's independence in 1947. At the heart of their differences was one man—Mohandas Karamchand Gandhi—who would be declared 'Mahatma' or the holy soul of India.

In this chapter, we shall see how these political Hinduism views interacted with the Congress, led by Gandhi and Nehru, and how they grew and morphed parallelly to the nonviolent resistance movement against the British administration that Gandhi propagated.

But before we get into the differences between these two streams of ideation within the Indian freedom movement, two contradictions must be highlighted because these give a sense of the reasons for the resilience of the ideas of political Hinduism. First, it is worth noting that there was a significant overlap of vocabulary between the men whose ideas fuelled political Hinduism and others who are considered their 'secular' alternatives, primarily Gandhi.

Consider, for instance, the use of 'Hindu iconography and concepts'. If there is one that connects Bal Gangadhar Tilak, Vinayak Damodar Savarkar, Aurobindo Ghosh (Sri Aurobindo) and Mohandas Karamchand (Mahatma) Gandhi, it is that they all spoke about 'sanatana dharma'. They were all concerned with upholding this eternal code as a fundamental pillar of Indian nationalism.

In 1906, Tilak gave his famous speech asking for Hindu political and social unity at Varanasi, where he said, among other things:

'The term Sanatana Dharma shows that our religion is very old—as old as the history of the human race itself . . . But you all know no branch can stand by itself. Hindu religion as a whole is made up of different parts co-related to each other as so many sons and daughters of one great religion. If this idea is kept in view and if we try to unite the various sections it will be consolidated in a mighty force. So long as you are divided amongst yourselves, so long as one section does not recognize its affinity with another, you cannot hope to rise as Hindus. Religion is an element in nationality . . . You might put on a different dress, speak a different language, but you should remember that the inner sentiments which move you all are the same. The study of the Gita, Ramayana and Mahabharata[3] produce the same ideas throughout the country. Are not these common allegiance to the Vedas, the Gita and the Ramayana—our common heritage? If we lay stress on it forgetting all the minor differences that exist between different sects, then by the grace of Providence we shall before long be able to consolidate all the different sects into a mighty Hindu nation. This ought to be the ambition of every Hindu.'[4]

In 1908, after he emerged from prison[5] and before he moved to distant Pondicherry to turn towards spirituality (with the British secret police keeping an eye on him), Aurobindo delivered a speech that became one of the most important documents in the political Hinduism universe. Echoing Tilak, Aurobindo said at Uttarpara in Bengal,

'I spoke once before with this force in me, and I said then that this movement is not a political movement and that nationalism is not politics but a religion, a creed, a faith. I say it again today, but I put it in another way. I say no longer that nationalism is a creed, a religion, a faith; I say that it is the Sanatan Dharma which for us is nationalism. This Hindu nation was born with the Sanatan Dharma, with it, it moves and with it, it grows. When the Sanatan Dharma declines, then the nation declines, and if the Sanatan Dharma were capable

of perishing, with the Sanatan Dharma[6] it would perish. The
Sanatan Dharma, that is nationalism. This is the message that
I have to speak to you.'[7]

Savarkar, the atheist with, a deep cultural conviction nonetheless,
also had detailed thoughts on what he believed to be the real
sanatan dharma. He concluded that the lessons of sanatan dharma
were contained in the Vedas and the Upanishads, the foundational
ancient scriptural texts of Hinduism, and any scripture that could
not pass the test of scientific reasoning was not worth following.
In short, spirituality fused with scientific reasoning, argued
Savarkar, was at the core of sanatana dharma. Savarkar was all for
consistently accommodating scientific progress within scriptures
(the Smriti texts[8]).

Gandhi thought long and deep about *swaraj*, which is a term
he, in a sense, inherited from Tilak, and the phrase 'sanatana
dharma' too. He said he was a 'sanatani Hindu' which, according
to him, meant, I call myself a Sanatani Hindu, because:

'I believe in the Vedas, the Upanishads, the Puranas and all that
goes by the name of Hindu scriptures, and therefore in avataras
and rebirth;

I believe in the varnashrama dharma[9] in a sense, in my
opinion, strictly Vedic but not in its present popular and crude
sense;

I believe in the protection of the cow in its much larger
sense than the popular;

I do not disbelieve in idol-worship.'[10]

There were other commonalities too, especially in the conception
of Indian nationhood. This is particularly evident from the

early imaginings of two characters who are today considered antithetical to one another: Jawaharlal Nehru and Vinayak Damodar Savarkar.

Perhaps no two political figures in modern Indian history have been considered more antithetical to one another than Jawaharlal Nehru and Vinayak Damodar Savarkar. The self-professed admirer of socialism, Nehru, the first prime minister of India, is seen as an emblem of pluralism while Savarkar, with his sectarian fusing of the Hindu religion with nationalism, is considered parochial and divisive.

But that is an oversimplification of the complex lives of these men. As we saw above with Tilak, Aurobindo, Savarkar and Gandhi, so it is with Savarkar and Nehru. There are ideational, if not ideological, overlaps between them especially in conceptualizing Indian nationhood—they start at the same conceptual points, even though they arrive at different destinations.

This is most apparent in their two seminal texts, Nehru's *The Discovery of India* (1946), and Savarkar's *Hindutva* (1923), both composed when the writers were imprisoned by the British government for participating in the freedom movement. These show how, while the two leaders built differing, even antagonistic political projects, the ideas they used in conceptualizing an independent homeland contained areas of significant convergence, even though their 'takeaways' are divergent.

Embedded in these texts are themes that are considered key to the world view of political Hinduism but, as a careful comparison shows, these views were perhaps part of a broader consensus, in some ways, of thinking about the nation at that time. There is a reference to a 'sacred geography'[11] which holds, for these men, the 'hidden heart of national identity'[12], the shared narrative of masculinity, a framing through the 'Eastern nationalism'[13] lens where they feel compelled to contest a sense of cultural inadequacy, and a need to address caste discrimination.

This comparison between *Discovery* and *Hindutva* shows how the modern Indian nation was created through an ideological tussle whose dispute is well-documented but its commonalities at origin are often ignored. In doing so, it depicts a key argument in this book: the reason for political Hinduism's sustenance is its historical longevity and the consensus around many of its ideas even though the political manifestations may be vastly different.

What bridges the vision of Nehru and Savarkar in *Discovery* and *Hindutva* is a permeating sense of devotion, a language of piety, to a spatial topography that they imbibe with metaphysical meaning. For two men who declare aesthetical disinterest in religion (Nehru, like Savarkar, was famously averse to organized religion and its traditional customs), neither can construct the idea of a nation without theological tropes.

'I wandered over Himalayas, which are closely connected to old myth and legend . . . the mighty rivers of India that flow from this great mountain barrier into the plains of India . . . The Indus or Sindhu from which our country came to be called India or Hindustan . . .' says *The Discovery of India*[14], echoing Savarkar's, '. . . the great Indus was known as Hindu to the original inhabitants of our land and owing to the vocal peculiarity of the Aryans it got changed into Sindhu . . . [15].' The ancients, argued Savarkar, were looking to find a word 'comprehensive enough . . . to express the vast synthesis that embraced the whole continent from the Indus to the sea and aimed to weld it into a nation'.[16]

If nationalism is made up of 'cultural artefacts of a particular kind'[17], then these artefacts are to be found, for both Nehru and Savarkar, in geography. If for one, 'The story of the Ganges, from her source to the sea, from old times to new, is the story of India's civilization and culture'[18], for the other, the sense of the nation is created 'out of their gratitude to the genial and perennial network of waterways that ran through the land like a system of nerve threads and wove them into a Being.'[19] Both men emphasize the interweave of co-related geographies, a mountain range here, a river there, all of them in conversation with one another, using the idea that 'geography is a science of relationships'.[20]

Their imagined communities[21] are plotted in scriptural terms with Nehru pointing to 'vast numbers of common folk were continually travelling to the numerous places of pilgrimage . . . All this going to and fro and meeting people from different parts of the country must have intensified the conception of a common land and a common culture . . .'[22] and Savarkar claiming to quote from the ancient Vishnu Purana, 'The land which is to the north of the sea and to the south of the Himalaya mountain is named Bharata'.[23]

But using this shared conception, they arrive at divergent destinations. Nehru talks of an India built as an 'ancient palimpsest on which layer upon layer of thought and reverie had been inscribed, and yet no succeeding layer had completely hidden or erased what had been written previously'.[24] But for Savarkar, assimilation (and not coexisting layering) is the key to nationhood. For instance, for Muslims, he wants 'worship as heroes our ten great avatars only adding Muhammad as the eleventh'[25] as the criterion for entry into the embrace of nationhood. This difference is stark, for instance, in describing Mahmud of Ghazni's invasion of India. 'Mahmud was far more a warrior than a man of faith and like many other conquerors he used and exploited the name of religion for his conquests . . . He enrolled an army in India and placed it under one of his noted generals, Tilak by name, who was an Indian and a Hindu. This army he used against his own co-religionists in central Asia'[26], while '. . . where religion is goaded by rapine and rapine serves as a handmaid to religion . . . such were the forces, overwhelmingly furious, that took India by surprise the day Mohammad [Mahmud] crossed the Indus and invaded her'.[27] While they can agree with why their homeland is glorious, Nehru and Savarkar part ways in defining the enemies of India and their attributes.

In Nehru's imagination of India, there is no defined 'other' whereas the 'other' for Savarkar is acutely established. For Savarkar, India is defined by influences that it must repel, while for Nehru, even in the most repellent of experiences, India is constructed of that which it absorbs—even from those that attack it.

In their imagining of India, there is also a shared sense between Nehru and Savarkar of Eastern nationalism.[28] The Oxford political philosopher John Plamenatz (1912–75) spoke of two kinds of nationalism: Western and Eastern. Western nationalism, according to Plamenatz, is seen among Western countries that may have gone into decline but are sure of their cultural apparatus, whereas Eastern nationalism in places like Asia and Africa comes from 'peoples recently drawn into a civilization hitherto alien to them'[29] and deals with a feeling of cultural inadequacy.

The Discovery of India has tracts of the questioning of such alien culture with undertones of a pushback against the inadequacy of the native culture.

'Ancient Greece is supposed to be the fountainhead of European civilization, and much has been written about the Orient and the Occident. I do not understand this . . . India, it is said, is religious, philosophical, speculative, metaphysical, unconcerned with this world, and lost in dreams of the beyond . . . So we are told, and perhaps those who tell us so would like India to remain plunged in thought . . . so that they might possess this world . . .[30]'

Savarkar has even more emotive fare: 'The Indians saw that the cherished ideals of their race . . . were trampled underfoot, the holy land of their love devastated and sacked by hordes of barbarians.'[31]

Nehru disagreed with poet Matthew Arnold's description of the East ('The East bow'd low before the blast; In patient, deep disdain; She let the legions thunder past; And plunged in thought again'[32]) in *The Discovery of India*, writing, 'But it is not true that India has ever bowed patiently before the blast or been indifferent to the passage of foreign legions. Always she has resisted them, often successfully, sometimes unsuccessfully, and even when she failed for the time being, she has remembered and prepared herself for the next attempt.'[33] Savarkar makes a similar point of forgotten valour, when attacked, he argued, '. . . the enlightened would perhaps remain as unaffected as ever . . . But the rest of the Hindus could not then drink with equanimity this cup of bitterness and political servitude at the hands of those whose barbarous violence could still be soothed by the mealy-mouthed formulas of ahimsa (non-violence)'.[34]

(It is important to note here the divergence. Savarkar was writing against 'mealy-mouthed ahimsa' barely two years after Gandhi, in a sense, took over the reins of the Congress and started his first mass movement of non-violent civil disobedience against the Rowlatt Act[35], which gave the police powers to arrest anyone on suspicion and without evidence.)

Both Savarkar and Nehru were using and reinforcing, in their respective texts, a vision of nationalism based on 'an ancient civilizational entity'[36], consistently used as a counterbalance to the cultural inadequacy Nehru and Savarkar seem to sense around them.

Perhaps it is because of this feeling of insufficiency that both men seep into their description of India strong undertones of masculinity. (Political Hinduism would pick up and develop this idea of masculinity and make it a core value in the years to come.)

Underlining both texts, there is a sense of romanticist masculinity, a portrayal of adventure—theoretically, this is their journey to become 'men of consequence'[37]. Nehru has an effusive description of the moon seen from his jail room at the beginning of *The Discovery of India*, 'The moon, ever a companion to me in prison, has grown more friendly . . . a reminder of the loveliness of this world . . .'[38] His portrayal of prison life as a romantic ideal started early and stayed on. 'Nehru thrilled in jail-going, and there is, in his letters and diaries of the early twenties, the glow of virginal suffering and self-indulgent sacrifice.'[39] In *Discovery*, for instance, Nehru highlights how he bravely spurned an invitation to meet Mussolini despite being on a visit to Rome and surrounded by immense diplomatic pressure.[40] On his part, Savarkar's self-imagery and positioning are lucid. He mentions, 'Forty centuries, if not more' have gone by as 'prophets and poets, lawyers and law-givers, heroes and historians, have thought, lived, fought and died'[41] to establish the legitimacy of the word 'Hindutva'. There is no confusion about his self-placement in that pantheon—Savarkar is, in his own assessment, the latest in the list of historical figures battling to establish the credentials of Hindutva. Then, for all the talk of non-violence, Nehru hastens to explain in *Discovery* that non-violence did not prevent the Congress from formulating the creation of a military or police force in independent India.[42] Savarkar has a more aggressive ideology and displays an 'anxious Hindu masculinity'[43] as he pushes forth the idea of sangathan (organization), 'The numerical strength of our race is an asset that cannot be too highly prized'[44]. In his world view, every enemy of India is defined in terms of 'bitter haters of Hindus'[45] and every hero as 'you are the restorer of the Hindu religion and the destroyer of the Mlechchas (foreigners)[46]'.

Nehru and Savarkar also denounced caste—Nehru in a Gandhian vein, Savarkar, more unequivocally. India may have had caste discrimination, but this was better than the slave labour in ancient Greece, argues Nehru. 'Within each caste there was equality . . . each caste was occupational and applied itself to its own particular work. This led to a high degree of specialization and skill . . .'[47] Savarkar is more strident, '. . . pull down the barriers that have survived their utility . . . of castes and customs . . . Let this ancient and noble stream of Hindu blood flow from vein to vein.'[48]

While the comparison between these texts does not, of course, give us a full ideological comparative analysis between the two men, it does give us a sense that even though contemporary imagination pitches them as irreconcilable adversaries, the men were products of their class and milieu. Though the two differed in their conclusions, it is because of the early commonalities that Savarkar's monochromatic viewpoint never disappeared. If Nehru's subsequent leadership of independent India established his version of a mosaic society, Modi's ongoing stint as prime minister is, in a sense, a glimpse of the alternative, the anti-Nehruvian, Savarkarite, if you will, idea of India.

It is important to affirm, though, that the two men are not merely extensions of their ideological fountainhead—Nehru was a political innovator in his own right, not merely an acolyte of Gandhi, and Modi, while reverential towards Savarkar, is much more than a simple implementer of Savarkar's ideals.

When Gandhi and Savarkar met in 1906 in London[49], it was probably Savarkar, though the younger of the two[50], who was better known in anti-colonial circles in India than Gandhi who was experimenting in South Africa. The day they met, Savarkar had been cooking prawns, which shocked Gandhi, a devout vegetarian, who expected Savarkar, a Brahmin, to reject non-vegetarian food too. Savarkar, who rejected caste discrimination, and indeed caste and many other Hindu dos and don'ts, is said to have told Gandhi, scornfully perhaps, 'If you cannot eat with us, how on earth are you going to work with us? Moreover, this is just boiled fish; while we want people who are ready to eat the British alive!'[51] These differences would become more acute with the creation of the Muslim League in 1906 and the British government's allowing of a separate Muslim electorate in 1909[52], in keeping with the demands of the Muslim League.

These differences between the two men are explicitly clear through the reading of, again, Savarkar's *Hindutva*, and the book Gandhi published in 1909 called *Hind Swaraj*. In these texts, both men put forward what they believe is the essence of India and what could take the country towards its manifest destiny. In a nutshell, for Gandhi, it is the rejection of 'Western civilizational', and for Savarkar, it is the embrace of 'innate Hindu culture'.

Denouncing everything from Western medicine ('I have indulged in vice, I contract a disease, a doctor cures me, the odds are that I shall repeat the vice [he mentions overeating]. Had the doctor not intervened, nature would have done its work, and I would have acquired mastery over myself, would have been freed from vice and would have become happy[53]') to the railways and lawyers, Gandhi argues,

'I believe that the civilization India has evolved is not to be
beaten in the world. Nothing can equal the seeds sown by our
ancestors. Rome went, Greece shared the same fate; the might
of the Pharaohs was broken; Japan has become Westernized;
of China, nothing can be said; but India is still, somehow or
other, sound at the foundation. The people of Europe learn
their lessons from the writings of the men of Greece or Rome,
which exist no longer in their former glory. In trying to learn
from them, the Europeans imagine that they will avoid the
mistakes of Greece and Rome. Such is their pitiable condition.
In the midst of all this, India remains immovable and that is
her glory. It is a charge against India that her people are so
uncivilized, ignorant and stolid, that it is not possible to induce
them to adopt any changes. It is a charge really against our
merit. What we have tested and found true on the anvil of
experience, we dare not change. Many thrust their advice upon
India, and she remains steady. This is her beauty: it is the sheet
anchor of our hope.'[54]

For Savarkar, the antidote to India's upliftment is altogether
different. Radically, in an age where caste divides are sharp and
prominent, Savarkar says,

'What of interdining?— but intermarriages between provinces
and provinces, castes and castes, be encouraged where they
do not exist . . . Let the minorities remember they would be
cutting the very branch on which they stand. Strengthen every
tie that binds you to the main organism, whether of blood or
language or common Motherland. Let this ancient and noble
stream of Hindu blood flow from vein to vein, from Attock to
Cuttack till at last the Hindu people get fused and welded into

an indivisible whole, till our race gets consolidated and strong, sharp as steel.'[55]

Savarkar's prescription is for people and specifically Hindus to understand that

'the future of India is bound up in the last resort, with Hindu strength. We are trying our best, as we ought to do, to develop the consciousness of and a sense of attachment to the greater whole, whereby Hindus, Mohammedans[56], Parsis, Christians, and Jews would feel like Indians first and every other thing afterwards. But whatever progress India may have made towards that goal one thing remains almost axiomatically true—not only in India but everywhere in the world—that a nation requires a foundation to stand upon and the essence of the life of a nation is the life of that portion of its citizens whose interests and history and aspirations are most closely bound up with the land and who thus provide the real foundation to the structure of their national state.'[57]

Savarkar is at pains to explain that his concept of Hindutva is not Hinduism, the religion, but that the religion is a subset of the broader notion of Hindu culture common to all who live on the land, and who consider it their *pitrubhu* (land of their forefathers) and *punyabhu* (sacred ground or holy land), 'as the land of his prophets and seers, of his godmen and gurus, the land of piety and pilgrimage'[58].

Savarkar's Hindutva came on the heels of Gandhi's Khilafat Movement where, controversially and to the dismay of many of his supporters, he pushed the Congress to support the demand for the restoration of the Caliphate in Turkey where the Ottoman

Empire was collapsing, having sided with the losing camp in
World War I. For the Muslim leaders of India who started the
movement, it was a show of pan-Islamism; some even claimed
that to allow the Caliphate to fall would take away Muslim control
from Islam's holiest sites, Mecca and Medina, which could not be
allowed. For Gandhi, it was an attempt to bring together Muslim
participants in large numbers to his satyagraha campaigns, along
with Hindus and others, against British rule along with the Hindus
and others—this was to be the campaign that would bring the two
communities together.

In spite of severe reservations, including from the most
prominent barrister in India, the Muslim Congress leader
Muhammad Ali Jinnah, Gandhi went ahead with the movement.
It quickly collapsed when Turkey itself threw off the Caliphate
under Mustafa Kemal Ataturk's secular revolution.

But the damage was done. Jinnah, till then a dual member
of the Muslim League and the Congress, had defended Bal
Gangadhar Tilak as his lawyer in two major cases of sedition
in 1909 and 1916[59], and had brokered a major Hindu-Muslim
agreement of cooperation against the British Raj with Tilak called
the Lucknow Pact in 1916, which promised separate electorates
for Muslims in provincial councils for Muslim participation in
the wider struggle for freedom from British rule. In the Congress,
this pact brought together the so-called 'extremists' or people
such as Tilak and others, who were unwilling to compromise
on their demand for absolute freedom by any means necessary,
and 'moderates', who advocated a slower approach starting with
some autonomy under British rule and who were represented by
leaders such as Gopal Krishna Gokhale. Gokhale's death in 1915
and Tilak's in 1920 had given Gandhi complete leadership of the
Congress, which, under him, leaned towards the moderate side.

Gandhi had written in *Hind Swaraj* that 'If the Hindus believe that India should be peopled only by Hindus, they are living in dream-land. The Hindus, the Mahomedans, the Parsis and the Christians who have made India their country are fellow countrymen, and they will have to live in unity, if only for their own interest. In no part of the world are one nationality and one religion synonymous terms; nor has it ever been so in India.'[60]

He had also made it clear that he was willing to compromise considerably to bring about peace between the two communities. On cow protection, dear to Gandhi, he said:

'I myself respect the cow, that is, I look upon her with affectionate reverence. The cow is the protector of India because, being an agricultural country, she is dependent on the cow. The cow is a most useful animal in hundreds of ways. Our Mahomedan brethren will admit this. But, just as I respect the cow, so do I respect my fellow-men. A man is just as useful as a cow no matter whether he be a Mahomedan or a Hindu. Am I, then, to fight with or kill a Mahomedan in order to save a cow? In doing so, I would become an enemy of the Mahomedan as well as of the cow. Therefore, the only method I know of protecting the cow is that I should approach my Mahomedan brother and urge him for the sake of the country to join me in protecting her. If he would not listen to me, I should let the cow go for the simple reason that the matter is beyond my ability. If I were overfull of pity for the cow, I should sacrifice my life to save her but not take my brother's. This, I hold, is the law of our religion. When men become obstinate, it is a difficult thing. If I pull one way, my Moslem brother will pull another. If I put on a superior air, he will return the compliment. If I bow to him gently, he will do it much more so; and if he does not, I shall not be considered to have done wrong in having bowed.'[61]

Even Savarkar, who scoffed at notions of cow worship, said, 'I criticized the false notions involved in cow worship with the aim of removing the chaff and preserving the essence so that cow protection may be better achieved. A worshipful attitude is necessary for protection. But it is improper to forget the duty of cow protection and indulge only in worship. The word "only" used here is important. First, protect the cow and then worship it if you so desire'[62]. He mentioned in his *Hindutva* an incident of local people from one part of Maharashtra complaining to Shivaji about the oppression under Aurangzeb's legionaries who 'oppresses the women and the children, commits atrocities and even resorts to such reprehensible misdeeds as the slaughter of cows. We are so disgusted that we can no longer live under him.'[63]

Savarkar had envisioned good relations between Hindus and Muslims using the following example:

'. . . take the case of a patriotic Bohra or a Khoja[64] countryman of ours. He loves our land of Hindusthan as his Fatherland which indisputably is the land of his forefathers. He possesses—in certain cases they do— pure Hindu blood; especially if he is the first convert to Mohammedanism[65] he must be allowed to claim to inherit the blood of Hindu parents. He is an intelligent and reasonable man, loves our history and our heroes; in fact the Bohras and the Khojas as a community, worship as heroes our great ten Avatars[66] only adding Mohammad as the eleventh . . . He may differ as regards a few festivals or may add a few more heroes to the pantheon of his supermen or demigods. But we have repeatedly said that difference in details here or emphasis there, does not throw us outside the pale of Hindu Sanskriti.[67] The sub-communities amongst the Hindus observe many a custom, not only contradictory but even conflicting with the customs of other Hindu communities. Yet both of them are Hindus. So also in the above cases of a patriotic Bohra or a Christian or a Khoja, who could satisfy the required qualifications of Hindutva to such a degree as that, why should he not be recognized as a Hindu?'[68]

Gandhi had gone much further in *Hind Swaraj*. He argued:

'Am I to dislike a Mahomedan because there are passages in the Koran I do not understand or like? It takes two to make a quarrel. If I do not want to quarrel with a Mahomedan, the latter will be powerless to foist a quarrel on me; and, similarly, I should be powerless if a Mahomedan refuse his assistance to quarrel with me. An arm striking the air will become disjointed . . . A clay pot would break through impact, if not with one stone, then with another. The way to save the pot is not to keep it away from the danger point but to bake it so that no stone would break it. We have then to make our hearts of perfectly baked clay. Then we shall be steeled against all danger. This can be easily done by the Hindus. They are superior in numbers; they pretend that they are more educated; they are, therefore, better able to shield themselves from attack on their amicable relations with the Mahomedans . . . There is mutual distrust between the two communities. The Mahomedans, therefore, ask for certain concessions from Lord Morley[69]. Why should the Hindus oppose this?'[70]

The reference to 'concessions from Lord Morley' of course are separate electorates granted to Muslims under the Minto-Morley Act of 1909 and Gandhi seemed to be acquiescing.

A decade later, the Khilafat Movement would first demonstrate to what other, and to what degree of, concessions Gandhi was willing to accommodate to broker peace between the two communities.

A furious Jinnah told the journalist Durga Das in 1920, 'I will have nothing to do with this pseudo-religious approach to politics. I part ways with the Congress and Gandhi.'[71] Das recorded, 'Jinnah particularly deplored the Khilafat agitation, which had brought the reactionary mullah element to the surface . . . encourage the Pan-Islamic sentiment . . . and dilute the nationalism of the Indian Muslim.'[72]

Babasaheb Bhimrao Ambedkar[73], who was emerging as the key critic of Gandhi on the issue of caste (he accused Gandhi of wanting to maintain the status quo insidiously) and Hindu-Muslim relations (where he felt that Gandhi was appeasing hardline Muslim interests), was appalled that Gandhi continued to support the Khilafat cause even though many Muslim leaders of that movement were hatching plans to invite the Emir or King of Afghanistan to attack the British and force the hand of the British on Turkey. 'Can any sane man go so far, for the sake of Hindu-Moslem[74] unity? But Mr Gandhi was so attached to Hindu-Moslem unity that he did not stop to inquire what he was really doing in this mad endeavour.'[75]

Whatever it was that Gandhi was trying to achieve failed to bear fruit. Hindu-Muslim tensions and clashes that had been going on since the late 1880s had grown steadily since the partition of Bengal in 1905. In 1920–21, one of the worst incidents of bloodshed took place in the Malabar region of Kerala, which would come to be known as the Moplah riots, where efforts by the British government to quell Khilafat-related agitations turned into a massacre as the majority Muslim peasantry turned on the British administrators and the Hindu landlords murdering hundreds, and converting thousands more forcibly to Islam.

Ambedkar, ever the astute observer, noted,

'Beginning with the year 1920 there occurred in that year in Malabar what is known as the Mopla[76] Rebellion. It was the result of the agitation carried out by two Muslim organizations, the Khuddam-i-Kaba (servants of the Mecca Shrine) and the Central Khilafat Committee. Agitators actually preached the doctrine that India under the British Government was Dar-ul-Harab[77] and that the Muslims must fight against it and if they could not, they must carry out the alternative principle of Hijrat. The Moplas were suddenly carried off their feet by this agitation. The outbreak was essentially a rebellion against the British Government. The aim was to establish the kingdom of Islam by overthrowing the British Government. Knives, swords and spears were secretly manufactured, bands of desperadoes collected for an attack on British authority. On 20th August 1920, a severe encounter took place between the Moplas and the British forces at Pinmangdi. Roads were blocked, telegraph lines cut, and the railway destroyed in a number of places. As soon as the administration had been paralysed, the Moplas declared that Swaraj had been established . . . Khilafat flags were flown, and Ernad and Wallurana[78] were declared Khilafat kingdoms. As a rebellion against the British Government, it was quite understandable. But what baffled most was the treatment accorded by the Moplas to the Hindus of Malabar. The Hindus were visited by a dire fate at the hands of the Moplas. Massacres,

forcible conversions, desecration of temples, foul outrages upon
women, such as ripping open pregnant women, pillage, arson
and destruction—in short, all the accompaniments of brutal
and unrestrained barbarism— were perpetrated freely by the
Moplas upon the Hindus until such time as troops could be
hurried to the task of restoring order through a difficult and
extensive tract of the country.'[79]

Gandhi, though, responded by saying, 'Hindus must find out
the causes of Moplah fanaticism. They will find that they are not
without blame. They have hitherto not cared for the Moplah.
They have either treated him as a serf or dreaded him. They have
not treated him as a friend and neighbour, to be reformed and
respected. It is no use now becoming angry with the Moplahs
or the Mussulmans in general. Whilst Hindus have a right to
expect Mussulman aid and sympathy, the problem is essentially
one of self-help, i.e., development of strength from within.'[80]
When a senior Muslim leader of the Congress, and a personal
friend of Gandhi, Maulana Hasrat Mohani, defended Muslim
actions in the Malabar as jihad or holy war, Gandhi seemed
to defend him. 'The Maulana considers that the Moplahs had
started a jehad and, according to the rules of jehad, those
who help the enemy become enemies themselves . . . I do not
blame the Maulana. He looks upon the British Government as
an enemy. He would defend anything done in fighting it. He
thinks that there is much untruth in what is being said against
the Moplahs and he is, therefore, not prepared to see their
error. I believe that this is his narrowness, but it should not
hurt the Hindus. The Maulana speaks what is in his mind. He
is an honest and courageous man. All know that he has no ill
will against the Hindus.'[81]

Many disagreed. Annie Besant, one of the most prominent women members of the Congress who was elected the Congress president in 1917, wrote:

'The fourfold programme was begun formally on August 1, 1920; Swaraj was to be attained in a year, and on August 1, 1921, the first step was taken in the Malabar Rebellion; the Musalmans (Moplas) of that district after three weeks of preparing weapons, rose over a definite area in revolt, believing, as they had been told, that British Rule had ceased, and they were free . . . They established the Khilafat Raj, crowned a King, murdered and plundered abundantly, and killed or drove away all Hindus who would not apostatize. Somewhere about a lakh[82] people were driven from their homes with nothing but the clothes they had on, stripped of everything.'[83]

Some of the most biting criticism came from a partly fictional book called *Moplah*, released to great reader response in 1924, which described the incident as an anti-Hindu genocide and was released to great reader response in 1924. The author of the book was Savarkar who saw in these killings every warning he had ever given come true.

The late 1800s and the early 1900s had already seen a revival of Hindu ideas and ideals coming together in new organizations such as the Brahmo Samaj and neo-Vedantins in Bengal, and with major revival and reform movements such as the Arya Samaj and its ideological offspring such as the Hindu Sabhas in Punjab and other parts of north India, both regions with significant Muslim populations (Punjab, in fact, had a Muslim majority). An early leader of the Hindu Sabha in Punjab, R.B. Lal Chand, a disciple

of Swami Dayanand Saraswati, the founder of the Arya Samaj,
wrote soon after the Minto-Morley Reforms in 1909:

'. . . In replying to the Mohammadan Deputation Lord
Morley said: "I know very well that any injustice, or suspicion
that we are capable of being unjust to Mohammadans in
India, would certainly have a severe and injurious reaction in
Constantinople" . . . that seems to me to form the crux of the
whole situation. Mohammadans have Constantinople behind
their back, not to speak of other Mohammadan independent
states with which more or less British statesmanship have to
deal . . . On the other hand, the Hindus have to fall back on
their gullibility. They have no independent state to support
their cause, not even to cheer them with sympathy for their
grievances. They are circumscribed within the four walls of
Hindustan and have no outside assistance to influence the
attitude of their rulers. They might cry themselves hoarse over
this Charter and that Proclamation, but words and protests do
not make up for the inherent weakness of their position . . .
To add to this natural misfortune the Hindus have got a self-
inflicted one in what is called and known as the Congress. This
has proved a veritable source of weakness for purely Hindu
interests. If there is one thing which is strictly forbidden within
the precincts of the Congress it is the term "Hindu".'[84]

By 1915, the Hindu Mahasabha had come into being as a
common interest pressure group within the Congress. At its first
conference in Haridwar during the famous Kumbh Mela, Gandhi
himself was present, along with another champion for Hindu
causes, Swami Shraddhanand, another disciple of Dayanand
Saraswati.[85]

Swami Shraddhanand is important because of the role he played in the 1920s in bringing together a cohesive political Hinduism movement, which had support from key Congress leaders such as Madan Mohan Malaviya and Lala Lajpat Rai. In Shraddhanand's mind, the two most important causes were eradicating caste discrimination, especially prejudice against the so-called untouchables, and 'shuddhi'[86] or reconversion of Muslims and Christians back into the Hindu fold. By 1922, Ambedkar considered him 'the greatest and most sincere champion of the untouchables'.[87]

It was Shraddhanand, among others, who spoke forcefully about the need for 'sangathan' or the coming together to form a unified body, as it were, in defence of Hindu causes. Reconversion, interdining between castes to remove untouchability, inter-caste marriage, the propagation of Sanskrit and even more importantly, Hindi—these ideas to bring Hindus together were preached extensively by the early missionaries of Hindu unity. It is from men such as Dayanand Saraswati, Shraddhanand, Lal Chand and others that Savarkar's ideas interacted and were refined to three primary aspects: Hindi, Hindu, Hindustan. Language, faith and nationalism provided the unity the nation needed, according to them.

But Shraddhanand's success in converting Muslims brought him into the crosshairs of Muslim clerics and in 1926, a Muslim assailant, Abdul Rashid. Gandhi, a champion of Shraddhanand's work in removing untouchability 'deplored the murder of Swamiji [Shraddhanand]. But Swamiji's death could be turned to good account, if both the Hindus and the Muslims cleansed their hearts with his blood. That would be the work of purification, that would be a real *shuddhi* work. What was the duty of the Hindus? They should not seek to retaliate. The teaching of all religions was not to return evil for evil but good for evil. All the religions taught that the greatest conquest was the conquest of one's own self. The Hindus should attain that self-possession. Abdul Rashid was a poor creature; he alone was not responsible for this diabolical deed. The bulk of the Muslim Press in Delhi and all those who had been holding up Swami Shraddhanand, Lala Lajpat Rai and Pandit Madan Mohan Malaviya as the enemies of Islam collectively contributed to the murder. The results of those things were before them. The whole atmosphere of the country demanded purification.'[88]

Said Gandhi, 'If the Hindus forgive Abdul Rashid, what can be more welcome than that?'[89]

Many Hindus were no longer willing to listen. This would be a constant feature for the rest of his life. Gandhi's statements would be held up again and again, and even today in political Hinduism, to showcase what is perceived as either his bias or his irrational need to bring Hindus and Muslims together no matter what the cost to Hindus.

The political Hinduism movement was promulgating its own literature, for instance, *Hindu Superiority* by Har Bilas Sarda, another Arya Samaj disciple, first published in 1906, which argued that 'The Varnashrama was not the same as the caste system of the present day—a travesty of its ancient original. No one was a brahman by blood nor a sudra by birth, but everyone was such as his merits fitted him to be . . . The son of a Brahman sometimes became a kshatriya, sometimes a vaishya, and sometimes a sudra.[90] At the same time, a sudra as certainly became a brahman or a kshatriya.'[91] To argue his case, Sarda pointed out that Valmiki and Vyasa, the two authors of the Ramayana and Mahabharata, were shudras and quoted authoritative sources to explain that there were instances cited even in the Vedas of so-called 'lowly' born people achieving the highest levels of scholarship and considered saints.[92]

Sarda was a civil servant. He had been influential in his activism against child marriages and as a member of the Central Legislative Assembly, and had even sponsored the Child Marriage Restraint Act in 1925 (which was referred to as the Sarda Act).

It merits highlighting here that even though political Hinduism has been considered 'conservative' by some scholars, many of the ideas and champions, whose thoughts and beliefs created political Hinduism, were, in fact, radical in their time. Whether it was fighting untouchability, complete access to temples and all public spaces for all castes including untouchables, striking at child marriage, or promoting widow remarriage, inter-caste dining and marriage—all these were radical, volatile ideas deeply contested, and often resented, by orthodox Hindus during the time that these thinkers were propagating them. People such as Swami Vivekananda, Sri Aurobindo, Dayanand Saraswati, Swami Shraddhanand and even Savarkar, were constantly going against the grain of conservatism, shedding rituals and customs that they thought were inimical to political Hinduism and indeed, Hinduism at large. This is why many of them have been considered 'reformers', which is what they were. Their instincts were to change, alter and better, and throw out where necessary, rather than merely to preserve.

But that's not all. It was not just the domestic that these thinkers of political Hinduism were starting to be concerned with, they were also concerned about the world. In a section titled, 'Foreign Relations', Sarda says:

'When such brilliant national character combines with such happy social organization of the people as to excite the

admiration of all who study it, one can easily conceive what
noble achievements of peace and war the ancient Hindus must
have accomplished. It is true, "peace hath her victories no less
renowned than war"; still a peculiar halo of glory attaches
to military achievements. The achievements of the Hindus
in philosophy, poetry, sciences and art prove their peaceful
victories. But their military achievements were equally great,
as will appear from their mastery of the science of war . . .
Their civilizing missions covered the globe, and Hindu
civilization still flows like an undercurrent in the countless
social institutions of the world.'[93]

The idea that there was something unique Hindu India had to
contribute to the world was not confined to political activists,
ascetics or lawmakers. In 1916, the Bengali scholar Benoy Kumar
Sarkar, who founded several institutes in Calcutta such as the
Bengali Institute of Sociology, the Bengali Asia Academy, the
Bengali Dante Society and the Bengali Institute of American
Culture, published *The Beginning of Hindu Culture as a World
Power (A.D. 300–600).* An original thinker, he wrote in five
languages (Bengali, English, German, Italian and French) the
same year Sarkar also published *Chinese Religion through Hindu
Eyes: A Study in the Tendencies of Asiatic Mentality,* one of the
earliest analyses of China through Indian eyes. In 1918, he
produced a book called *Hindu Achievements in Exact Science: A
Study in the History of Scientific Development.* By 1919, he had
published a seminal paper in the *American Political Science Review*
called 'Hindu Theory of International Relations'.[94] In this, Sarkar
dug deep into ancient Hindu texts to explain 'the doctrine of
mandala (sphere of influence)'.

Sarkar wrote:

'The conception of "external" sovereignty was well established in the Hindu philosophy of the state. The Hindu thinkers not only analysed sovereignty with regard to the constituent elements in a single state. They realized also that sovereignty is not complete unless it is external as well as internal, that is, unless the state can exercise its internal authority unobstructed by, and independently of, other states.[95] The doctrine of independence (*svarajya*[96], *aparadheenatva*[97]) implied in this conception of external sovereignty was obviously the foundation of the theory of the state in relation to other states. And it gave rise to certain categories of droit des gens or jus gentium which normally influenced Hindu political thinking from at least the fourth century B.C. These concepts can more or less be grouped under the doctrine of mandala, that is sphere or circle (of influence, interests, ambitions, enterprise, and what not). This doctrine of mandala, underlying as it does the Hindu idea of the "balance of power", pervades the entire speculation on the subject of international relations.'[98]

As Martin Bayly has argued:

'Sarkar's work demonstrates that envisaging the "international" was not just the preserve of imperial powers seeking a new framework for international co-operation—as with ideas of "Greater Britain". Nor was it solely the product of a rising American great power delineating a strategy for the enacting of its prestige and power in what would become known as the "American Century". The activity of "thinking the international" was forged in global projects of imperial power and anti-imperial resistance. In India, this reimagining of

international order would resonate in the theory and practice
of India's foreign policy long after independence, and in many
ways leave a legacy that exists to this day.'[99]

Sarkar was not the only one constructing Hindu theories. The
Father of Indian Chemical Science, Prafulla Chandra Ray, had, in
the early 1900s, produced two seminal volumes called *A History of
Hindu Chemistry*, the first volume in 1902 and the second in 1909.

The stage was set for deeper interventions from political
Hinduism and the push came from multiple sources. Since the
1920s, two highly influential and firebrand leaders within the
Congress were championing the cause of political Hinduism—
Madan Mohan Malviya (1861–1946) and Lala Lajpat Rai (1865–
1928). Both had trained as lawyers. Both founded prominent and
feisty newspapers. Malviya is today remembered as the founder
of the Benaras Hindu University while Rai is remembered for his
slogan 'Simon, go back!' This was against the all-British Simon
Commission which came to India to study constitutional reform
in 1928. Indian nationalists demanded that Indians should
be included in any such study. Leading a protest against the
Commission, Rai was bludgeoned severely and responded by
saying, 'I declare that the blows struck at me today will be the last
nails in the coffin of British rule in India.' He died soon afterwards.

These two men championed many of the causes of political
Hinduism from within the Congress. In 1923, in a Hindu
Mahasabha speech, Malviya said, 'I solemnly affirm before God
I never mean to hurt Muslims or have the supremacy of Hindus
over Muslims. If that be the sentiment in me, God may give me the
greatest punishment, but I wish that my Hindu brethren be wiped
off this earth if they cannot protect their sisters, daughters and
others, cannot save the honour of our religion. We are responsible

for our weakness. We have forgotten our duty. We should not fight shy of being called Hindus.'[100] Malviya was with Gandhi but perhaps not quite ready to go as far as Gandhi to push for Hindu-Muslim peace. On his part, Rai said in a meeting in 1925, 'There is some apprehension in the mind of a certain section of our Muslim countrymen that the Hindus are working for a Hindu Raj. It is to be deplored that some Hindus, too, should have taken to that line of argument in retaliation to the Mohammedan cry for Muslim Raj. We know that all Mohammedans do not want a Muslim Raj, and we also know as a fact that the bulk of the Hindus do not want a Hindu Raj.'

But in the same speech, he also added, '. . . Hindus are very much obsessed by a fear of the Indian Mohammedans making a common cause with the Mohammedan Powers beyond the North West Frontier to establish Mohammedan dominions in India . . .' He adds that such opinions had been expressed by influential leaders[101] from the northern frontiers [and] 'I have reasons to believe that this opinion is shared by a large number of Mohammedans in the Frontier Province and the Punjab and Sindh. In light of this evidence, the Hindu apprehension cannot be dismissed as entirely unfounded. The question of the Frontier is very important to the whole of India and it especially concerns the safety and security of the Hindu community.'[102]

Why did Rai have reason to believe this? Perhaps because as early as 1887, the Muslim educationist Syed Ahmad Khan, the founder of the Muhammadan Anglo-Oriental College (which later became Aligarh Muslim University), had declared in a speech in Meerut what would become famous as the 'two nation theory'. It must be added here that one of the earliest conceptions of separate parts of Indian history that could be termed 'Hindu' and 'Muslim' comes from the Scottish historian James Mill who looked at Indian history, and especially the Hindus, in quite disparaging and racist terms, including a dismissal of Hindu culture and traditions, and divided the history in three phases: Hindu, Muslim and British. Khan said:

> 'Now, suppose that all English, and the whole English army, were to leave India, taking with them all their cannon and their splendid weapons and everything, then who would be rulers of India? Is it possible that under these circumstances two nations— the Mahomedans and the Hindus—could sit on the same throne and remain equal in power? Most certainly not. It is necessary that one of them should conquer the other and thrust it down. To hope that both could remain equal is to desire the impossible and the inconceivable. At the same time, you must remember that although the number of Mahomedans is less than that of the Hindus, and although they contain far fewer people who have received a high English education, yet they must not be thought insignificant or weak. Probably they would be by themselves enough to maintain their own position. But suppose they were not. Then our Mussalman brothers, the Pathans, would come out as a swarm of locusts from their mountain valleys, and make rivers of blood flow from their frontier in the north to the extreme end of Bengal. This thing—who, after the departure of the English, would be conquerors—would rest on the will of God. But until one nation had conquered the other and made it obedient, peace could not reign in the land. This conclusion is based on proofs so absolute that no one can deny it.'[103]

Subsequently, such an idea had appeared in the writings of a prominent proponent of political Hinduism, the social reformer, Bhai Parmanand, in the 1920s.

Thus, keeping this context in mind, Rai defended the movement towards Hindu sangathan: 'Every religious community is trying to unify itself and organise itself in different ways. It is true that the Hindus have so far neglected that work, but if they have learnt the lesson from the example of other communities and are doing the right thing towards their own community, no one has a right to find fault with them on that ground.'[104]

Savarkar's monograph on Hindutva was released in 1923. He was released from prison (though under the condition that he would remain confined to the Ratnagiri region in Maharashtra) from his fifty-year jail sentence, after promising to stay away from political activity, in 1924. In many minds, including that of the young revolutionary Bhagat Singh, he was a hero. Singh, under a pseudonym, wrote about Savarkar in 1924, 'The one who loves this world is that braveheart, whom we don't feel ashamed to call as a fierce insurgent and a fanatic anarchist—this is the Veer (brave) Savarkar'.[105] In 1925, Savarkar published a deeply researched history of the Maratha Empire called *Hindu Padshahi*. The monograph *Hindutva* not only had much to say about the nature of nationhood and political Hinduism in India but it also added an international dimension that has been a critical foreign policy pillar of political Hinduism: support for Israel. Savarkar wrote in *Hindutva*, 'If the Zionists' dreams are ever realized—if Palestine becomes a Jewish State and it will gladden us almost as much as our Jewish friends.'[106] While today, many of political Hinduism's critics suggest that it might have 'fascist' leanings—and we will see going forward in this book where that idea comes from—the far more resolute idea that political Hinduism has always had, and which is seen even today in the rapid advancement and friendship between India and Israel under BJP governments, is friendship and admiration for Israel. It is easy to see why. Political Hinduism considers Hindus as embattled as the Jews, facing countless invasions and conflicts with Islam.

In 1925, a doctor based in the western city of Nagpur in Maharashtra, Keshav Baliram Hegdewar, who had been influenced by B.S. Moonje[107], who in turn was once a follower of Tilak but had distanced himself from the Congress after Tilak's death and the rise of Gandhi, started a voluntary organization dedicated to cultural nationalism using Hindu emblems and ideas called the Rashtriya Swayamsevak Sangh (RSS).

Hegdewar had studied medicine in Calcutta where he became part of a lot of the secretive revolutionary work, including that of Anusilan Samiti led by Aurobindo and Barindra, and was deeply influenced by the writings of Bankim Chandra Chattopadhyay. Later, in Maharashtra, Savarkar's writing impressed Hegdewar, who even met Savarkar before the founding of the RSS in September 1925.

Savarkar's brother and Moonje were among the five people present at the founding day of the RSS; the organization chose as its flag, the triangular saffron-coloured flag of the Maratha Empire. The declared intention was to strengthen Hindu society and unite it. Hegdewar had been exposed to the ideas of the desire for strength, including physical strength, in the revolutionary thinking of everyone from Bankim to Aurobindo and Savarkar, and conceptualized a system where young men would come together, play games, usually kabaddi, sing patriotic songs, wear a uniform, play in a military-style band and conduct a march-past.

While political Hinduism has had an admiration for European militaristic traditions, this has been interpreted by some analysts to suggest that its uniform (white shirt and khaki shorts[108]) was borrowed from fascist groups. But the uniform had much more in common with something Hegdewar and others saw and experienced locally; it mirrors the look and colour scheme of the colonial police, which was a lived reality for the founders of the RSS. The 'paramilitary' training that RSS gatherings, called *shakhas* ('branches') in Hindi, provided, were mainly old Indian martial skills, such as wielding a wooden stick as a weapon and some sword-and-dagger fighting, and shooting practice using air guns. The quest was to awaken, as Vivekananda had said, the martial spirit, which in turn would instil values of courage and sacrifice.

Moonje had visited military academies across Europe in 1931 as he had been keen on military training for boys and young men. He also met Italian Prime Minister Benito Mussolini in March 1931 and expressed admiration for such training schools—though not for Mussolini or his politics but specifically for the organizational methods and disciplined training of young men, which Moonje thought was necessary in a country like India fighting colonial rule, including through revolutionary methods.

'Every aspiring and growing Nation needs such organisations. India needs them most for her military regeneration. During the British Domination of the last 150 years Indians have been waved away from the military profession but India now desires to prepare herself for under-taking the responsibility for her own defence and I am working for it. I have already started an organisation of my own, conceived independently with similar objectives. I shall have no hesitation to raise my voice from the public platform both in India and England when occasion may arise in praise of your Balilla and Fascist organisations. I wish them good luck and every success.'[109]

This meeting between Moonje and Mussolini has been interpreted by some researchers as a showcase of organized political Hinduism's ideological, and not only institutional, reference points,[110] whereas others have argued that Moonje drew inspiration from other sources as well, not only from military training schools across Europe and not just Germany and Italy, and in 1931, 'not many Indian leaders knew or cared much about the real face of fascism'.[111] Gandhi, in fact, met Mussolini the same year, about six months previously, and wrote about the meeting in admiring terms:

> 'Mussolini is an enigma to me. Many of the reforms he has made attract me. He seems to have done a great deal for the peasantry. Of course the iron glove is there. But allowing that force is the basis of Western society, Mussolini's reforms deserve an impartial study. His care of the poor people, his opposition to over urbanization, his attempt to bring about co-ordination between capital and labour seem to me to demand very careful attention. I would like you to enlighten me on these matters. My own fundamental doubt of course abides in that these reforms are forced. But that is true even of democratic institutions. What strikes me is that behind Mussolini's ruthlessness is the motive of serving his people. Even behind his bombastic speeches there is a ring of sincerity and burning love for his people. It also seems to me that the bulk of the Italians like Mussolini's iron rule.'[112]

Hegdewar, who had once been expelled from school for singing 'Vande Mataram' and spent time in prison as a member of the Congress, had not built the RSS as a political outfit; for that, there was the Congress, the Hindu Mahasabha and others. The focus of the RSS was to be a society—building people, better Hindus, stronger Hindus—who could take their rightful place in the nation. Accordingly, Hegdewar himself participated in Gandhi's Dandi March and Salt Satyagraha[113] but kept his organization out. Members of the RSS participated in various anti-colonial movements but mostly as individuals.

In the meantime, after a decade in England, Jinnah, who left the Congress in 1920 and remained a member only of the Muslim League, returned to India. He had spent large parts of the previous decade in England as a successful barrister with a home in Hampstead.

But by the mid-1930s, Jinnah was back in India and was the undisputed leader of the Muslim League. A year before Jinnah's return to India, a Cambridge-trained Muslim nationalist, Chaudhary Rahmat Ali, presented a pamphlet to delegates of the Third Round Table Conference.[114] The document demanded for the first time, a homeland only for Muslims—Pakistan—carved out of five northern parts of India: Punjab, Afghan Province or North-West Frontier Province, Kashmir, Sindh and Balochistan. It said:

'Our brave but voiceless nation is being sacrificed on the altar of Hindu Nationalism not only by the non-Muslims, but to the lasting disgrace of Islam, by our own so-called leaders, with reckless disregard to our future and in utter contempt of the teachings of history. The Indian Muslim Delegation at the Round Table Conference have committed an inexcusable and prodigious blunder. They have submitted, in the name of Hindu Nationalism, to the perpetual subjection of the ill-starred Muslim nation. These leaders have already agreed, without any protest or demur and without any reservation, to a Constitution based on the principle of an All-India Federation. This, in essence, amounts to nothing less than signing the death-warrant of Islam and its future in India. In doing so, they have taken shelter behind the so-called Mandate from the community. But they forgot that that suicidal Mandate was framed and formulated by their own hands. That Mandate was not the Mandate of the Muslims of India.'[115]

Soon after Jinnah returned as the leader of the Muslim League to India, someone more heavyweight, the scholarly poet Iqbal, wrote two letters to Jinnah (one in May and the other in June 1937). Iqbal spelt out in less emotional, but in much greater detail, the argument for Pakistan. In the first, Iqbal argued that the only solution to poverty among Muslims in India is:

'. . . the enforcement of the Law of Islam and its further development in the light of modern ideas. After a long and careful study of Islamic Law I have come to the conclusion that if this system of Law is properly understood and applied, at last the right to subsistence is secured to every body. But the enforcement and development of the Shariat of Islam is impossible in this country without a free Muslim state or states. This has been my honest conviction for many years and I still believe this to be the only way to solve the problem of bread for Muslims as well as to secure a peaceful India . . . If such a thing is impossible in India the only other alternative is a civil war which as a matter of fact has been going on for some time in the shape of Hindu Muslim riots.'[116]

The second letter, in which Iqbal starts by apologizing for writing so frequently to Jinnah, describes some of these riots. 'During the last few months, there has been a series of Hindu-Muslim riots in India. In North-West India alone there have been at least three riots during the last three months and at least four cases of vilification of the Prophet by Hindus and Sikhs. In each of these four cases, the vilifier has been murdered . . .'[117] Iqbal goes on to say that he believes, '. . . In the Hindu-majority provinces, the Hindus have of course absolute majorities, and can ignore Muslims altogether. In Muslim majority provinces, the Muslims are made entirely dependent on Hindus. I have no doubt in my mind that this constitution is calculated to do infinite harm to the Indian Muslims. Apart from this, it is no solution of the economic problem which is so acute among Muslims.'[118] Iqbal also said in the second letter that he considered the Hindu Mahasabha to be the 'real representatives of the masses of the Hindus' and believed that it did want a shared homeland for Hindus and Muslims.

As Jinnah consolidated the influence of the Muslim League in the country and his own leadership of the League, the very year that Iqbal wrote his letters to Jinnah and identified the Hindu Mahasabha as its primary antagonist, Savarkar was finally given the freedom to move out of Ratnagiri, where he had been confined after his return from the Cellular Jail in the Andaman Islands. Like Jinnah, he started expansive work to expand the Mahasabha's footprint. And not only would Iqbal talk about two nations in 1937 but so would Savarkar: 'India cannot be assumed to be an unitarian and homogenous nation, but on the contrary there are two nations in the main [sic], the Hindus and the Muslims in India.'[119]

But in the same speech, Savarkar also said,

'Let the Indian State be purely Indian. Let it not recognize any invidious distinctions whatsoever as regards the franchise, public services, offices, taxation on the grounds of religion and race. Let no cognizance be taken whatsoever of man being

Hindu or Mohammedan, Christian or Jew. Let all citizens of that Indian State be treated according to their individual worth irrespective of their religious or racial percentage in the general population . . . If such an Indian State is kept in view, the Hindu Sanghatanists will, in the interest of Hindu Sangathan itself, be the first to offer their whole-hearted loyalty to it. I for one and thousands of the Mahasabhaites like me have set this ideal of an Indian State as our political goal ever since the beginning of our political career and shall continue to work for its consummation to the end of our life. Can any attitude towards an Indian State be more national than that?'[120]

This contradiction notwithstanding, the lines were swiftly hardening. As the winds of Pakistan blew rapidly, so did the Hindu Mahasabha's. In 1937, at the Lucknow session of the Muslim League, Jinnah declared:

'. . . the majority community have clearly shown their hand: that Hindustan is for the Hindus; only the Congress masquerades under the name of nationalism, whereas the Hindu Mahasabha does not mince words. The result of the present Congress Party policy will be, I venture to say, class bitterness, communal war, and strengthening of the imperialistic hold as a consequence . . . I find that a very tense feeling of excitement has been created, and the British Government, out of sheer desperation, are resorting to repressive measures and ruthlessly dealing with the public opinion of the Arabs in Palestine. The Muslims of India will stand solidly, and will help the Arabs in every way they can in their brave and just struggle that they are carrying on against all odds . . . Eighty millions of Musalmans in India have nothing to fear. They have their destiny in their hands, and as a well-knit, solid, organised, united force can face any danger; and withstand any opposition to its united front and wishes.'[121]

Savarkar responded by saying,

'We, though we form the overwhelming majority in the land, do not want any special privileges for our Hindudom; nay more, we are even willing to guarantee special protection for the language, culture and religion of the Mohammedans as a minority if they also promise not to infringe on the equal liberty of other communities in India to follow their own ways within their own respective houses and not try to dominate and humiliate the Hindus. But knowing full well the anti-Indian designs of the pan-Islamic movement, with a link of Moslem nations from Arabia to Afghanistan bound by their recent offensive and defensive alliances and the ferocious tendencies of the frontier tribes to oppress the Hindus out of religious and racial hatred, we Hindus are not going to trust you any longer with any more blank cheques.'[122]

What had long been antagonistic in history, and in rhetoric, was once again becoming a battle in the trenches. Both sides now found themselves facing one another as political organizations, and to the adherents of political Hinduism, here was what had always been feared: the idea come alive that Muslims would not accept anything but their own rule in India.

Under Savarkar's leadership, the Mahasabha was becoming a national party for the first time, the RSS was steadily growing as a cultural force focused on expanding the network of shakhas, while with Jinnah at its helm, the Muslim League had never been as potent. But the fear of 'the other' seemed to be heightening with each speech. Both Jinnah and Savarkar felt that independence without adequate protection for their communities would be disastrous. Additionally, in Savarkar's opinion, '. . . our countrymen belonging to the Parsi, Jew and Christian communities have extended their readiness to abide by the safeguards laid down as reasonable for the minorities which the Hindu Mahasabha also is ever willing to guarantee. The fact is that it is not a question of minorities, but of one minority, the Moslem minority alone.'[123]

1937 was also a defining year for both the Muslim League and the Hindu Mahasabha because, in spite of their efforts, the Congress swept most of the seats in the provincial elections and created government bodies with small pockets of Muslim winners. In no region had the Muslim League been able to clearly form a majority government. Jinnah and Tilak had once hoped for separate electorates but Gandhi's ideal of unified electorates of Hindus and Muslims, and Hindu symbolism including bhajans, prayer meetings and talk of Ram Rajya, had ended that plan. Now the Congress, with its claims of representing all communities, was winning elections with large majorities but not really managing to get the Muslim votes, which were widely divided between the League and other local political parties. The Hindu votes were clearly mostly going to the Congress. This version of things seemed very much like political powerlessness to Jinnah and his followers. For Savarkar, just freed from Ratnagiri, this was just the right motivation to launch a countrywide campaign and movement.

One major campaign that Savarkar took up in the late 1930s was pushing for greater freedom and representation for Hindus under the rule of the Nizam of Hyderabad, then one of the wealthiest men in the world. The Nizam, a seventh-generation ruler, governed a minority Muslim population state with around 85 per cent Hindu population. But Hindus were a tiny part of his administration, Urdu was the official language of the state even though most did not speak it[124] and explicit rules were created to prevent the creation, or even upkeep, of Hindu temples.[125] A year-long civil resistance movement fronted by Savarkar spread the news of the plight of Hindus, including the mass torture of protestors, and led to the announcement of administrative reforms including far-reaching civil liberties for Hindus and reservations in certain categories of jobs.

Savarkar's run-in with the Nizam and his views about the radical Islamism in the Hyderabad ruler's ranks would, in a few years, be echoed by the powerful party chief of the Congress, and India's first deputy prime minister and home minister, Sardar Vallabhbhai Patel.

In the meantime, Savarkar's popularity was attracting talent from different parts of the country. One of these was another England-trainer lawyer and educationist from Bengal, Syama Prasad Mookerjee. Mookerjee had started his political career with the Congress and was inspired by Savarkar to join the Mahasabha, horrified by what he saw as excesses of Muslim parties including the Muslim League in Bengal and Congress inaction. So, when Savarkar came touring to Calcutta, a major conference of Hindu leaders was held in December 1930 in the city,[126] and Mookerjee presided over it. Savarkar had said, 'It is you [the Congress] who have initiated the Moslems into the belief that the more they demand the more you yield, the more they frown the more you placate, the more they pocket the more you offer, the more thankless they grow the more afflicted you are with craving for their thanks.'[127] Soon, Mookerjee was persuaded to join the Mahasabha, with, it seems, the sotto voce blessings of Gandhi, who told him, 'Somebody was needed to lead the Hindus after Malviyaji[128] . . . Patel is a Congressman with a Hindu mind, you be a Hindu Sabhaite with a Congress mind.'[129]

The comparison with Sardar Vallabhbhai Patel is worth detailing at this juncture. A farmer's son who worked up the ranks as a lawyer, funded his training as a barrister in England, he then returned to become one of the most prominent lawyers in the country. Until, inspired by Gandhi, he joined the freedom movement in 1920. While devoted to Gandhi, Patel was the most pragmatic among the trio of Gandhi, Nehru and himself. He had the responsibility of raising funds for the party and ensuring that their campaigns were properly organized on the ground. Patel is also usually credited for being the pivotal force in the negotiations of the union of more than 500 'princely states', or royal kingdoms, which had hereditary rulers who had governed under British overlordship into the new democratic union of the Indian republic. It was Patel who had spearheaded efforts to merge these princely states peacefully with the erstwhile British government to create the united independent India.

Patel was a lifelong believer in the need for Hindu-Muslim unity, and in the early years, believed this was inevitable. For instance, in 1921, Patel was telling a gathering[130], 'Even today, our Muslim brothers continue to believe that since the Hindus are in a majority, they, the Muslims would be able to defend their rights so long as the British Government continues to rule India. But those very Muslims have started believing Hindus are their friends.'[131] Later that same year, he was saying[132], 'We have tried to overcome our weaknesses honestly and in a definite manner. The proof, if any proof is needed, is Hindu Muslim unity . . . Similarly, we have established cordial relations with Parsis, Christians and other citizens of the country.'[133]

This continued in the 1930s too, with Patel taking the kind of stance Nehru would, declaring in 1931[134]:

'Having removed from within us our weaknesses, we have seen to it that we do procure the purity of heart with a true conscience and earnestness. The most direct evidence of this is (in) the Hindu-Muslim unity. Up to this time we never had faith in each other, and we used to take each other (Hindus and Musalmans[135]) to be the natural enemies of each other, but now we have commenced to love each other and have been living on terms of complete intimacy . . . On similar terms of friendship have we been living with Parsees[136], Christians and other countrymen. Let those who talk of communal representation and seats in the Council come with me to rural India where there was no communal problem to solve. The only problem faced by that part of India was the problem of hunger and of bread.'[137]

But the Lahore session of the Muslim League in 1940 was a definitive moment in the history of India's freedom movement. In a terse short set of bullet points, it laid out its main demand:

'that no constitutional plan would be workable in this country or acceptable to Muslims unless it is designed on the following basic principle, namely that geographically contiguous units are demarcated into regions which should be so constituted, with such territorial readjustments as may be necessary, that the areas in which the Muslims are numerically in a majority as in the North-Western and Eastern Zones of India, should be grouped to constitute "Independent States" in which the constituent units shall be autonomous and sovereign.'[138]

The demand for Pakistan had been formally placed. In his speech at the Lahore session, Jinnah explained why this was the main demand of the League and why he was so adamant about it:

'It is extremely difficult to appreciate why our Hindu friends fail to understand the real nature of Islam and Hinduism. They are not religions in the strict sense of the word, but are, in fact, different and distinct social orders; and it is a dream that the Hindus and Muslims can ever evolve a common nationality; and this misconception of one Indian nation has gone far beyond the limits and is the cause of more of our troubles and will lead India to destruction if we fail to revise our notions in time. The Hindus and Muslims belong to two different religious philosophies, social customs, and literature[s]. They neither intermarry nor interdine together, and indeed they belong to two different civilizations which are based mainly on conflicting ideas and conceptions. Their aspects on life, and of life, are different. It is quite clear that Hindus and Mussalmans derive their inspiration from different sources of history. They have different epics, their heroes are different, and different episode[s]. Very often the hero of one is a foe of the other, and likewise their victories and defeats overlap. To yoke together two such nations under a single state, one as a numerical minority and the other as a majority, must lead to growing discontent, and final destruction of any fabric that may be so built up for the government of such a state.'[139]

This changed everything. What had been discussed, deliberated and argued upon, was now laid down on paper, in concrete shape and form.

After the declaration of the final demand for Pakistan by Jinnah and the Muslim League, in 1942, we found Patel responding to Gandhi[140] who told him in a letter, 'You should try to learn Urdu.'[141]

Patel responds, 'Sixty-six years are over and this earthen vessel is near to cracking. It is very late to learn Urdu but I will try. All the same, your learning Urdu doesn't seem to have helped. The more you try to get close to them [Muslims], the more they flee from you.'[142]

In this statement of Patel, we hear the echo of Savarkar's viewpoint expressed in around the same period, '. . . Nehru says that they accepted Pakistan to avoid bloodshed. On the contrary, they will again use threats of bloodshed in order to press their additional demands. If you do not stop them, there would come about 14 Pakistans. They will demand Mayostan near Alwar, in the South they will demand Moplahstan in Kerala and in Hyderabad they will demand Nizamistan. Their demands will have to be crushed by the policy of reciprocity.'[143] In time, it would fall upon Patel to prevent this in Hyderabad and elsewhere.

This hardened tone is apparent in many of Patel's statements and decisions from that point. He was not the only one hardening their views.

Savarkar and the Hindu Mahasabha were determined to make the nation see what the motivations for Pakistan really were—not merely a geographical ambition, but a deep-seated religious divide, grounded in theological difference, as B.R. Ambedkar explained in his book *Pakistan, or the Partition of India*.[144] Ambedkar wrote:

'The real explanation of this failure of Hindu-Muslim unity lies in the failure to realize that what stands between the Hindus and Muslims is not a mere matter of difference, and that this antagonism is not to be attributed to material causes. It is formed by causes which take their origin in historical, religious, cultural and social antipathy, of which political antipathy is only a reflection. These form one deep river of discontent which, being regularly fed by these sources, keeps on mounting to a head and overflowing its ordinary channels. Any current of water flowing from another source, however pure, when it joins it, instead of altering the colour or diluting its strength, becomes lost in the mainstream. The silt of this antagonism which this current has deposited, has become permanent and deep. So long as this silt keeps on accumulating and so long as this antagonism lasts, it is unnatural to expect this antipathy between Hindus and Muslims to give place to unity.'[145]

Jinnah told his supporters in July 1946, 'Today we have said goodbye to constitutions and constitutional methods. Throughout the painful negotiations, the two parties with whom we bargained held a pistol at us; one with power and machine guns behind it, and the other with non-cooperation and the threat to launch mass civil disobedience. This situation must be met . . . Today we have also forged a pistol and are prepared to use it.'[146]

It is important to note here that despite their very significant differences, the Hindu Mahasabha joined the Muslim League to run several provincial governments including in Sindh, the North-West Frontier Province and Bengal between 1939 and 1943 under the leadership of Savarkar and Syama Prasad Mookerjee. When the Congress gave the call of 'Quit India' in 1942 in the middle of British war efforts in the Second World War, the Hindu Mahasabha did not participate as its leaders felt that it would not lead to any gains, and it would be better to take the opportunity to build military capabilities instead among Hindus. But all this would change with the bloodletting in August 1946.

The Muslim League was to observe 'Direct Action Day' on 16 August 1946. On 2 August 1946, faced with what he saw as intransigence from the Muslim League and its supporters, Patel is found saying, 'Much can be done by love, but nothing by holding a pistol to our heads. You [Muslim League] cannot get your object by threats. If you are still keen on freedom, come, let us sit together like two brothers and arrive at a settlement.'[147]

Massive riots broke out in Bengal on Direct Action Day with the epicentre being Calcutta and within seventy-two hours, by conservative estimates, around 4000 had been slaughtered and one lakh rendered homeless.

Patel was deeply critical of what had happened, and at the end of August, he was saying, 'Unfortunately, the Muslim leadership of today has chosen to take a different course. We all feel ashamed of what has happened in Calcutta. No Indian can help feeling sorry about it. It has brought discredit to the country and has disgraced the League all over.'[148] Lord Wavell, the then viceroy and governor-general of India, would later claim that Gandhi had told him at the end of August, 'If India wants blood bath she shall have it . . . if a bloodbath was necessary, it would come about in spite of non-violence.'[149]

By November of that year, Gandhi himself would have to travel and stay in Bengal—even at the risk of his own safety—to try and bring peace after a massacre of Hindus at Noakhali, including around 5000 murdered[150] and hundreds more raped or converted forcefully[151]. In November, Patel responded to the killings: 'They can ask for Pakistan; they can ask for all India. But this method would not pay . . . Poison would produce poison and the sword would ultimately have to be met by the sword.'[152] It is as Savarkar said, 'the spirit of reciprocity'.

The incident was mentioned as a complaint to Gandhi— it is unclear by who, but Patel suspected it was someone close to Nehru. Gandhi wrote to Patel, 'Your speeches are inflammatory . . . You make no distinction between violence and non-violence . . . You are teaching people to meet the sword by the sword. All this is very harmful if true.'[153] Patel replied by saying, '. . . it is my habit to tell people very unpalatable truths.'[154]

The echoes of Savarkar in Patel should not be read to suggest that the two men were ideologically identical to one another. Far from it. Patel was a Congressman through and through and devoted to Gandhi no matter what his differences with the Mahatma. Savarkar had never cared much for Gandhi and was lucid in his criticism: 'The [British] Government has nothing to fear while the Congress is led by men like Gandhiji who have been, as I am aware, not only pro-Government but sincerely pro-English throughout their lives.'[155]

Like Patel, Savarkar, too, had a penchant for telling what he saw as uncomfortable truths, especially about Gandhi. Savarkar had been a revolutionary for a large part of his life, and therefore considered that the Gandhian policy of 'absolute non-violence is so far from being a virtue that it is absolutely sinful because it is anti-humanitarian.'[156]

It was Savarkar's firm belief, and indeed this is a belief that goes to the ideological heart of political Hinduism, that the unqualified offering of non-violence, even when faced with violence, is understood by most as cowardice. And true freedom cannot be a by-product of cowardice.

Savarkar asserted:

'... that even if the Congress, the Hindu Mahasabha, the League produce a united demand signed by all the crores[157] of Indian citizens and ask for independence, Britain will never give it for the mere asking simply because it was united! The superstition that if but the Congress and the League demanded with one voice anything in the world, the demand would immediately be irresistible is responsible for making the value of the League inflated beyond all proportions. As soon as the League does join the Congress and even if the whole of India goes to England with a common demand, England will say, "Well, boys, you have behaved wonderfully. Hindus, Moslems—all united in common demand for independence, but as all of you united are still unitedly helpless, disarmed and unable to protect yourselves against armed aggression of the Axis Powers, moral obligation compels Great Britain to continue to rule India for your own protection."'[158]

This is why Savarkar advocated taking advantage of military training rather than non-violent non-cooperation, Congress-style, during the British war efforts during the Second World War. Savarkar argued:

'There is no question of co-operating or non-co-operating with the British Government in their war-efforts. The only question that you have before you is to find out how best you can turn this inevitable co-operation with the British as profitable to your own country as it is possible under our present circumstances to do. Because let it not be forgotten that those who fancy that they can claim not having co-operated with the Government and helped the war-efforts either on account of the demoralizing and hypocritical fad of

absolute non-violence and non-resistance even in the face of
an armed aggression or as a matter of policy simply because
they do not join the fighting forces, are but indulging in self-
deception and self-complacency. They pay taxes, serve in the
railway, postal, legal and even police department and are
openly out to pool up as much profit as they can in supplying
directly to the military departments clothing, blankets, food
and all other articles. Thus they too provide the Government
with the very sinews of war. For all practical purposes they
too cannot but cooperate with the British Government with
this only difference that their policy of boycotting the army
deprives the nation of the only outstanding benefit it could
have received in return for this inevitable co-operation. But
if we Hindusabhaites utilize this opportunity to the largest
measure possible by extending military co-operation with
the British Government in a responsive spirit and measure,
we shall do a double service to Hindudom. The first being
that we shall be able to defend our own country, hearths
and homes, if we are actually attacked by alien forces from
outside or by an internal anti-Hindu anarchy, secondly in
addition to this immediate benefit we shall be able to press on
the Hindu Militarization movement to such an extent as to
secure permanently a dominant position for the Hindus in the
Indian army, navy and air-force wherein today the Moslems
are almost monopolizing and the Hindu element is woefully
subordinated as a result of the criminal negligence towards
and even a downright condemnation of military life which
the Congress under the Gandhist lead had been guilty of.'[159]

Why was militarization so important to Savarkar? One part, of
course, was that he was a revolutionary, a believer in armed rebellion

against the injustice of colonial rule. The other was something that came from the statistical composition of the British Indian armed forces at that time and its repercussions. Once again, Ambedkar explained this most lucidly and courageously. Courageous because his book on Pakistan was published in 1945 amidst a tidal wave of friction between Hindus and Muslims.

Ambedkar wrote:

'. . . the Indian Army today is predominantly Muslim in its composition. The other is that the Musalmans who predominate are the Musalmans from the Punjab and the N.W.F.P. [North-West Frontier Province]. Such a composition of the Indian Army means that the Musalmans of the Punjab and the N.W.F.P. are made the sole defenders of India from foreign invasion. So patent has this fact become that the Musalmans of the Punjab and the N.W.F.P. are quite conscious of this proud position which has been assigned to them by the British, for reasons best known to them. For, one often hears them say that they are the "gatekeepers" of India. The Hindus must consider the problem of the defence of India in light of this crucial fact. How far can the Hindus depend upon these "gate-keepers" to hold the gate and protect the liberty and freedom of India? The answer to this question must depend upon who comes to force the gate open. It is obvious that there are only two foreign countries which are likely to force this gate from the North-West side of India, Russia or Afghanistan, the borders of both which touch the border of India. Which of them will invade India and when, no one can say definitely. If the invasion came from Russia, it may be hoped that these gate-keepers of India will be staunch and loyal enough to hold the gate and stop the invader. But suppose the Afghans singly or in combination with other Muslim States march on India, will these gate-keepers stop the invaders or will they open the gates and let them in? This is a question which no Hindu can afford to ignore. This is a question on which every Hindu must feel assured, because it is the most crucial question. It is possible to say that Afghanistan will never think of invading India. But a theory is best tested by examining its capacity to meet the worst case. The loyalty and dependability of this Army of the Punjabi and N.W.F.P. Muslims can only be tested by considering how it will behave in the event of an invasion by the Afghans. Will they respond to the call of the land of their birth or will they be swayed by the call of their religion, is the question which must be faced if ultimate security is to be obtained. It is not safe to seek to escape from these annoying and discomforting questions by believing that we need not worry about a foreign invasion so long as India is under the protection of the British. Such a complacent attitude is unforgivable to say the least. In the first place, the last war has shown that a situation may arise when Great Britain may not be able to protect India, although, that is the time when India needs her protection most. Secondly, the efficiency of an institution must be tested under natural conditions and not under artificial conditions. The behaviour of the Indian soldier under British control is artificial. His behaviour when he is under Indian control is his natural behaviour. British control does not allow much play to the natural instincts and natural sympathies of the men in the Army. That is why the men in the Army behave so well. But that is an artificial and not a natural condition. That the Indian Army behaves well under British control is no guarantee of its good behaviour under Indian control. A

Hindu must be satisfied that it will behave as well when British control is withdrawn.'[160]

This again does not imply that Ambedkar agreed fully with Savarkar's solution, even though he saw the problem similarly. Savarkar argued that the only way for Hindus and Muslims to coexist was to keep the country united and undivided, give only proportional representation based on population to different communities, allocate public services only on the basis of merit and ensure that every citizen has the fundamental right to worship, to their own language and other such rights.[161] Ambedkar thought this was merely pushing the real problem aside, which according to Ambedkar was:

> 'According to the Muslim Canon Law, the world is divided into two camps, Dar-ul-Islam (abode of Islam) and Dar-ul-Harb (abode of war). A country is Dar-ul-Islam when it is ruled by Muslims. A country is Dar-ul-Harb when Muslims only reside in it but are not rulers of it. That being the Canon Law of the Muslims, India cannot be the common motherland of the Hindus and the Musalmans. It can be the land of the Musalmans—but it cannot be the land of the Hindus and the Musalmans living as equals.'[162]

Ambedkar believed that Savarkar's path of allowing religious, language and cultural separateness and then insisting on one nation would 'give the Hindus an empire over the Muslims and thereby satisfy their vanity and their pride in being an imperial race. But it can never ensure a stable and peaceful future for the Hindus, for the simple reason that Muslims will never yield willing obedience to so dreadful an alternative.'[163]

Before we proceed further, perhaps it is important to highlight that seventy-five years later, it is Savarkar's vision that has come true. The Muslim population in India from 1947 onwards has remained broadly consistent and even rose consistently for many years, for instance, from 35 million to 172 million between 1951 and 2011.[164] On the contrary, in Muslim-majority Pakistan[165] and in Muslim-majority Bangladesh[166], which was created when the eastern part of Pakistan broke away in 1971, the fall of the Hindu population has been precipitous.

Here, it is vital to note how antagonists in this turbulence fed off the same narrative, though, of course, from different ends. People like Iqbal and later Jinnah and others in the Muslim League, and other Muslim leaders, built on the storyline that the religious affinity between the Muslim world especially from Afghanistan and beyond, and the Muslims in India, would ensure that these two groups would seamlessly merge to form one unified front, the former defending the latter in any time of crisis. The reason behind this argument, of course, was clear: the Indian Muslim was not only bound to their north/north-western cousins by faith but also by history. The undercurrent here is the Islamic conquest of India and subsequent Mughal rule, a history of nearly a thousand years which weighs heavily on the minds of all the interlocutors.

So, the violence/non-violence debate during this period and afterwards (in fact, even today) is intrinsically linked to history and the writing of history, and who got a chance to tell the story and in which way.

In the political Hinduism narrative, non-violent resistance became the sole story of how India freed itself from colonialism because it was promoted ideologically and institutionally by the Congress party, led by Gandhi, and Nehru, who took charge first of independent India (and remained in power for a long time), and thus, had the opportunity to establish the contours of the narrative of popular history about the freedom movement. But the truth, argued political Hinduism, is more complicated, and the role of violent rebellion and revolutionaries was as critical, in fact, if not more, to the British, leaving their 'jewel in the crown'.

There was support for this view of Savarkar from fellow revolutionaries early on. In 1937, Rash Bihari Bose, one of the most daredevil revolutionaries of the time, wrote to Savarkar saying, 'I do not think India can ever achieve independence though the Congress methods. I fear that the Congress leadership is playing into the hands of the British knowingly or otherwise seems to have strengthened the position of the British Government in India. I was delighted by your criticism and rebuttal of the Congress ideas and politics. This gives me hope and fills me with excitement.'[167]

This view has increasingly become more prominent in recent years. In 2022, at the annual Independence Day speech given by the incumbent prime minister, Modi took the opportunity to highlight the revolutionary history of the independence movement.[168] Modi's closest aide in government, Home Minister Amit Shah, who considers Savarkar one of the two biggest influences in his life,[169] has asked for India's independence history to be rewritten and offered as an example that without Savarkar's history of the 1857 revolt, describing it as the 'first war of independence', it would have forever been known as merely a mutiny.

But this argument is not confined to the proponents of political Hinduism. The advance in the examination of historical records has meant that others, like international affairs scholar Brahma Chellaney, have argued that Gandhian non-violent protest succeeded because the British were already spent after the

devastation of the Second World War and what really frightened
them to leave was a revolt in the British Indian navy off the shores
of Bombay[170] in 1946[171]. The British had held India using mostly
Indian soldiers who took orders from a handful of British officers.
But when they realized that the soldiers could perhaps no longer
be trusted, it was time to go. What added to British fears was
that one Indian revolutionary, Subhas Chandra Bose, a one-
time follower of Gandhi who fell out bitterly with the Mahatma,
managed to raise an army, the Indian National Army (INA), and
attack British India in 1944.

As one Cambridge scholar has written,

'After the Second World War, many British officials were
unsettled by fear of the Indian National Army, a military
organization made up of Indian prisoners of war released from
Japanese custody and led by the famous nationalist Subhas
Chandra Bose . . . Despite being defeated militarily, the INA
strengthened British unease that the continued occupation of
India would be met by violent resistance. Following the end of
the war, the trial of INA prisoners provided a serious problem
for colonial legitimacy and helped to stoke the mass nationalism
that forced Britain to withdraw in 1947.'[172]

Simply, without this history, the argument goes that Gandhian
non-violence would not have achieved much except a litany of
failed promises.

The years of the Second World War also introduced within
political Hinduism that which is asked of it even today: How
influenced was political Hinduism and its organizations of
fascism, and of Adolf Hitler? Certainly in the early years, before
the concentration camps and the gas chambers, many leaders

of anti-colonial movements saw the militaristic determination and cadre-building ability of early ultra-nationalist and fascist movements as the only effective counter to their lived experience of brutal colonial force. In Indonesia for instance:

'. . . fascism was seriously contemplated as such an "alternative" by Indonesian nationalists whose sympathies did not lie with socialism. That being said, fascism was more of a practical than an intellectual influence, a point that has been entirely missed in studies of illiberal and authoritarian trends in Indonesia . . . Fundamental elements such as organizational principles (e.g., the fascist ideal of the 'cadre' or 'squad') and sets of values (e.g., militarism) are essential building blocks of any political movement, and it is in this realm of performative politics and mass-mobilization that historians can detect a strong fascist imprint.'[173]

In India, Subhas Chandra Bose, the most famous of revolutionary activists, fled British imprisonment from Calcutta and travelled first to Germany to seek the support of the Third Reich to raise an army against the British, and even met Hitler once. Gandhi, as we have noted before, was willing to give Mussolini a chance in the early years. The case of Savarkar is similar, though in some parts more complicated.

From his own statements, it is clear that Savarkar did not see any difference in the early years of the war between the colonial oppression of Britain and that of Nazi Germany. He said:

'Pandit Jawaharlalji was characteristically vehement and declared in a number of public speeches that while the "Great Democracies, that is, of course, England and France, were

fighting for their very life, the only duty of India consisted
in extending unconditional help to Great Britain in this war
against those enemies of mankind—the Nazis." The fun of it
all was that, at that time, the Russians whom Jawaharlalji[174]
and the Congressites of his persuasion have ever been
worshipping as saviours of mankind were themselves hand
in glove and in open alliance with those very enemies of
mankind: the Nazis!'[175]

In *Hindutva*, that is as early as the 1920s, Savarkar wrote, 'If
the Zionists' dreams are ever realized—if Palestine becomes a
Jewish State and it will gladden us almost as much as our Jewish
friends.'[176] That the Hindus and the Jews were natural allies, in
fact, was established early in political Hindu ideology.

In 1940, we find Savarkar saying:

'We should neither hate nor love Nazists [sic] or Bolshevists
[sic] or Democrats simply on the ground of any theoretical
or bookish reasons. There is no reason to suppose that Hitler
must be a human monster because he passes off as a Nazi or
Churchill is a demi-God because he calls himself a Democrat.
Nazism proved undeniably the saviour of Germany under the
circumstances Germany was placed in; Bolshevism might have
suited Russia very well and we know what English democracy
has cost us.'[177]

Later, he would add, '. . . there is very little difference between
the imperialism of Great Britain and the authoritarian cult of the
Nazis so far, at any rate, as India is concerned.'[178]

In 1941, at the Bhagalpur session of the Hindu Mahasabha,
Savarkar reiterated:

'Under whatever label their principles are trotted out whether as Bolshevism or Nazism or Fascism or Republicanism or Parliamentarianism their armed domination over other peoples they have conquered or wish to conquer does not and cannot savour of anything else but autocratic tyranny . . . The sanest policy for us which practical politics demand is to befriend those who are likely to serve our country's interests in spite of any 'ism' they follow for themselves and to befriend only so long as it serves our purpose.'[179]

Savarkar's views focused on eradicating British colonial rule in India. Any force that weakened British power to him seemed worthy of admiration. But with time, as the reality of Nazi rule emerged, he seemed to have accommodated in his views the new authoritarian reality. The views of the Hindu Mahasabha as the main body representing political Hinduism were also offered by Nirmal Chandra Chatterjee, vice president of the Hindu Mahasabha, who had organized Savarkar's talks in Bengal. Chatterjee said in 1941, 'Our passionate adherence to democracy and freedom is based on the spiritual recognition of the Divinity of man. We are not only non-communal but we are nationalists and democrats. The Anti-Fascist Front must extend from the English Channel to the Bay of Bengal.'[180] Notably, it was Chatterjee who disagreed with Subhas Bose and argued that a Japanese invasion would be a calamity for Bengal.[181] As Hitler's crimes became more common knowledge, Chatterjee, on behalf of the Mahasabha, became more strident. In 1942, Chatterjee argued, 'In the conflict of ideologies, the Hindus have made their position perfectly clear. We hate Nazism and Fascism. We are the enemies of Hitler and Mussolini. We are longing and struggling for our own emancipation, and we want to repel any dictator who would try to reduce sections of humanity to slavery to serve the whims of his own megalomania.'[182] And by December 1943, Chatterjee was firm, 'We are wholeheartedly anti-Fascist. Every anti-Imperialist must be anti-Fascist.'[183]

But questions about Savarkar and fascism persisted because of a few sentences in a book called *We or Our Nationhood Defined*. This book was written by a man who took over the RSS when its founder, Hegdewar, died in June 1940. Before his death, Hegdewar selected his successor as the chief or the sarsanghachalak of the RSS. The man he chose dressed and lived like an ascetic with flowing hair, intense eyes and the simplest robes. Madadev Sadashivrao Golwalkar had a degree in marine biology and left his studies to become a monk at Vivekananda's Ramakrishna Mission. He had found a guru in Swami Akhandananda, one of the original founding monks of the mission and brother sages to Vivekananda. But the death of his guru had left Golwalkar a bit lost. He had found solace in the RSS and the mentorship of Hegdewar, who even got Golwalkar to train as a lawyer. It was Golwalkar who translated what was said to be the Marathi writings of Ganesh Savarkar, the brother of Vinayak Damodar Savarkar, and one of the founding members of the RSS, made lucid in English as *We or Our Nationhood Defined*. This book has a paragraph that reads,

'To keep up the purity of the race and its culture, Germany shocked the world by her purging the country of the Semitic Races—the Jews. Race pride at its highest has been manifested here. Germany has also shown how well nigh impossible it is for races and cultures, having differences going to the root, to be assimilated into one united whole, a good lesson for us in Hindustan to learn and profit by.'[184]

This paragraph had been read by many as Golwalkar's support for Nazis, but in recent times, more complex questions have emerged. In the same book, Golwalkar is admiring of the Jews who he says '. . . had maintained their race, religion, culture and language: all they wanted was their natural territory to complete their Nationality. The reconstruction of the Hebrew Nation in Palestine is just an affirmation of the fact that Country, Race, Religion, Culture and Language must exist unavoidably together to form a full Nation idea.'[185] The elements mentioned are what Golwalkar calls 'five continuities', necessary for a 'people' to constitute a 'nation'.

Thus, in the same text, Golwalkar seems to be admiring of the Jews and supportive of the Jewish nation, while sounding sympathetic to Nazism. That sounds improbable and perhaps the problem lies with the word 'highest' which could also mean 'most severe' or 'most extreme'. Also, Golwalkar was writing at a time of extreme Hindu-Muslim friction, and with talk of the breaking away of a 'Muslim nation', as we have seen earlier, prominently around him.

The probability of confused words also increases since Golwalkar wrote *We or Our Nationhood Defined* not as his original text but as a translation of Ganesh Savarkar's Marathi text *Rashtra Mimhansa* (Reflections on Nationhood).

To avoid this controversy perhaps, in 2006, the RSS said that it did not consider *We or Our Nationhood Defined* as part of their critical texts as it was a translation, and because it was written before M.S. Golwalkar became sarsanghachalak.[186]

This distancing from this text comes from an RSS monograph called *Shri Guruji and Indian Muslims* (2006) by the RSS ideologue Rakesh Sinha. It says:

'In spite of his open and liberal perspective on the question of nationalism and secularism, he [Golwalkar] has been treated most unfavourably by Islamic scholars and secularist social scientists. Selective and out of context citation of his views is unparallel in Indian academic. They largely quoted a treatise *We or Our Nationhood Defined* which was published in 1939. A baffled and elusive domestic and international politics certainly influenced the contents of the book. Not much water has flown down the river of Ganga since Guruji was introduced in the ideological mission of the RSS. The fact is that the book *We . . .* neither represents the views of the grown Guruji nor of the RSS.'[187]

Apart from the distancing from *We . . .*, the assertion that the most influential chief leader of the RSS in its history, who led the organization for three decades till his death in 1973, was liberal and indeed secular is striking in the study of the self-narrative of the organization.

The book Golwalkar wrote which is canonical within the RSS is called, simply, *Bunch of Thoughts* (1966). In this, Golwalkar detailed his thoughts on what a Hindu *rashtra* or a nation built on Hindu values would look like and what its relations with its minorities would be. It also takes care to underline its separation from fascism.

Golwalkar used a comparative analysis with Semitic faiths, namely Christianity, Islam and Judaism to make his argument. He believes that each of these faiths has tried to argue that they alone possess the final and most authentic spiritual answer and therefore have the right to deny others the right to exist. This argument is one of the most longstanding in the political Hinduism universe. That political Hinduism is reacting to the world, to the assault from Semitic faiths, and ideologies (Marxism, for instance, also described 'by the book' and the 'messenger'), and that the political Hinduism alternative represents a better, more evolved methodology of coexistence, an acceptance of 'all paths', a rejection of the idea of 'one true God' and therefore a diluted focus on 'saving souls' or religious conversion. Born of the reading of a history of iconoclastic attacks and created amidst religious massacre and bloodshed that led to the break-up of a country, demography is of vital concern to political Hinduism. Its overarching concern was, and is, the cultural and social protection of Hindu values.

'The first Semitic religion was Judaism, an intolerant faith. It was this intolerance that nailed Christ on the Cross. Then came Christianity, the child of the former. That too was equally intolerant. Doubtless Christ was a great saint. But later, what went on in the name of Christ had nothing to do with him. It was no Christianity but only "Churchianity". The saying "There was but one true Christian and he died on the Cross" is true to the letter. The Christians committed all sorts of atrocities on the Jews by giving them the label "Killers of Christ". Hitler is not an exception but a culmination of the 2000-year-long oppression of the Jews by the Christians. Then came Islam—a long story of "Sword and Koran" written in the tears and blood of millions of innocent human beings. It's latest chapter of "Pakistan", the self-declared theocratic Islamic State, is no different with the entire Hindu population butchered and driven out from its western wing and the same process continuing in its eastern wing. All these have ingrained in their blood intolerance of other faiths. The fear that Hindu Rashtra will imperil the existence of other religious groups arises by applying the above Semitic yardstick to it and imagining that the concept of Hindu Rashtra in analogous to that of the Semitic states notorious for their religious bigotry and persecutions.'[188]

But there is a solution in Golwalkar's mind. The Semitic and non-Semitic faiths can live together in India. It needs a certain reframing of notions of majority and minority. Golwalkar says:

'. . . all that is expected of our Muslim and Christian co-citizens is the shedding of the notions of their being "religious minorities" . . . As far as the national tradition of this land is concerned, it never considers that with a change in the method of worship, an individual ceases to be the son of the soil and should be treated as an alien. Here, in this land, there can be no objection to God being called by any name whatever. Ingrained in this soil is love and respect for all faiths and religious beliefs. He cannot be a son of this soil at all who is intolerant of other faiths.'[189]

To explain his point, Golwalkar gives the example of three countries—Turkey, Indonesia and Iran.

'Even now a Persian will remember his forefathers, will speak of Rustom[190] with great respect and honour. Rustom was not a Muslim. Kamal Pasha[191], "the Maker of Modern Turkey", restored the age-old national pattern of life and limited the role of Islam to personal worship of God. The example of Indonesia is extremely revealing. A majority of the Indonesians profess Islam. However, Saraswati and Ganesh are the presiding deities of their learning and knowledge. Children start their ABC in education with the pictorial Ramayana. One of our countrymen was amazed to see this when he had gone there. He asked a leading Indonesian, "How is it, though you are Muslims, you teach Ramayana to your children?" The Indonesian replied with pride, "Because. Sri Ramachandra[192] is our national hero par excellence. We very much desire that our children should emulate his lofty ideal. No doubt we belong to the Islamic faith. But that does not mean that we should give up our precious national heritage and values of life." What an excellent lesson for our Muslim friends here! There the names too are hundred per cent Hindu. Their previous President was Sukarna. His son, Kartikeya. The present President is Suhrida (distorted as Suharto in English) meaning "a true friend". Women too bear the proud names of Sita, Savitri, Damayanti, etc. Garuda[193], the mount of Vishnu, adorns the name of their airways.'

Golwalkar argues that rather than any harm to the minorities, the Hindu Rashtra offers them the best defence. He argues that pluralism of Hindu thoughts ensures that no belief system is discriminated against, or attacked, and points to the Jews and the Parsis.[194] He calls Hindutva:

'. . . the real and abiding cornerstone of national harmony and integration, subscribing to common national ideals irrespective of personal religious creeds . . . As such, the so-called minorities living here have nothing to lose but everything to gain by the rejuvenation of Hindu Rashtra. It is the Hindu thought alone which, in this wide world, has recognized the immanence of one Supreme Power in the entire humanity and has respected and even protected and encouraged all types of cults and creeds to grow and blossom to their fulfillment. All these factors point

to the fact that it is only a strong and resurgent Hindu Rashtra
that can stand guarantee to the free and prosperous life of the
so-called minorities here sharing equal opportunities.'[195]

It was under Golwalkar's relentless focus and ascetic temperament
that the RSS grew multifold to become, swiftly, one of the
biggest public organizations in the county and started to spread
around the world. Golwalkar discovered that, apart from the
traditional antagonists in competing religions and religious
ideologies that political Hinduism had been worried about for
the disintegration of the nation, there was also Marxism which
had its own variety of disintegrative forces against nationhood.
With Golwalkar's push as early as 1940, the RSS started a
branch in Kashmir, run by Balraj Madhok. Golwalkar himself
went to Kashmir in 1946. It is because of the success of the
RSS in spreading a network across Kashmir that in October
1947, Sardar Vallabhbhai Patel, as the first deputy minister and
interior minister, sought the help of Golwalkar to be an emissary
and convince Maharaja Hari Singh, the then ruler of Kashmir,
to accede his kingdom to India.

While Patel was encouraging of the role the RSS and its
leaders could play under certain circumstances[196], Nehru was a
strong critic. He warned chief ministers of various new states in
December 1947 that:

'We have a great deal of evidence to show that the RSS is
an organization which is in the nature of a private army . . .
The fact that the RSS is definitely and deliberately against
the present central and provincial governments need not be
considered enough for any action to be taken against them
and any legitimate propaganda might certainly be allowed. But

their activity more and more goes beyond these limits and it is desirable for provincial governments to keep a watchful eye and to take such actions as they may deem necessary.[197]'

Some of Nehru's objections about the Sangh also came from collisions on the ground between the expanding network of Sangh shakhas. A secret intelligence note on the RSS in 1942 mentioned that while the Sangh was first confined mainly to Maharashtra, its operations had spread to Punjab, Delhi, the United Provinces, Madras, Sindh, Bombay, Bihar, Berar, Gwalior, Indore, Bengal, Hyderabad, Mysore, the Central Provinces and even the North-West Frontier Province.[198]

The difference in tonality, if not always the institutional approach, between Patel and Nehru was not limited to the RSS or the Hindu Mahasabha but stretched across many other issues in the wider political Hinduism framework. The men had differing approaches on the issue of Kashmir, with Nehru often advocating the arguments of Sheikh Abdullah, the firebrand Kashmiri leader who complained of oppression by the Hindu ruler of the Muslim-majority state, Maharaja Hari Singh. Singh had a better relationship with Patel and was inclined to deal with him. Patel took the decision to send the Indian Army to defend Kashmir after it was attacked by Pakistani forces in the autumn of 1947 and registered his deep unhappiness about Nehru's decision to take the Kashmir issue to the United Nations[199], stating: 'You have seen what price we are paying in Kashmir. We went to the United Nations in order to bring the dispute to an early end. For six months we were maligned all over the world by the representatives of Pakistan and by people who had never seen this country and who did not understand what the problem of India or Pakistan or Kashmir was.'[200]

So fraught had become relations between Nehru, then the first prime minister of independent India, and Patel, the first deputy prime minister and home minister, that after a clash of views on Hindu-Muslim riots in Ajmer, both men offered to resign not only to one another but also via detailed notes to Mahatma Gandhi between December 1947 and early January 1948.[201]

These divergent views were soon to be tested when, on 30 January 1948, Mahatma Gandhi was murdered by a Hindu assassin, Nathuram Vinayak Godse, who had once been a devoted pupil of Savarkar[202] and had worked closely with the RSS and Golwalkar but had distanced himself from both because he felt they were not radical enough. Pledged to a monk-like austerity, including celibacy, Godse, the son of a minor postal department employee, was devoted to the revolutionary cause and to the Savarkarite ideals of political Hinduism—and fiercely against the creation of Pakistan. He had staged protests and heckled Gandhi and the Congress. Savarkar had stepped away from official duties of the Hindu Mahasabha in 1942 saying that he was exhausted from endless responsibilities as the only real crowd-puller of the Mahasabha recognized across the country at that time. But he remained active as a public intellectual and a politician, and mentor to revolution-minded young activists, writing often on topics he deemed worthwhile and constantly challenging the Congress status quo.

Now what Savarkar knew of Godse's plans to assassinate Gandhi remains fiercely debated as does the question of Godse's formal affiliation with the RSS. He did not have a designated post and the organization is by its nature made up as a voluntary association. But by the time he shot Gandhi, he was disillusioned by what he saw as the inefficacy of the Hindu Mahasabha and the RSS in being able to stop the creation of Pakistan. On 30

January 1948, Godse wrote in a letter to his co-conspirators, 'My mental condition is inflamed in the extreme, so that it has become impossible to find out any reliable way out of the political atmosphere[203]. I have therefore decided for myself to adopt a last and extreme step.'[204]

The murder of Mahatma Gandhi unleashed violent protests across the country; Maharashtrian Brahmins were attacked, many were killed and many more rendered homeless. Savarkar himself narrowly escaped a mob attack, and he and Golwalkar, along with thousands of Hindu Mahasabha and RSS workers, were arrested across the country.

In court, in his statement on his chargesheet, Nathuram Godse declared that Savarkar had no knowledge about his plans, and it was not true that Savarkar had blessed him and his mission. He also said:

'In my writings and speeches I have always advocated that the religious and communal consideration should be entirely eschewed in the public affairs of the country. At elections, inside and outside the legislatures and in the making and unmaking of Cabinets I have throughout stood for a secular State with joint electorates and to my mind this is the only sensible thing to do.'[205]

In the tradition of political Hinduism, Godse believed real secularism, perhaps it is better to say, fair secularism, was advocated by Savarkar, the Hindu Mahasabha and the RSS, and the Congress, especially under Gandhi, had done little to stop the divisiveness that began with the demand for separate electorates for Hindus and Muslims. 'What was the thin end of the wedge in the beginning became Pakistan in the end. The mistake however was begun with the laudable object of bringing about a united front amongst all classes in India in order to drive out the foreigner and it was hoped that separatism would eventually disappear.'[206] Godse remarked that he was not opposed to separate electorates but insisted that they had to be based proportionally on the percentage of population for each community. But despite this accommodation, the failure of the Congress to prevent Partition and the role of Gandhi, as Godse saw it, in consistently supporting Muslim arguments and demands, had caused the division of the country—'the image of our worship'[207], as Godse put it—and this was not acceptable to him. In this statement, Godse not only considered the history of his time but also noted the contributions of the ideal heroes in the pantheon of political Hinduism—from Shivaji to Savarkar.

'I am prepared to concede that Gandhiji did undergo sufferings for the sake of the nation. He did bring about an awakening in the minds of the people. He also did nothing for personal gain ... But I do maintain that even this servant of the country had no right to vivisect the country . . . I felt that this man should not be allowed to meet a natural death so that the world may know that he had to pay the penalty of his life for his unjust, anti-national and dangerous fanaticism towards a fanatical section of the country.'[208]

After his trial, Godse was sentenced to death. He was hanged on 15 November 1949. During his trial and time in prison, Godse noted with satisfaction that the Indian government had used military force to stop the attacks of the Muslim paramilitary forces, the Razakars, on Hindus in Hyderabad after long negotiations between the Nizam of Hyderabad and the Indian government led by Sardar Vallabhbhai Patel had failed. The Nizam ruled over a Hindu-majority population and tensions between his administration and his subjects had brewed for years. After Independence, he had been negotiating with Jinnah to join Pakistan or ostensibly remain independent, with Pakistani support. While Nehru was severely opposed to military action, Patel took the decision to roll in the army for Operation Polo, which led to Hyderabad joining the Indian Union. Godse noted his strong approval for what was codenamed 'Operation Polo'.[209]

With Gandhi's assassination and the death of Jinnah from lung cancer in September 1948, two of the main antagonists in the political Hinduism story disappeared. But the impact of their legacies had only just begun, and therefore the struggle between the two, their legacies and the proponents of political Hinduism had in a sense only just begun.

On 15 November 1949, at 7.15 a.m., just before he was hung, Nathuram Godse noted in the prison records that he had donated 101 rupees for the reconstruction of the Somnath temple in Gujarat. It was a project that had been taken up by Sardar Vallabhbhai Patel and would, in time, become an insignia of resistance in the world of political Hinduism.

4

The Third Way

The princely state of Junagadh in Gujarat was inhabited mostly by Hindus but was ruled over by a Muslim, animal-loving nawab, Sir Mahabatkhan Rasulkhanji, fond of conducting weddings for his dogs,[1] who preferred to accede to Jinnah and join Pakistan.

When the nawab of the landlocked kingdom wanted to accede to Pakistan despite the will of his people and protestations from India, in the middle of the stalemate, he fled to Karachi[2] with all his money, dogs and harem.

When Sardar Vallabhbhai Patel reached Junagadh, after a plebiscite overwhelmingly chose India, he saw the dilapidated Somnath temple, whose endless wealth had been looted countless times by Islamic marauders. He gave instructions to begin its rebuilding and upon his death in December 1950, his close aide, his fellow Gujarati lawyer and litterateur, K. M. Munshi, took up the task as he had been instructed by Patel.

Munshi recorded that Prime Minister Nehru tried to dissuade him from the task saying, 'I don't like you trying to restore Somnath. It is Hindu revivalism.'[3] Munshi refused to be stopped and completed the restoration of Somnath. Nehru also advised the first President Rajendra Prasad not to inaugurate the rebuilt Somnath, but the President refused to listen to him too. Interestingly, the other Nehru acolyte who was furiously opposed to the reconstruction of Somnath was K.M. Panikkar, India's ambassador to China, whom Vallabhbhai Patel once described as being fooled by Chinese intentions and being overly apologetic on behalf of the Mao government.

Somnath, since then, has become an emblem in political Hinduism, and it appears at critical junctures of our story as we move forward.

Meanwhile, both Savarkar and Golwalkar had condemned and mourned Gandhi's murder in explicit terms publicly. Both were arrested and their organizational work disbanded. Tens of thousands of activists of the Hindu Mahasabha and the RSS were arrested and many others were attacked in various parts of the country, especially in Maharashtra.

In court, the evidence was too weak to incriminate Savarkar and he was released one year later. Golwalkar was released in six months but the RSS activities remained banned. The Hindu Mahasabha, with a strong presence as a political party with leaders like Savarkar and Syama Prasad Mookerjee, was not banned, even though Godse and his co-conspirators were identified as members of the Hindu Mahasabha. This would, in time, underline to the RSS the need for their own people in Parliament, to speak for them. This would be a turning point moment for the RSS, which under both Hegdewar and Golwalkar had hitherto refused to join overtly political activities, preferring to remain in the 'cultural' domain. But the RSS, it occurred to Golwalkar and others, needed a political voice, and yet the RSS, built on ideas of austerity and a moral positioning, could not 'become political'. The middle path was to 'depute' people from the RSS to join political bodies. Syama Prasad Mookerjee, Atal Bihari Vajpayee, Lal Krishna Advani and others were first groomed in the RSS and then sent to the Jana Sangh (then BJP). This is true, of course, of Narendra Modi too. Sometimes, after a designated period working with the BJP, RSS members return to the parent body, as did Ram Madhav, who was groomed in the RSS since his teenage years, rose to become the national spokesperson of the RSS between 2003 and 2014, moved to the BJP to become national general secretary between 2014 and 2020, and then moved back to the RSS as a member of its national executive.

In 1948, during investigations that were overseen by Patel himself, an exchange of letters between Nehru and Patel shows the difference in perspective between the two men about the RSS. Nehru wrote to his deputy on 26 February 1948:

'More and more I have come to the conclusion that Bapu's[4] murder was not an isolated business but part of a much wider campaign organized chiefly by the RSS. A large number of RSS men have been arrested, probably many of them more or less innocent. But a considerable number of their key men are still abroad or underground or even sometimes flourishing in the open . . . The Delhi police has apparently a goodly number of sympathizers with the RSS . . . I have little doubt that the RSS organization is still fairly active in many ways and will hit back when it can.'[5]

To this, Patel replied:

'I have kept myself almost in daily touch with the progress of the investigation regarding Bapu's assassination case . . . the

RSS was not involved in it at all. It was a fanatical wing of the
Hindu Mahasabha directly under Savarkar that [hatched] the
conspiracy and saw it through . . . I have come to the conclusion
that the conspiracy of Bapu's assassination was not as wide as is
generally assumed, but was restricted to a handful of men who
have been his enemies for a very considerable time . . .'[6]

Despite Patel's early convictions on Savarkar's association with
the crime, the trial for Gandhi's murder acquitted Savarkar for
lack of evidence.[7] Patel had assured Syama Prasad Mookerjee
that the case against Savarkar would be 'approached purely from
a legal and judicial standpoint and political considerations should
not be imported into the matter.'[8] In the case of the RSS, it was
banned till July 1949 and many things contributed to its release,
including several rounds of confrontations, via the exchange of
letters, between Golwalkar and Nehru-Patel, and the submission
by T.R. Venkatrama Shastri, former advocate general of Madras
and head of the Servants of India Society, of a written constitution
of the RSS, which had hitherto lacked a written constitution. The
RSS leader Eknath Ranade had even discussed a proposal for RSS
members to join the Congress, an idea Patel approved of, and RSS
members like Madhukar Dattatreya 'Balasaheb' Deoras, P.B. Dani,
and then Mauli Chandra Sharma, and Deendayal Upadhyaya had
participated in the writing of the Constitution.[9] But the plan failed
when the Congress, while initially seeming to agree, finally rejected
the idea of dual memberships for RSS men—in order to join the
Congress, they would have to stop being part of the RSS, and this
was not acceptable to the RSS people. So the coming together
collapsed—this saga would one day be repeated.

The main interlocutor on behalf of political Hinduism
in this period with the Congress of Nehru and Patel was the

Bengali lawyer Syama Prasad Mookerjee, then a noted leader of the Hindu Mahasabha. It was he who wrote many of the letters to Patel, who was amenable to at least some of his suggestions. For instance, on 6 May 1948, Patel replied to a letter from Mookerjee saying, 'I quite agree with you that the Hindu Mahasabha as an organization was not concerned in the conspiracy that led to Gandhiji's murder; but at the same time, we cannot shut our eyes to the fact that an appreciable number of the members of the Mahasabha gloated over the tragedy and distributed sweets . . .'[10]

There were many reasons why Mookerjee was influential; after Savarkar, he was the most renowned leader of the Hindu Mahasabha with significant popularity in many parts of the country. Not only was he a lawyer from England but he was also one of the most influential educationists in the country, having become the youngest-ever vice chancellor of the University of Calcutta at the age of thirty-three in 1934, and, under the advice of Gandhi, became the first industries minister of India in Nehru's cabinet.

In a sense, it was Mookerjee with a zeal for business and ideas of enterprise, which he shared with Patel but not Nehru. Nehru once told the most prominent industrialist of India, J.R.D. Tata of the Tata conglomerate, 'I hate the very mention of profit.'[11] An exasperated Tata told Nehru, 'I am talking of the need of the public sector making a profit!'[12] To this, an unrepentant Nehru, replied, 'Never talk to me about the word profit, it is a dirty word.'[13] It is because of issues like these, among others, that the BJP continues to venerate Patel even today.

It was Mookerjee who wrote independent India's first industrial policy, focusing it on creating large-scale industrial projects and triggering the creation of indigenous businesses.

'Dr. Mookerjee had very clear ideas on the role of private capital in India's industrial development as also on the relationship between capital and labour. He was in favour of giving full scope to private enterprise under suitable government regulation and control, to play its part in India's industrialization . . . Apart from the basic objections to total nationalization, he was convinced that India lacked the requisite resources, experience and trained personnel to nationalize all industries and still run them efficiently. He was, therefore, opposed to loose talk about nationalization of all industries which antagonized private capital.'[14]

Instead, Mookerjee devised a 'mixed economy' plan which also had, apart from private companies, joint stock companies and private entrepreneurs on their boards but where the government paid up most of the initial capital. Mookerjee's efforts created a number of mega industrial institutions that India needed to build capacity, such as the Chittaranjan Locomotive Works, the Hindustan Aircraft Factory, the Sindri Fertilizer Factory and the Damodar Valley Corporation. Organizations that Mookerjee conceptualized, such as the All India Handicrafts Board, the All India Handloom Board and the Khadi and Village Industries Board, are still some of the main pillars of India's vast handicrafts sector.

Mookerjee was also an advocate of something that was already a core element of political Hinduism, the promotion of Hindi. He gave a famous speech on this subject during his time as minister 'which is remarkable, because a substantial part of the social class he belonged to, namely that of the Bengali middle-class *bhadralok*[15], was one of the staunch anglophiles, and looked down upon Hindi.'[16]

Mookerjee said in his speech on 13 September 1949:

'India has been a country of many languages . . . Some of my
friends spoke eloquently that a day might come when India shall
have one language and one language only. Frankly speaking, I
do not share that view . . . If it is claimed by anyone that by
passing an article in the Constitution of India, one language
is going to be accepted by all, by a process of coercion, I say,
that will not be possible to achieve. Unity in diversity is India's
keynote and must be achieved by a process of understanding
and consent . . . Left to myself, I would have certainly preferred
Sanskrit . . . Why do we accept Hindi? . . . It is for the main
reason that that is the one language which is understood by
the largest single majority in this country today. If 14 crores[17]
people out of the 32 today understand a particular language,
and it is also capable of progressive development, we say, let
us accept that language for the purposes of the whole of India,
but do it in such a way that in the interim period it may not
result in the deterioration of our official conduct of business or
administration and at no time retard true advancement of India
and her other great languages.'[18]

But for all of Syama Prasad Mookerjee's innovative views, he was not
destined to remain in Nehru's cabinet for too long. Syama Prasad
had cut his political teeth protesting the Government of India Act
of 1935, awarding separate electorates to Muslims and had been
at the forefront of the activism against the Noakhali massacre of
Hindus. Now, in 1950, the dreaded pogrom began again when,
between January and March 1950, tens of thousands of Hindus
were murdered in the eastern parts of Bengal—which were under
Pakistan after the partition of India—and many more forcefully

converted to Islam. Under encouragement and incitement from Islamabad, the Muslims of East Pakistan turned on the Hindus, who were mostly from the professional class, or landowners, and the bloodletting dramatically changed the demographics of the region, including major cities such as Dhaka. During this period, one of the most illustrative incidents was the return of Jogendranath Mandal, the lower-caste politician from India who had joined the Muslim League, encouraged by Jinnah's promises of a better future for the lower castes, who had become the first law and labour minister of Pakistan. But in 1950, Mandal returned horrified and heartbroken by the persecution and prejudice that he had seen and experienced. Jinnah had once professed to support a separate homeland for India's lower castes, apart from Pakistan for Muslims, but the only prominent lower caste who bought into his vision was soon ostracized and had to flee Pakistan.

Despite persistent entreaties to Nehru from Mookerjee who was supported by Patel, about the need for severe political, and even military action, in eastern Pakistan to stop the butchering of the Hindus, Nehru chose not to intervene strategically to stop the attacks against Hindus in east Pakistan. Instead, after considerable strategic inaction, Nehru finally signed a pact with the prime minister of Pakistan, Liaqat Ali Khan, which spoke about restoring minority rights, returning abducted women and property, and de-recognizing forced conversions.

But Mookerjee argued that this was farcical. The damage had long been done, and vast numbers of Hindus had already fled to India. From both parts of Pakistan, the east and the west, minorities, especially Hindus, had been ethnically cleansed. Mookerjee argued with Nehru that such agreements had no validity and would never be implemented on the ground—as history showed. When that argument failed to move the prime minister, he asked for 'the insertion of a penal clause to provide for sanctions against whichever country failed to honour the agreement.'[19] Nehru refused and the incident caused a major rift between the two men, and Syama Prasad Mookerjee resigned from the cabinet. In the Sardar Vallabhbhai Patel Papers in the National Archives, the detailed exchange between Nehru and Syama Prasad Mookerjee on the subject of the latter's resignation—with Patel as a sort of intermediary—can be found. While Nehru attempted to dissuade Mookerjee from resigning because it would send the wrong signal about the government, Mookerjee defended his position on 10 April 1950, by saying, 'From the very beginning I have tried to convince you that a pact of the kind you had in contemplation, or the one that you have now arrived at, will be no solution at all. It ignores the basic problem all together.'[20] This long exchange of letters shows Nehru trying to avoid what he believes would be a bit of a scandal with the resignation of Mookerjee coming side-by-side with the pact with Liaqat Ali Khan, but Mookerjee remains adamant and argues that not only does he not agree with Nehru's views on tackling Pakistan in the context of the Bengal violence, he does not agree with Nehru's broad outlook towards Pakistan. 'I can under no circumstances be party to it. Apart from the fact that it will bring little solace to the sufferers, it has certain features that are bound to give rise to fresh communal and political problems in India, the consequences of which we cannot foresee today. In my humble opinion, the policy you are following will fail. Time alone can prove this.'[21]

In his resignation speech to the Lok Sabha, the lower house in the Indian Parliament, on 19 April 1950, Mookerjee said:

'. . . the Bengal problem is not a provincial one. It raises issues of an all-India character and on its proper solution will depend the peace and prosperity, both economic and political, of the entire nation . . . There is an important difference in the approach to the problem of minorities in India and Pakistan. The vast majority of Muslims in India wanted the partition of the country on a communal basis, although I gladly recognize that there has been a small section of patriotic Muslims who consistently have identified themselves with national interests and suffered for it. The Hindus on the other hand were almost to a man definitely opposed to partition . . . if anyone analyses the course of events in Pakistan since its creation, it will be manifest [sic] that there is no honourable place for Hindus within that State.'[22]

The echoes of these arguments have never died out and they remain prominent today in the Modi government's plans to apply the Citizenship Amendment Act (CAA) that was passed by the Indian Parliament in 2019, which seeks to protect, through granting citizenships, minorities in Pakistan, Afghanistan and Bangladesh, namely Hindus, Sikhs, Jains, Buddhists, Parsis and Christians who have been in India on or before December 31, 2014. Faced with protests that such a rule discriminates specifically against Muslims, the government argued that minorities who have been traditionally persecuted in these countries must be able to count on India to provide refuge. The Indian Ministry of External Affairs regularly points out atrocities on minorities in Pakistan[23] and India protested in 2021 when Hindus in Bangladesh were attacked during the autumnal Durga Puja festival of Hindus, including urging condemnation and action from Bangladeshi prime minister Sheikh Hasina.[24] Indian Home Minister Amit Shah has also raised the issue of attacks on Hindus with his Bangladeshi counterpart in late 2022.[25]

One of the things that Mookerjee pointed out was the change in demographics in India, meaning the rise in the Muslim population vis-à-vis Hindus and others, and this is an issue that continues to be an integral part of political Hinduism and its concerns even today. In Assam and Bengal, regions neighbouring Bangladesh (erstwhile East Pakistan), this is still a contentious topic. As recently as March 2022, the incumbent chief minister of Assam, from the BJP, noted that since the Muslim community in Assam now represented 35 per cent of the population, it could not be considered a minority any more.[26] The chief minister has also noted that 'According to the census of 2001 and 2011, the Muslim population of Assam grew constant at a rate of 29% while the growth rate of Hindus dipped from 15% in the 2001 census to 10% in the 2011 census. One can gauge how dangerous the difference between 29% and 10% is.'[27] These concerns have seeped into policy, with Home Minister Amit Shah asking for greater vigilance on the borders to stall demographic change via infiltration,[28] and the jurisdiction of India's Border Security Force (BSF) has been expanded in 2021 to control demographic change through illegal immigration.[29]

In his speech, Syama Prasad Mookerjee said something that has echoed through the years and is particularly pertinent to the present moment in the subcontinent. He said:

'Today there is a general impression that there has been a failure both on the part of India and Pakistan to protect their minorities. The fact however is just the reverse of it. A hostile propaganda has been also carried on in some sections of the foreign press. This is a libel of India and truth must be made known to all who desire to know it.'[30]

In September 2022, Indian Minister for External Affairs, S. Jaishankar, told an audience in America,

> 'There are some newspapers, you know, exactly, what they are going to write . . . 'There are biases, efforts really to determine . . . Look, the more India goes its way and the people who believe that they were the custodians and the shapers of India lose ground in India, the more actually, some of these debaters gonna [sic] come outside . . . This is something which we need to be aware of. It is important to contest. It isn't because most Americans will not know what sort of nuances and complexities are back home, so, it's important not to sit back, not to let other people define me. That is something which I feel as a community is very important for us.'[31]

The state of minorities also remains a debating point between India and Pakistan. While former prime minister of Pakistan Imran Khan has argued that extremists were targeting minorities in India[32], India has responded with figures that the number of minorities has only grown in the country since Independence, highlighting that Pakistan in recent years has stopped publishing data about its minorities.[33]

Syama Prasad Mookerjee realized that the issues he was so concerned about would not be resolved under the Congress in a manner he would have liked (for instance, adding sanctions and a penalty clause in the Nehru-Liaqat Pact for violations in ensuring minority protection). There was only one route to take.

Mookerjee decided to start his own political party, which would be, in his ideation, a sort of umbrella body for anyone opposed to the Congress under Nehru. About eight months after Mookerjee left the Congress, in December 1950, the only real ally he had in the Congress, died. Before his death, Sardar Vallabhbhai Patel wrote two letters, one to Girija Shankar Bajpai, the Secretary-General in the External Affairs Ministry, and the other to Jawaharlal Nehru. In these letters, Patel, naturally circumspect, expresses his reservations about Mao's China. Patel makes a set of points in these letters, which has consistently been at the top of India's security concerns and headlines any strategic discussion in political Hinduism even today.

Having fought colonial imperialism all his life, Patel now warned in these letters that India had to be as worried about Communist imperialism as it has been about colonial imperialism. Having seen the way Mao's army swept across Tibet, Patel wrote, 'We cannot be friendly with China and must think in terms of defence against a determined, calculating, unscrupulous, ruthless, unprincipled and prejudiced combination of powers, of which the Chinese will be the spearhead.'[34]

From warning about unrestrained missionary activity in India's north-east, parts of it bordering Tibet, to complaining that India's approach to China was replete with 'a lack of firmness and unnecessary apology,'[35] Patel noted all the issues that were about to surface in the years to come. He warned that Nehru's idea that the Himalayas were a natural barrier for India may not be as secure as had been imagined. This too would come true when India lost its first major war to China under Nehru's rule in 1962. All these ideas have been fundamental to the way political Hinduism constructs the security dialogue of the country.

In fact, even in December 1950, Syama Prasad Mookerjee's views on China echoed the warnings of Patel:

'. . . what is the reply that China sent to India, when India asked China not to proceed on the path of violence in the matter of Tibet? The reply that China has sent has shocked, surprised and has given sorrow to the Government of India. I do not know whether it has made any difference with regard to China's settled policy in respect of Tibet, but here again, what is the definite policy of the Government of India with regard to Tibet? The Prime Minister just glossed over it. He said, "We have sent another request asking them to be peaceful, but has that made any difference?"'[36]

These views would be underlined by Savarkar in 1954 when, writing in the *Kesari* newspaper, he critiqued Nehru's attempt at peacemaking with China through the Panchsheel (Five Principles of Peaceful Coexistence) Agreement:

'When China, without even consulting India, invaded the buffer state of Tibet, India should at once have protested and demanded the fulfilment of rights and privileges as per her agreements and pacts entered into with Tibet. But our Indian Government was not able to do any such thing. We closed our eyes in the name of world peace and co-existence and did not even raise a finger against this invasion of Tibet. Neither did we help this buffer state of Tibet when her very existence was at stake. Why? The only reason that I visualise is our unpreparedness for such an eventuality and/or war . . . That is the reason why after swallowing the whole of Tibet the strong armies of China and Russia are now standing right on our borders in a state of complete preparedness and on the strength of the above, China is today openly playing the game of liquidating the remaining buffer states of Nepal and Bhutan . . . We have not been able to put before her an army which can match the strength of her armies on these borders of ours even today. This is precisely the reason why China dares come forward with such an unabashed claim on our territories.'[37]

Such were the ideas that Mookerjee sought to propagate when he aimed at creating a new political party. But where would the right partners with ample organizational skills and a dedicated cadre base be found? Some would come from the old Hindu Mahasabha but that had limited uses considering how discredited the Sabha had become after Gandhi's assassination. To tap into a new and growing source of energy, Mookerjee consulted Golwalkar, who, after his struggles at rehabilitating the RSS following Gandhi's assassination, had also understood the need for access to political power.

The coming together of Mookerjee's individual appeal and the RSS's cadre strength and ideological conviction created a new political force, which Mookerjee had first wanted to call the Young India Party or the All-India People's Party. But Hindi won the day and it was called the Bharatiya Jana Sangh (or the Indian People's Party).

The RSS sent some of its most hardworking, diligent and astute minds to help build and run the Jana Sangh, among them Balraj Madhok and Deendayal Upadhyay.

In the history of political Hinduism, in this phase, it was Mookerjee and then Upadhyay, who were the most influential and it is their ideals and ideas that made political Hinduism the force it would become. Madhok, who described Mookerjee as 'my guru', noted that Mookerjee wanted to build a 'nationalist alternative to the Congress'.[38]

One of the first hard stances Mookerjee took with his new party was to reiterate that Partition was a great failing and any dealing with Pakistan would have to be strictly on the basis of reciprocation, and the Kashmir dispute had only one solution: a reiteration that Kashmir is an inalienable and indivisible part of India. No UN resolution, no plebiscite, no special regulations or laws. Kashmir had been granted a sort of semi-autonomous status, which was noted as part of temporary measures under the new Indian Constitution. But Mookerjee was clear from the beginning, as the Jana Sangh, and then the BJP reiterates even today, there should not be special rules for any part of India.

It was a slogan from Syama Prasad Mookerjee which would become a slogan that is repeated by the BJP even today: '*Ek desh mein do bidhan, do pradhaan aur do nishaan nahi chalega*' (In one country, there cannot be two Constitutions, nor two prime ministers, and two national emblems or flags)—all of which had initially been allowed for Kashmir.[39]

But despite tireless efforts by Mookerjee and the discipline of the RSS men in the first general elections, held in 1951, the Jana Sangh could win only three seats,[40] one of which was won in Bengal by Mookerjee himself. The good news for Mookerjee and his supporters was that on the basis of the number of votes received, the Bharatiya Jana Sangh was declared a national party.

Back in Parliament, the key issues raised by Mookerjee are significant and we shall see later in the book how they remain fundamental to the BJP even today. Two issues are worth highlighting: Kashmir and the Hindu Code Bill.

It was Mookerjee who said about Nehru's Pakistan policy:

'I have never known this extraordinary spectacle of any self-respecting country being at war with another country and at the same time hugging that country to its bosom when the people of that country are preparing to wage war . . . If I am not mistaken, every day about 250 wagons are moving from India to West Pakistan carrying coal. What for? Not only to enable Pakistan to carry on her industries or other useful occupations but also to get ready to attack Kashmir . . . Does any country follow such a suicidal policy?'[41]

Syama Prasad Mookerjee was one of the first to demand economic sanctions against Pakistan.

On the Hindu Code Bill,[42] a social reform law that was introduced by the Nehru government only for Hindus, and no other community, Mookerjee objected that such measures were being taken only for one community and in a secular state, it should be applied to all. 'Stand for one social doctrine. If you believe that monogamy as a social system is the best that India should have then do not try to look at it through the Hindu door[43]. Look at it through the human door and make it applicable to all. Behave like a secular State at least in this instance . . .'

In Kashmir, the National Conference, led by Nehru's dear friend and Maharaja Hari Singh's rival, Sheikh Abdullah, was completely in charge and was responsible for the region's autonomy—but faced with incessant protests of neglect from the non-Muslim majority areas of Kashmir, such as Jammu and Ladakh. Mookerjee also objected to the fact that a special permit was needed to enter Kashmir and was a strong critic of Article 370, which emphasized Kashmir's separateness, including having its own flag, its own Constitution and, of course, its own prime minister and head of state.

When Abdullah arrested Pandit Prem Nath Dogra, from the same community as Maharaja Hari Singh, the last king of Kashmir and a respected Dogra leader, the protests against Sheikh Abdullah intensified and so did Mookerjee's criticism.

In May 1953, Syama Prasad Mookerjee decided to defy the rules and march into Kashmir without a permit. Among the men from his party who went with him were Balraj Madhok and a young journalist-poet named Atal Bihari Vajpayee. Mookerjee was immediately arrested and would spend forty days imprisoned by the government of Sheikh Abdullah. The persistent pain in his leg worsened and he received only boiled vegetables to eat. The medical treatment, by all accounts, seemed to have been rudimentary even though he was known to have had a heart attack before. He suffered a second heart attack and was then taken to a gynaecology hospital in a taxi instead of an ambulance and made to walk up a flight of stairs.[44] In June, even though doctors had recently assured that he was starting to feel better, Mookerjee died. His family and his party, and many others, have believed that there was an element of negligence, if not conspiracy, in the treatment of Mookerjee in Kashmir and his death. The questions regarding his death, including Nehru's refusal of an official inquiry about the death of Mookerjee, have cast a long shadow. Mookerjee's mother wrote to Nehru questioning the fact that even though the prime minister had visited Kashmir during Mookerjee's incarceration, he did not visit the opposition leader. N.C. Chatterjee, a barrister of repute, and a Hindu Mahasabha politician, who had first introduced Savarkar to Mookerjee, said in Parliament:

> 'what adds poignancy to the tragic death, that one of the greatest sons of India was robbed of his freedom, not by a government run by alien usurpers, but by a government which was manned by the children of the soil. The greatest tragedy was that he was kept as a prisoner behind prison bars, without any trial and he was treated like an ordinary criminal despite his serious illness because he loved his motherland deeply and passionately and because he sought in his way to maintain the unity of the country, and, if possible, to intensify and strengthen that unity and solidarity.'[45]

Syama Prasad Mookerjee's death has remained a pivot in Hindu politics, a sore point between the BJP and the Congress that has never been satisfactorily resolved.

With Mookerjee gone, the baton passed to a man who had entered politics from the RSS, and in many ways was the antithesis of Syama Prasad Mookerjee. Deendayal Upadhyaya had been a dedicated and promising student of English literature but could not study beyond the bachelor's level due to financial constraints. Directly influenced by Hegdewar, he had become the most rigorous kind of RSS *swayamsewak* or part-time volunteer; he became a *pracharak*, with a vow of celibacy and non-materialism (even personal bank accounts are discouraged) and devoted to the single cause of spreading the message about the ideology of the RSS. Reticent by nature, Upadhyaya was the perfect foil to Mookerjee, who was a flamboyant speaker and an activist at heart who was skilled in legal debate. Upadhyaya was scholarly and an organization man, devoted to the nitty-gritty of constructing a political base ground up.

In the analysis of political Hinduism,[46] few have considered with any depth the impact of Upadhyaya, who was the general secretary of the Bharatiya Jana Sangh for sixteen years from its inception in 1951 to 1967, then becoming its president in 1968. He died soon afterwards in a mysterious way. The Bharatiya Jana Sangh after Syama Prasad Mookerjee was shaped more by Upadhyaya, as general secretary, than the many illustrious men who became its president after Mookerjee, including Prem Nath Dogra, Balraj Madhok and one renowned Indologist and Leiden University PhD, Raghu Vira, who was part of the team of scholars that produced the definitive English critical edition translation of the great Indian epic, the Mahabharata.[47]

Upadhyaya's great contribution to the Jana Sangh was a brick-by-brick building of a political party that could embody the values of the RSS and also be able to build bridges with a larger political community. He was instrumental in nurturing leaders such as Atal Bihari Vajpayee and Lal Krishna Advani and taking the seat count of the party from three in 1951 to thirty-five in 1967.[48] For all his ideological impetus, Upadhyaya, quite like Savarkar and Mookerjee, was not averse to joining broad political coalitions against the Congress even when they included parties antithetical to the Jana Sangh and its politics, such as the Muslim League. Thus, the Jana Sangh under Upadhyaya joined the Samyukt Vidhyak Dal, a coalition of all anti-Congress political parties, both on the Left and the Right, after the 1967 national elections when the Congress fared much worse than expected.

But perhaps Upadhyaya's most seminal contribution was in developing what became the core intellectual ideology of political Hinduism, as represented by the BJP and the RSS. He called it 'integral humanism'. It has become the cornerstone of the political philosophy of political Hinduism.

The ideology of integral humanism was expounded by Upadhyaya to members of the Jana Sangh in April 1965 through four lectures. In these, Upadhyaya explained a world view that he explained was different from the prevailing polarities of his time, Nazism and communism. He had been influenced by what was happening in Europe and also the work of French philosopher Jacques Maritain, who had written a book called *Integral Humanism* in 1936. In this book, Maritain had proposed the idea that it is spiritual development that ought to lie at the heart of building a society, though, for him, this was spirituality rooted very much in Christian values and his Catholic beliefs, and finding meaning, contentment and happiness finally with Christ.

Deendayal Upadhyaya took these ideas and created a broader philosophical framework, including some ideas that had been propagated by Gandhi, such as *antodaya* or thinking above all else about the poorest or the least privileged, the 'last person', so to speak.

Like Gandhi, Upadhyaya was concerned about mindless adoption of Western ways and cultural mannerisms, but his main concern was a lack of what he called 'national identity' in independent India. Upadhyaya explained:

'It is essential that we think about our national identity. Without this identity there is no meaning of independence, nor can independence become the instrument of progress and happiness. As long as we are unaware of our national identity, we cannot recognize or develop all our potentialities. Under alien rule this identity is suppressed. That is why nations wish to remain independent so that they can progress according to their natural bent and can experience happiness in their endeavor. Nature is powerful. An attempt to go against nature or to disregard her leads to troubles. The natural instincts cannot be disregarded but it is possible to elevate this nature to the level of culture. Psychology informs us how by suppression of various natural instincts different mental disorders ensue. Such a person remains restless and dejected. His abilities slowly deteriorate and become perverted. The Nation too like the individual becomes a prey to numerous ills when its natural instincts are disregarded. The basic cause of the problems facing Bharat is the neglect of its national identity.'[49]

Deendayal Upadhyay fundamentally argued that India had a unique way of looking at its problems and would have to find its unique solutions. Borrowing any 'ism' and cut-pasting it on Indian conditions is not particularly useful. This is something repeated by top RSS functionaries such as RSS chief Mohan Bhagwat even today, He has said, 'Hinduism is a wrong word. "ism" is a closed concept. Hindutva, Hinduness is not any "ism" but a dynamic process.'⁵⁰ What he recommended was a deep dive into India's own culture, history and tradition to find ways of thinking and solutions that would be rooted in Indian culture.

Upadhyaya's ideal was a state that follows the principles of dharma.

'Thus the fundamental law of human nature is the standard for deciding the propriety of behavior in various situations. We have termed this very law as "Dharma". The nearest equivalent English term for Dharma can be "Innate law", which, however, does not express the full meaning of Dharma, since "Dharma" is supreme, our ideal of the state has been "Dharma Rajya". The king is supposed to protect Dharma. In olden times at the coronation ceremony the king used to recite three times: "There is no authority that can punish me" . . . Upon this, the Purohit⁵¹ used to strike the king on his back with a staff saying, "No, you are subject to the rule of Dharma. You are not sovereign." The king used to run around the sacred fire and the Purohit would follow him striking him with the staff. Thus after completing three rounds, the ceremony would come to an end. Thereby the king was unambiguously told that he was not an unpunishable sovereign. Dharma was above him, that even he was subject to Dharma. Can the people do whatever they please? It may be contended that democracy means just that. The people can do what they please. But in our country, even if people wish, they are not free to act contrary to Dharma . . .'⁵²

This would give rise to the question of what happens to minorities who do not believe in the principle of dharma, which is taken from Hinduism. Upadhyaya had an answer. He claimed that there would be a state based on the principles of dharma, which would be fundamentally non-discriminatory, and values would be, in the natural course, accommodative of everyone. He said:

'Dharma Rajya does not mean a theocratic state. Let us be very clear on this point; where a particular sect and its prophet or Guru, rule supreme, that is a theocratic state. All the rights are enjoyed by the followers of this particular sect. Others either cannot live in that country or at best enjoy a slave-like, secondary citizen's status . . . This does not happen in a Dharma Rajya. Rather, there is freedom to worship according to one's religion. In a theocratic state, one religion has all the rights and advantages, and there are direct or indirect restrictions on all other religions. Dharma Rajya accepts the importance of religion in the peace, happiness and progress of an individual. Therefore the state has the responsibility to maintain an atmosphere in which every individual can follow the religion of his choice and live in peace. The freedom has its inherent limits. I have the freedom to swing my hand, but as soon as there is conflict between my hand and someone else's nose, my freedom has to be restricted. I have no freedom to swing my hand so as to hit another person's nose. Where another person's freedom is likely to be encroached upon, my freedom ends. The freedom of both parties has to be ensured. Similarly every religion has the freedom to exist. But this freedom extends only as far as it does not encroach upon the religion of others. If such encroachment is carried on, it will have to be condemned as misuse of freedom and will have to be ended. Such limitations will be required in all aspects of life. Dharma Rajya ensures religious freedom and is not a theocratic state. Now-a-days the word 'secular state' is being used as opposed to theocratic state. The adoption of this word is mere imitation of the Western thought pattern. We had no need to import it. We called it a secular state to contrast it with Pakistan. There is some misunderstanding arising out of this. Religion was equated with Dharma and then secular state was meant to be a state without Dharma. Some said ours is a state (without Dharma), whereas others trying to find a better-sounding word called it Dharmanirkshepa (indifferent to Dharma state). But all these words are fundamentally erroneous. For a state can neither be without Dharma nor can it be indifferent to Dharma just as fire cannot be without heat. If fire loses heat, it does not remain fire any longer. A state which exists fundamentally to maintain Dharma to maintain law and order, can neither be *Needharma* nor *Dharmanirpeksha*. If it is *Needharma* it will be lawless state, and where there is lawlessness, where is the question of the existence of any state? In other words, Dharma and State are self-contradictory. State can only be Dharma Rajya (rule of Dharma) nothing else. Any other definition will conflict with the reason of its very existence. In a Dharma Rajya, the state is not absolutely powerful. It is subject [to] Dharma. We have always vested sovereignty in Dharma. Presently there has arisen a controversy. Parliament is sovereign or the Supreme Court? Legislature is higher or judiciary? This quarrel is like a quarrel whether left hand is more important or right hand? Both are limbs of the state, the Legislature is well as Judiciary. Both have distinct functions to perform in their individual sphere, each is supreme. To consider either one above the other would be mistake. Yet the legislators say, "we are higher", on the other hand, members of the Judiciary assert that they have a higher authority, since they interpret the laws which the Legislature makes. The Legislature claims to have given powers to the Judiciary. If necessary, the Legislature can change the Constitution. Hence it claims sovereignty. Now since powers are bestowed by the Constitution, they are talking of amendment to the Constitution. But I believe that even if by a majority the Constitution is amended, it will be against Dharma. In 'reality' both the Legislature and the Judiciary are on an equal plane. Neither the Legislature is higher nor the Judiciary. Dharma is higher than both. The Legislature will have to act according to Dharma and the Judiciary will have to act according to Dharma. Dharma will specify limits of both. The Legislature, the Judiciary or the people, none of these is supreme, Some will say, "Why! People are sovereign. They elect", but even the people are not sovereign because people too have no right to act against Dharma. If an elected government allows people to go against Dharma and does not punish, then that government is in reality a government of thieves. Even the general will cannot go against Dharma. Imagine the situation if by some manoeuvring, thieves gain a majority in the government and send one of their ranks as an executive! What will be the duty of the minority if the majority is of thieves and elects a thief to rule. The duty clearly will be to remove the representative elected by the majority. During the second world war when Hitler attacked France, the French army could not stall the onward march of Nazi troops. The then Prime Minister of France, Marshal Petain decided to surrender. The French public supported the decision, but De Gaulle escaped to London where he declared that he did not accept the surrender. France is independent and will remain so. From London, he formed a Government of France in Exile and eventually liberated France. Now if the majority rule is to be considered supreme, then De Gaulle's action will have to be condemned. He had no right to fight in the name of

independence. De Gaulle derived his right from the fact that
the French nation was above the majority public opinion. The
national Dharma is above all. Independence is Dharma of every
nation. To preserve independence, and to strive for regaining it
when lost is the duty of every citizen.'[53]

What remained sotto voce in this explanation was who would
be the defining authority in deciding whether something was
following dharmic principles or not? The answer for the RSS has
always been building or constructing a better quality of people—
as the organization is fond of saying, it does not, in reality, do
any other work than creating the right kinds of people—and
those people go on to do what is necessary. As is apparent, such a
definition can best be applied if *sangh* and *samaj* or the RSS and
the broader society become indistinguishable.

Deendayal Upadhyaya also had detailed thoughts on India's
political economy as communism had been considered a major
threat to the unity and integrity of India by political Hinduism. It
is important to remember that men like Upadhyaya were products
of a time when major, violent agitations had sprung up in various
parts of newly independent India demanding separate Pakistan-
style homelands, including on the basis of language and religion.
They were also surrounded by ideas of revolution, including
the communist revolution, and Western ideas of individual
freedom, which many saw as having a disintegrating effect on
the traditional family. When Upadhyaya was talking about his
theories, the old 'joint family' style of living in India where many
generations would live under the same roof was crumbling with
the rise of nuclear families. It was also a period when the Sangh[54]
had gone through a significant crisis after the assassination of
Gandhi and the rise of Nehru to near absolute power, with no

real competitor after the deaths of Vallabhbhai Patel and Syama Prasad Mookerjee. This meant that the Sangh had to operate constantly to avoid adverse scrutiny and yet consistently grow its networks and membership. M.S. Golwalkar was focused on spreading the RSS and its shakhas to every part of the country in this period while avoiding any direct confrontation with Nehru and the Congress. The political activity was left to Deendayal Upadhyaya and the Jana Sangh.

Nehru died in 1964 after the debacle of the war against China in 1962, the loss of which haunted him until the end. His faith in the India-China friendship had been dashed and it has been speculated[55] that the humiliating defeat and the failure of his dream of 'Asian unity' and 'Hindi-Chini-bhai-bhai'[56] drove him to his death.

In 1966, M.S. Golwalkar published a book called *Bunch of Thoughts*, which contained his speeches and thoughts about the world view of the RSS and the broader Sangh Parivar or organizations that were affiliated through the broad belief in political Hinduism. At the heart of the message that *Bunch of Thoughts* offers is the idea that India has something unique to offer in the discourse pitting capitalism versus communism and that it is a society built on attaining national strength on the basis of 'dharmic values'. Golwalkar also detailed all the places from where he saw threats to the nation: Muslim sub-nationalism and other kinds of sub-nationalisms (he points to the connections between Christian missionaries and Naga rebels demanding a separate homeland carved out of Assam[57]), and India's failure to understand the threat from communism and China.

The solution to all of society's and the nation's problems, says Golwalkar, comes from two sources, which he defines as 'competition', and 'permissiveness'. He says:

'The first aspect of this pursuit of pleasure is the process of never ending competition. Each one competes with the other in amassing objects of enjoyment. The second aspect is what is nowadays described as the "permissive society" . . . In simple words, "permissiveness" means, the individual is left free to indulge in whatever way he chooses to enjoy himself. There is no restraint of any kind on him. It is unbridled licentious behaviour with respect to sex, food, drinks, family life, social intercourse and all such aspects. This is also reflected in their talk, writing and thinking as well. Will this type of permissiveness be conducive to the real happiness of man? The first and foremost effect of this trend would be the destruction of social fabric. The social contract theory on which the Western societies are based cannot stem this tide, because the theory is essentially one of mutual understanding between the individual and the society to protect each other's interests. But when the individual begins to assert that it is after all a contract between individuals, that basis of social integrity itself falls to the ground. The entity called the "society" will then disrupt and dissipate. And it requires not much of intelligence to guess what kind of fate awaits the pursuit of happiness by the individual where the society has disintegrated. It is only when the society is looked upon as a living corporate body of which the individual is a limb that the real unifying social consciousness will be ingrained in him. Then alone will he be able to restrain his erratic impulses and harmonise them with the interests of the society. And this is exactly what the Hindu philosophy propounds . . . The other element of the modern society is "competition". It is claimed that healthy competition is necessary for progress. But it is a matter of common experience that competition will not remain healthy for long. By its very nature it cannot remain healthy. Very soon, it degenerates. Competition, which implies bettering one's performance over the other, soon gives place to the urge to become better by pulling down the other. These days, such a trend is becoming more and more pronounced even in sports. After all, sports is played for pure joy and for increasing one's skill and efficiency. It should not matter much, who wins or loses. But we find that even there the atmosphere has no more remained cordial. The craze for winning by any means, fair or foul, and unwholesome rivalry are beginning to vitiate that field. If this could happen in the case of sports, then what to speak of other fields where material interests are directly involved! Now, what is all this competition intended for? It is, according to them, to "raise the standard of living" . . . Since their concept of happiness centres entirely round the satisfaction of the desires of senses, the term "raising the standards of living" has only come to mean more and more amassing of the objects of physical enjoyment, which becomes the major preoccupation of the individual to the exclusion of all other thoughts and aspirations. In order to procure the objects of physical pleasures, accumulation of wealth follows. To achieve more and more wealth, power becomes necessary. But the insatiable hunger for physical enjoyment does not allow one to stop within one's own national boundaries. On the strength of its state power, the stronger nation tries to subdue and exploit the other in order to swell its own coffers. This leads to conflicts and conflagrations. And once this process starts there is no end to it. Moral bonds are all snapped. Normal human emotions are dried up. The values and virtues, which ought to distinguish man from the rest of the animal kingdom, vanish. And it is this process of degeneration of man that is clothed in attractive terms such as "competition" and "raising the standard of human living"'.[58]

All of these are core attributes of the way of dharma, according to Golwalkar, which he believes should be the foundation on which any sense of self or nationhood for an Indian must emerge.

According to Golwalkar, national integration comes from a common or shared emotion.

> 'But what is that "common emotion", that common basis on which all can come together? What are those eternal life-springs of our national life that go to make it unified, resurgent and glorious? In the first place, feeling of burning devotion to the land, which, from times immemorial, we have regarded as our sacred Matrubhoomi[59]; in the second place, the feeling of fellowship, of fraternity, born out of the realisation that we are the children of that one great common Mother; in the third place, the intense awareness of a common current of national life, born out of a common culture and heritage, of common history and traditions, of common ideals and aspirations, this trinity of values or, in a word, Hindu Nationalism, forms the bedrock of our national edifice.'[60]

The question of what this means for minorities in India is also answered. The answer is a kind of cultural assimilation with what Golwalkar describes as the sort of mainstream. He says:

> '. . . we should make it clear that the non-Hindu who lives here has a rashtra dharma (national responsibility), a samaja dharma (duty to society), a kula dharma (duty to ancestors), and only in his vyakti dharma (personal faith) he can choose any path

which satisfies his spiritual urge. If, even after fulfilling all those various duties in social life, anybody says that he has studied Quran Sherif[51] or the Bible and that way of worship strikes a sympathetic chord in his heart, that he can pray better through that path of devotion, we have absolutely no objection. Thus he has his choice in a portion of his individual life. For the rest, he must be one with the national current. That is real assimilation. That is how we had conducted ourselves in the past. We had always been hospitable. Any one was welcome to stay here. But all of them were required to act up to our national codes and conventions. Several centuries ago, when barbaric hordes of Arabs and Turks invaded Persia, some Parsis left their motherland and sailed forth with their Holy Fire and Holy Book and landed at Surat. King Yadava Rana welcomed them with open arms and consulted the Shankaracharya of Dwaraka Math as to how to accept them. They were asked to give up beef-eating, respect mother-cow as an object of national faith and live here in peace. These followers of Zaratushtra have kept up their promise even to this day. They live here with their religion intact but have merged themselves wholly in the mainstream of national life . . . This is our concept of Hindu Nation and our attitude towards the non-Hindus residing here—the only rational, practical and right approach. In spite of this rational and positive approach, there are some who imagine that the concept of Hindu Nation is a challenge to the very existence of the Muslim and the Christian co-citizens and they will be thrown out and exterminated. Nothing could be more absurd or detrimental to our national sentiment. It is insult to our great and all embracing cultural heritage. Do we not know, for example, that even in the latest powerful expression of Hindu resurgence under Shivaji, one of his army officers was a Ranadulla Khan? Later on, on the battlefield of Panipat in 1761, in that life-and-death struggle for the rising Hindu Swaraj, the key position of the Artillery Chief was held by one Ibrahim Gardi. With such historical evidence and national traditions for the past thousands of years staring in our eyes, how strange that some persons still say that the non-Hindus live in peril if the Hindu Nation comes into its own!'[62]

It is important to note that Golwalkar takes the same examples that had been cited as examples of the multiculturalism of India (the consistent appearance of Shivaji in our story as well as Golwalkar's is noteworthy), but he analyses the issue from a different lens. He argues that successful assimilation required not merely the generosity of the hosts (the majority community), but also, importantly, the accommodation and adjustment of the minority communities. Golwalkar's *Bunch of Thoughts* would become—and remains—the definitive guide for RSS members, just as Deendayal Upadhyaya's *Integral Humanism* would become the guiding political philosophy for the Bharatiya Jana Sangh and its successor, the Bharatiya Janata Party.

By 1967, the Bharatiya Jana Sangh had become the third-largest political party in the country.

As it was for Golwalkar, in Upadhyaya's world view too, the idea of unity was paramount, as was the idea of mutual dependence, of a symbiotic relationship where none of the parts were greater than the whole.

His '. . . depiction of society as a living organism having a body, a mind, intelligence and a soul. So the progress of a human being and society means simultaneous progress of body, mind, intellect and soul . . . a society is a natural organism having limbs which cannot be created artificially, nor destroyed by man. The reason for its creation and destruction are the same as for the creation and destruction of the living world whether plant or animal. The relation of a society to its individuals is the same as that of an organism to its limbs or that of a tree to its branches, leaves and flowers. Under this concept both individual and society are not part of each other. One cannot conceive of a society without individuals and the individual has no value without society. According to our philosophy, a human being is born not only to meet material needs but a goal in life which is to get wisdom. This is the crux of Indian culture. So we have to view all issues in the frame of all perception of human life.'[63]

Beyond the political, social, cultural and religious arguments, Deendayal Upadhyaya also had a deeper economic heft. Like Golwalkar—and in fact, Gandhi—Upadhyaya asked questions critical questions about production and consumption, and satisfaction or contentment. Upadhyaya sought to ask, in *Integral Humanism*, what is the correct place for material well-being in a person's life?

He argued:

'Both these systems, capitalist as well as communist, have failed to take account of the Integral Man, his true and complete personality and his aspirations. One considers him a mere selfish being lingering after money, having only one law, the law of fierce competition, in essence the law of the jungle; whereas the other has viewed him as a feeble lifeless cog in the whole scheme of things, regulated by rigid rules, and incapable of any good unless directed. The centralization of power, economic and political, is implied in both. Both, therefore, result in dehumanization of man. Man. the highest creation of God, is losing his own identity. We must re-establish him in his rightful position, bring him the realization of his greatness, reawaken his abilities and encourage him to exert for attaining divine heights of his latest personality. This is possible only through a decentralized economy. We want neither capitalism nor socialism. We aim at the progress and happiness of "Man", the Integral Man. The protagonists of the two systems fight with "Man" on the state. Both of them do not understand man, nor do they care for his interests.'[64]

The economy was to be judged by the overall happiness of man, where progress and development meant upliftment of mind, intellect and soul. Instead of seeing citizens as individuals alone, Upadhyay advocated for understanding individuals in conjunction with family, nation and humanity at large. In his world view, too much wealth has as much of a distortionary effect as too little wealth.

'Both of the situations will cause for exploitation, suppression, and other related money and muscle power. Such happenings will destabilize and also destroy the societies. So the concentration of wealth by few and consumption of wealth by few is totally against the spirit of Dharma. Scarcity and unavailability of wealth in a society is also against the spirit of Dharma. So the economy of a society is to be kept free from both—lack (*Abhav*) of wealth and infatuation (*Prabhav*) of wealth. This equilibrium is connoted in the concept of *Arthayam* by Deendayal . . . His theory of Arthayam can be practiced in order to maintain equilibrium in production, distribution and consumption and the society itself has to promote various institutions and different forms of management system. The single role of the state is to regulate the economy from the standpoint of planning, direction, regulation and controls. It is needed to introduce self-regulatory discipline in the economy to reach the goals of satisfaction of basic needs of the people. The economic equilibrium causes the price factor and income factor in a society. Unlike western concept, Deendayal says that Nature itself is the wealth of human beings for their livelihood. But if the need for material wealth is exceeding natural limits, people will deviate from ethical behavior. So the material wealth is necessary for spiritual evolution so it should not go beyond the limit . . . [and emphasized that the] consumption of wealth should consider necessities and comforts and not luxuries. This discretion should govern the allocation of natural resources in the economy. So that people themselves have necessarily to work out their needs and wants by cultivating ethical principles and values . . . [65]'

Like Gandhi, Deendayal Upadhyaya was an early sceptic of endless natural exploitation to deliver productivity. He saw that the natural equilibrium was being disturbed. 'Nature renews its depreciation and losses by its own processes. However, man is destroying Nature as if the whole of its resources are meant for his own existence. The speed of destruction by man is not compensated by the speed of renewing resources in nature. The equilibrium cannot be sustained this way. In the mad race to produce maximum of agricultural and industrial commodities, we have lost the foresight.'[66]

But Upadhyaya, from a party which had received, and continues to receive, support from traditional business communities, was not in support of the abolition of private property. He understood that that too could cause suffering and imbalance—and destroy individual enterprise. Instead, quite like Gandhi, he advocated the propagation of a sense of trusteeship where the producers realize that they cannot produce without natural resources, and whatever they produce, they hold in trusteeship for generations to come rather than act as the sole exploiter and consumer. Material goals, to Upadhyaya, were deeply interconnected to the overall culture and its norms.

Deendayal Upadhyaya was not a big fan of the foreign investment-fuelled growth model. 'He was clear that dependencies on foreign import and foreign capital were detrimental for India. He averred that foreign investments would exploit domestic labour and also have the potential of influencing politics in the country. In his opinion, foreign capital would bring with it not just foreign money but also exploitative capitalist ideas. He feared that it would introduce all the evils of capitalism in society and play havoc with the social culture.'[67] He recommended a six-point formula for India's economic progress—a minimum standard of living for every individual and preparedness for the defence of the nation, an increase above the minimum standard of living whereby the individual and the nation acquire means to contribute to world progress on the basis of its own 'chiti'[68], meaningful employment to every able-bodied person and avoiding waste and extravagance, especially of natural resources, developing indigenous technological capability[69], protecting the individual and cultural, and other, values of life. The ownership, state, private or any other form of various industries, must be decided on a pragmatic basis.

Like Gandhi, Upadhyaya was an enthusiastic proponent of *swadeshi* or indigenous production and manufacturing, and 'decentralization'. This was a departure from the model that started with Nehru of large state-planned industrial development, which had progressively grown more and more centralized, especially after Nehru, and both Gandhi and Upadhyaya wanted to break free from this model. 'The concept of "Swadeshi" is ridiculed as old fashioned and reactionary. We proudly use foreign articles. We have grown over independent upon foreign aid in everything from thinking, management, capital, methods of production, technology, etc. to even the standards and forms of consumption. This is not the road to progress and development. We shall forget our individuality and become virtual slaves once again,'[70] said Upadhyaya, and soon we shall see how the Jana Sangh and more importantly, the BJP, would engage with and use these ideas, some to the letter and some creatively.

It isn't that there weren't defenders of business, entrepreneurship and free (or at least freer) markets within the world of political Hinduism. Certainly, Syama Prasad Mookerjee veered supporting greater, freer enterprise, and Balraj Madhok, one of the seminal people in the Jana Sangh, was even convinced enough to suggest a merger of the Jana Sangh with the main capitalism-supporting political outfit, the Swatantra Party, in 1967, but others in the Jana Sangh, including Atal Bihari Vajpayee, fervently opposed it and the RSS was unsure too. These ideas could emerge later but not quite in the way that Madhok had wanted.

All these commonalities of Upadhyaya's thinking with Gandhian economic thought are why, even today, the constitution of the BJP has Article IV, which commits the party to a 'Gandhian approach to socio-economic issues leading to the establishment of an egalitarian society free from exploitation'.[71]

In his *Integral Humanism*, Upadhyaya argued for a Dharma Rajya, or a state governed by dharma, and argued that 'Dharma Rajya ensures religious freedom and is not a theocratic state'.[72] In line with that thought, the BJP's Constitution states that it adheres to 'Positive Secularism, that is Sarva Dharma Sambhav[73] . . . [and it] stands for decentralization of economic and political power.'

Therefore, it was cultural change and self-reliance in the economy that had to be at the very core of the Jana Sangh's goals, as it was the RSS's. It must be highlighted here that intellectual work on political Hinduism was not being done only by members of the RSS and the Jana Sangh. Others, notably Sitaram Goel (October 1921–December 2003) and Ram Swarup (October 1920–December 1998), provided considerable intellectual firepower to the ideas of Hindutva. Both had been interested in communism in the beginning but came around to promoting the political Hinduism world view, especially through Voice of India, a publication house that published their work and the work of other like-minded authors. It was Swarup and Goel who published several monographs detailing for the first time the Hindutva perspectives on the interaction between Hinduism and other faiths, and, for instance, published an exhaustive list of scores of Hindu temples that had been destroyed by Islamic and other attacks, which provided scholarly argument to many of the revivalist ideas of the RSS, the Jana Sangh and then the BJP.

Nehru's death not only opened up space not only for the Jana Sangh and the RSS to grow but it also created space for other organizations to emerge to promote political Hinduism. In the year Golwalkar published *Bunch of Thoughts*, 1966, the universe of political Hinduism also expanded. In Maharashtra, a popular cartoonist, and the son of a man who had spearheaded the successful campaign for a state based on the Marathi language and Marathi speakers, created a feisty new political outfit. Bal Thackeray had been known in his early life as a biting cartoonist and the son of Keshav Sitaram Thackeray.[74] From his father's activism,

Bal Thackeray created a powerful political party that swore by protecting the rights of local Marathis, including ensuring jobs for them, and Hindutva. It declared as its foes local communist cadres looking to organize strikes at the cavernous textile mills of central Bombay[75], anyone depriving jobs to Marathis and later, Muslim gangsters. The name of his political party was Shiv Sena, or the army of Shivaji. Soon he would have a definitive role in the story of political Hinduism.

On 10 February 1968, when Deendayal Upadhyaya had been president of the Bharatiya Jana Sangh only for a few months, he was on a late-night train from Lucknow in Uttar Pradesh to Patna in Bihar. At around 2 a.m., his dead body was discovered a few hundred metres from the Mughalsarai railway station in Uttar Pradesh.

An initial police inquiry, and a subsequent judicial inquiry, both concluded that Deendayal Upadhyaya was probably pushed off the train after discovering two men trying to steal his belongings and threatening to call the police. Two men were arrested but murder charges could not be proved. Deendayal Upadhyaya's murder remains one of the great unsatisfactorily solved cases of India's political history—ironically quite like the death of Syama Prasad Mookerjee. Upadhyaya's family, quite like Mookerjee's family, remain unconvinced that these were open-and-shut cases.

But the death of these two men, both on suspicious grounds, gave the world of political Hinduism a certain air of martyrdom and anti-establishmentarianism. This often allowed the Congress to suggest that it had a 'historic role as the party of natural governance'[76]. This idea would start to be seriously challenged for the first time as two men now came to the forefront of the political Hinduism movement. Their names were Atal Bihari Vajpayee and Lal Krishna Advani.

5

The House of God

Atal Bihari Vajpayee[1] and Lal Krishna Advani came from very different worlds until the RSS discipline flattened their distinctions. Vajpayee was the son of a local schoolteacher from Gwalior in Madhya Pradesh in central India, whereas Advani was born in a relatively prosperous business family in Karachi, in the Sindh province of undivided India. While Vajpayee studied in Hindi, the medium of instruction at his local school, Advani was educated at the finest Catholic missionary school in Karachi, St Patrick's High School.

Both joined the RSS when they were little more than teenage boys. While Vajpayee cut his teeth working in the Hindi publications of the RSS with Deendayal Upadhyaya, and later became the aide of Syama Prasad Mookerjee when he was sent to work in the Jana Sangh, Advani pitched in with editing the RSS's English publications from the start.

During the partition of India, Advani's family had to flee Karachi, leaving behind the family's considerable prosperity.

Syama Prasad Mookerjee's death and Deendayal Upadhyaya's focus on institution-building created the space, and the need, for a rousing campaigner, someone who was a natural in the language of choice of the Jana Sangh and the RSS—Hindi.

To fill this gap, Upadhyaya turned to a twenty-nine-year-old amateur poet from Madhya Pradesh, who spoke movingly in Hindi, who had been an interlocutor for Syama Prasad Mookerjee in the Hindi-speaking areas such as Uttar Pradesh[2], and who, in his early twenties, had been the editor of *Panchajanya*. So, in 1954, at the age of twenty-nine, Atal Bihari Vajpayee contested his first election from the Lucknow parliamentary seat that had been vacated by Jawaharlal Nehru's sister, who was to become India's representative at the United Nations. When the votes were counted, he had come third.

But his oratory had hit a mark. In the next election, Vajpayee won his first seat, Balrampur in Uttar Pradesh. He was thirty-three and Upadhyaya made him the leader of the party in Parliament. And so it was Atal Bihari Vajpayee from Gwalior who arrived to make a new life in the heart of New Delhi, with his own bungalow as a member of Parliament in Lutyens Delhi. It is important to provide a quick aside here about what Lutyens Delhi is because it has an interesting side role later in the story.

Lutyens Delhi refers to a small area in the centre of the Indian capital and includes the presidential palace, the Parliament, and a range of single-storied bungalows built according to plans detailed by the British architect Edwin Lutyens, who was the leading light of colonial Delhi. This area also includes a famous bazaar, today full of chic coffee shops and restaurants, and high-end clothing and bookstores, called Khan Market. It is named after the freedom fighter Khan Abdul Jabbar Khan, also known as Dr Khan Sahib, the elder brother of the renowned politician and peacenik Khan Abdul Gaffar Khan, and the chief minister of the North-West Frontier Province between 1945 and 1947, and under whose watch, at a time of unprecedented bloodletting elsewhere, hundreds of refugees were able to move out without harm when the country was divided. A close friend of Mahatma Gandhi, and a fierce opponent of Partition, Khan, for his efforts at peace, was called 'the Frontier Gandhi'. The brothers considered Partition a deep betrayal of themselves and their people. Khan Market today is one of the most expensive commercial real estate in the world.

It is in such a world that Vajpayee found himself after his election victory. To help him navigate this world, the sophisticated, English-speaking, missionary-school-educated Lal Krishna Advani, who had proved his chops by then by going to jail with hundreds of other RSS men after the assassination of Gandhi, was sent to assist him. As Vajpayee had once helped Mookerjee with Hindi, Advani was to help him with English, and through the English-speaking culture of Lutyens Delhi.

The bond that the two men would start to build would last a lifetime.

In 1962, Vajpayee lost the election narrowly but was sent by Upadhyaya to the upper house of Parliament for nominated members, the Rajya Sabha. But that year, he and the RSS would have a game-changing role to play: support Nehru during the war in 1962 and sharply critique the loss. The 1962 war had another important pivot, in line with Savarkar's (and the RSS's) dream of greater military power. It allowed Vajpayee and the others to demand strongly that India get its own nuclear weapons when China conducted its first tests in 1964. For their vocal support during the war, the RSS was invited to be part of the Republic Day parade[3], where around 2000 RSS men marched in uniform[4].

The man who had most vociferously wanted the RSS banned had given the organization its biggest moment of legitimacy. So, it came to pass that when Nehru—who is said to have once described Vajpayee as a future prime minister[5] though some have disputed this[6]—died in 1964, Vajpayee said in Parliament, '. . . In spite of a difference of opinion we have nothing but respect for his great ideals, his integrity, his love for the country and his indomitable courage.'[7] To the exasperation of some of his Congress-opposing peers, Vajpayee also refused to directly call for Nehru's resignation after the war debacle[8].

While Vajpayee cut his teeth in electoral politics, Advani's first job was as a film critic for the RSS's English-language publication, the *Organiser*. While Advani married a young woman from Bombay, from an ousted Sindhi family like his own from Karachi, Vajpayee would meet a girl he had liked in his early youth in Gwalior again after many years in Delhi—as the wife of a middling philosophy professor—and would proceed to adopt the family as his own.

In 1964, the RSS facilitated the coming together of all sects and groupings of Hindus under one platform to create a new organization that would be its affiliate, the Vishwa Hindu Parishad (VHP) or World Hindu Council. The VHP's first agitation was to raise an old topic that had even found a place in the 'directive principles' in the Indian Constitution, the ban on cow slaughter. In November 1966, nearly three lakh people, including monks and ascetics from a wide range of Hindu organizations, supported by the RSS, the Vishwa Hindu Parishad and others marched to Parliament demanding a ban on cow slaughter. Soon the gathering turned into a mob threatening to storm Parliament. In response, the government of Indira Gandhi, the daughter of Nehru, who had by then become the prime minister, asked the police to open fire. Seven people were killed, underlining once again, in the minds of the adherents of political Hinduism, including many religious Hindu bodies, the old accusation that the Congress was against Hindus. It is an accusation that is repeated even today.

It was also a period when political Hinduism started to get support and resources from unprecedented places; for instance, through the very wealthy dowager queen of the princely state of Gwalior, Vijayaraje Scindia, who supported both the Jana Sangh and the Vishwa Hindu Parishad. The elections of 1967 gave the Bharatiya Jana Sangh its highest-ever tally of seats, and the Congress, while very much remaining in power, had its worst result ever. Vajpayee had won his seat again and Advani, demonstrating his organizational and election management skills, had helped the party win not only in the parliamentary elections but also the municipal corporation and metropolitan council of Delhi—and had become the chairman of the council. He was now a bona fide politician, no longer merely an admirer and aide of Vajpayee.

After the debacle of 1962, India and Pakistan fought a war in 1965 that ended in a ceasefire and a defeat for Pakistan, which had not been able to fulfil its main motivation to trigger a rebellion in Kashmir leading to its breakaway from India. 'Satisfied that it had secured a strategic and psychological victory over Pakistan by frustrating its attempt to seize Kashmir by force, when the UN resolution was passed, India accepted its terms . . . with Pakistan's stocks of ammunition and other essential supplies all but exhausted, and with the military balance tipping steadily in India's favour.'[9] To add to the injury, India managed to advance its troops deep inside Pakistani territory by the time the ceasefire was announced. 'The invading Indian forces outfought their Pakistani counterparts and halted their attack on the outskirts of Lahore, Pakistan's second-largest city. By the time the United Nations intervened on 20 September, Pakistan had suffered a clear defeat.'[10] Lal Bahadur Shastri, who succeeded Jawaharlal Nehru as prime minister, and who was at the helm during the 1965 war, had invited Golwalkar for meetings on civilian responses to the war, especially in relief and rehabilitation efforts for soldiers.[11]

So, when India entered the conflict in eastern Pakistan where people were rebelling against what was seen by the Bengali-speaking population as cultural and economic oppression of Urdu-speaking power centres in Islamabad and Lahore, the RSS cheered on Prime Minister Indira Gandhi as she sent in the army to support the Mukti Bahini or the guerilla force of Bangladeshis fighting the Pakistan army. When India won, and a separate Bangladesh was created, Vajpayee offered fulsome praise for Gandhi, though, contrary to popular belief, he never compared her to the Hindu Goddess Durga.[12] As president of the Jana Sangh, Vajpayee said, 'The prime minister must now lead the country to total victory over the enemy. If the government wanted to secure any more powers to handle the situation, this party would not hesitate to accord its fullest cooperation.'[13] It, of course, helped Indira Gandhi that months before going to war in 1971, she had won a massive victory, overturning the losses of 1967 and bringing down the Jana Sangh tally to twenty-two seats, down from thirty-five in the previous election, though Vajpayee managed to win his seat in Gwalior.

After this loss, Atal Bihari Vajpayee concluded that in order to win, the Jana Sangh would have to adopt a version of Indira Gandhi's socialist policies. Why did Vajpayee think this? Because of the way the Indian economy had been suffering and the responses that the Congress party had thrown up to tackle the challenges.

Since Independence, India had been drawing up five-year, Soviet-style economic plans to steer the economy, but the situation after the 1965 war, which had mopped up a lot of resources, had become so dire that the country abandoned five-year plans for annual plans as it became impossible to predict long-term resource generation. Food shortages and inflation soared, and the critical rains in a monsoon-dependent economy failed to arrive in adequate measure.

In response, Indira Gandhi nationalized fourteen private banks to heighten credit flow to agriculture that was in deep crisis and subsequently won a massive electoral victory. In a country, still one of the poorest in the world, with a per capita income of barely $100, anything done in the name of the poor made political sense.

That consideration for the poor also made sense to the RSS, and if Vajpayee was thinking of taking the Jana Sangh to new audiences, so would Balasaheb Deoras, who understood the need for strengthening political interaction and building deeper symbiosis. Thus, Deoras became the first RSS chief to speak at the annual gathering of the Jana Sangh.[14] It was Deoras who explained:

'Take the example of Congress. In the 1950s, Sardar Patel had got passed in the Congress Working Committee a resolution opening its doors to RSS Swayamsevaks. However, Pandit Nehru, who was abroad at that time, after his return, reversed the decision. And previous to that, a peculiar situation had developed. When the RSS was founded in 1925 and even later on, there was no discussion about the RSS relationship with political parties. When, however, Gandhiji was murdered in 1948, and the Sangh was banned . . . not a single Member of

Parliament or of any Assembly challenged the unjust ban . . .
Some of our Swayamsevaks felt that such an isolation is no
good and something must be done. They felt that though RSS
may have no politics, some members of the RSS, who have the
liking and ability, should take part in politics.'[15]

It was Deoras who also explained, and which is not well understood
even today, that the RSS was not opposed per se to their men
joining the Congress (as long as they could be members of the
RSS too). If Patel's resolution had held, even today, technically,
the RSS is not opposed to their men being part of any political
party that broadly aligns with their beliefs.

'I do want our Swayamsevaks to join different political parties.
The reason is, there is "political casteism" today in our country.
Just as there is social casteism, this political casteism is also
creating many nasty problems. This barrier of "casteism" can
be broken if RSS people join all political parties. Then, they
would be working in different parties, but in the morning or
in the evening they would be playing and singing together in
the shakha and imbibing the faith that all are patriots having
a common meeting-ground. So I say, let the other political
parties welcome the Swayamsevaks without any reservations.'[16]

This kind of viewpoint would soon prove handy because politics
was about to crash-land into the universe of the RSS again.

In 1974, the Gandhian Marxist civil rights leader and Congress
activist Jayaprakash Narayan, or 'JP', led the charge against the
mismanagement of the Indira Gandhi government. Under JP's
leadership, what had been disparate public protests and strikes
came together as one unified opposition to Indira Gandhi.[17] The

RSS had supported JP from the beginning of his efforts to bring the opposition together, and JP supported the Jana Sangh being part of his movement in the face of strong opposition from other groups, including the communists, even declaring, 'If the Jana Sangh is fascist, then Jayaprakash Narayan is also fascist.'[18]

In June 1975, around the same time as a state government of the Janata Front (the united opposition made up of parties that would later bring down the Congress at the national level) was being formed after an election win against the Congress in the state of Gujarat, the Allahabad High Court dismissed Indira Gandhi as prime minister on charges of corruption in electoral practices or rigging polls. The Supreme Court stayed her outright dismissal but ruled that the prime minister could not vote in Parliament. Soon afterwards at a protest rally of the unified opposition with one lakh people attending, JP told the police and military that they did not have to listen to Indira Gandhi's illegal orders because her government was illegitimate.

Hours later, Gandhi announced an 'emergency', suspending Parliament and elections, dismantling fundamental rights and enforcing governance only by prime ministerial order. Hundreds across the country immediately started getting arrested, including Vajpayee, Advani, Balasaheb Deoras and Jayaprakash Narayan. With unprecedented censorship at every news organization, an anguished Advani, a former journalist, would rail against the editors, later, 'You were asked to bend, but you began to crawl!'[19]

Tens of thousands more would be arrested and the RSS banned a second time. One of the people who escaped arrest was a young RSS pracharak who roamed around Gujarat with a thick beard to hide his identity and who would later write a book about his escapades—Narendra Damodardas Modi. But this time—unlike in the freedom movement—there would be no ambiguity that not only were members of the BJP and the RSS arrested en masse and spent time in jail but they were also on the frontlines of fighting what came to be known as the Emergency. But like before, the ban did not break the RSS or the Jana Sangh, and when the Emergency was lifted in 1977[20], the RSS made an exception and even its cadres campaigned against Indira Gandhi in the elections that followed. There was a palpable sense that her return to power would be an existential threat.

The unified Janata Party that had protested together and now fought the elections against Indira Gandhi won a landslide and a comfortable majority in Parliament. The Jana Sangh won 93 of the 298 seats secured by the Janata Party combined, becoming the largest party in the grouping.

But cognizant of the fact that many in the Janata Party combine were wary of them, the Jana Sangh would not seek the prime ministerial chair, as was due to them via numerical strength. Instead, Vajpayee became foreign minister, while Advani took the role of minister for information and broadcasting. It is in this role that Vajpayee would show himself as someone willing to find middle paths in even the most intractable challenges of Indian foreign policy, like trying to find common ground with Pakistan and reaching out to the influential Indian diaspora. The RSS had started reaching out to the diaspora for years and funds from them helped the organization during the Emergency as money was hard to raise in India—even though India's richest industrialist, who happened to be Jinnah's grandson, Nusli Wadia, supported the RSS and the Jana Sangh during the Emergency with considerable resources at great personal risk.

Vajpayee also tried mending fences with China through a visit in 1979, the first by an Indian foreign minister since 1962. But it was during his visit to China as foreign minister that the Chinese attacked Vietnam, a friend of India, underlining to Vajpayee and others that the warnings given by Patel and Savarkar about China were not to be forgotten.

For his part, Advani won praise for removing many of the roadblocks to press freedom imposed during the Emergency. A suggestion he made for more patriotic cultural content, including content based on the epics, the Ramayana and the Mahabharata, to film and television content makers, would bear fruit within the decade.

But the Janata Party experiment would be wrecked by constant fighting between its various leaders. Finally, the wheels turned on the RSS men on the question of 'dual membership' and whether the government was being impacted by having members and ministers who were both members of the Janata Party and the RSS. Vajpayee and Advani refused to give up their RSS membership. In his biography, Advani compared the bickering behaviour of the Janata Party politicians to lemmings, 'the only species, among all those created by God, which was believed to commit mass suicide. Those who were out to wreck the party knew that their conduct would certainly cause the downfall of the Janata government and pave the way for the political resurrection of Indira Gandhi. But they were simply beyond caring'.[21] Here, when told by some Janata members that Muslims might not like the RSS connection, Advani wrote that he pointed out that the RSS was:

'a non-political organization, dedicated to the cause of India's national renaissance based on our ancient culture and values . . . a reformist organization wedded to removing ills, such as untouchability, afflicting Hindu society . . . there are also others in the Janata Party who are linked to some other non-political organisations. Charan Singh, for instance, is a staunch Arya Samajist. One of the cardinal planks of the Arya Samaj is shuddhi or religious reconversion. Would it be right on that account to bar him from membership of the Janata Party?'[22]

A century after the various modern movements of political Hinduism had taken shape, here they were, in 1979, providing the rhetorical basis for another.

But something else happened through this process of the implosion of the Janata Party government and the accusation of 'dual membership'. Apart from rejecting any call to give up membership of the RSS, Vajpayee wrote an article in August 1979 in the *Indian Express* newspaper where he noted that the RSS had nothing to do with communal violence, nor was it trying to acquire political power. But he had three suggestions for the RSS: its journals should not offer opinions that took sides in a political argument, its youth members should not interact with political bodies or trade unions, and it should replace its vision of 'Hindu Rashtra' with 'Bharatiya Rashtra'.

Nothing like this had ever been offered as advice to the RSS by one of its very own, but if Vajpayee's opinion broke new ground, so did the clarity of the RSS response presented by Deoras in October 1979 at the annual Vijayadashami[23] rally. Deoras noted, 'It is said by some that the Sangh is changing and that it has to change further. All living things do change in their natural course. It is a sign of their evolution. That which does not change is not living, it is dead. But this change should not take place by cutting itself from the arteries of life-sap. The Sangh too has changed in keeping with the necessities of the times, and will keep changing in future too.'[24] The RSS was not going to blindly agree with

Vajpayee, never mind his charisma. Hindu rashtra as a goal and as terminology would not be ditched.

A few months later, the Janata Party voted to remove dual membership, and the very next day, 5 April 1980, Vajpayee and Advani announced the creation of a new party—the Bharatiya Janata Party (BJP). A major part of the funding came from Jinnah's grandson Nusli Wadia, and the chief guest was Mohammedali Carim Chagla, once Jinnah's legal junior who broke with Jinnah after the announcement of the demand for Pakistan and even created a Muslim Nationalist Party in Bombay. Chagla was Savarkar's dream of unity between Hindus and Muslims come true.

The BJP's new symbol was the lotus flower, and by adopting 'Gandhian socialism' as one of its guiding principles, no matter the history between political Hinduism and Gandhi, Advani argued that the new party wanted to:

'counter the communists' claim to be the sole champions of the poor. We wanted to demonstrate that the concept of "socialism", like the concept of "secularism", has Indian roots, and that only the Indian way of achieving economic and social justice would ultimately succeed. We wanted to reaffirm that all the great thinkers and social reformers in the Hindu tradition, including Swami Vivekananda and Mahatma Gandhi in the modern era, had been votaries of what can termed as "Spiritual Socialism". Our ancient seers did not regard man only as an economic being with purely material and physical needs. Rather, they had an integrated approach to life which urged the fulfilment of both material and spiritual needs of all human beings. The neglect and negation of the spiritual dimension of man had rendered the communist experiment, in country after country in Europe and Asia, utterly dehumanizing. Therefore, the BJP adopted Gandhian Socialism as a positive Indian alternative to communism.'[25]

Those who instinctively objected to 'socialism', such as Vijayaraje Scindia, finally chose to submerge their concern to the arguments of Vajpayee and Advani, described as an act of putting the nation, or at least the party, before self.[26]

At the inauguration of the BJP in Mumbai in December 1980, Atal Bihari Vajpayee gave one of his most memorable speeches which had a line which is still repeated and used. In Hindi he said,

अँधेरा छटेगा सूरज निकलेगा कमल खिलेगा

(The darkness will dissipate, the sun shall shine and the lotus will bloom)

This bloom would come from sources Vajpayee did not imagine in his focus towards countering communism. A combination of unsettling factors was creating a tumult among Hindu communities. A notoriously publicized mass conversion of Dalits to Islam at Meenakshipuram in Tamil Nadu in 1981, the rise of militant Sikh nationalism fuelled initially by the political impetus of the Congress in Punjab, a surging jobs and income crisis, simmering tensions on caste-based reservation and census data that showed the Hindu population falling while the population of minorities, especially Muslims, rising had created a volatile mood in many parts of India. In Gujarat, where some of these tensions were prominently playing out, one of the people grappling with them from the RSS was Narendra Damodardas Modi, who was soon joined by a man who would first be an aide and then a regular accomplice, Amit Anilchandra Shah.

From this tumult emerged a campaign that would transform the history of political Hinduism and the BJP. Several Islamic and colonial sources had noted that in the city of Ayodhya, sacred to the Hindus as the abode of the god-king Ram, a mosque existed which was often called 'Masjid Janmasthan' or the mosque of the birthplace that was said to have been built atop a temple marking the birthplace of Ram.[27] This temple was said to have been destroyed by the first Mughal king Babur and his army—specifically his general Mir Baqi—as they passed through the region. And the mosque, called the Babri mosque, was built over it. Sporadic skirmishes and clashes have happened on the issue since the 1800s. There had been evidence of a growing dispute between Hindus and Muslims in the area over the mosque. In between, a sharing arrangement for both Hindus and Muslims to pray at the site had been found but it brought only a temporary, uneasy peace. In 1949, Hindu idols were placed by locals inside the mosque, and it was the ruling Congress that agreed to keep the idols installed. A court judgement gave the Hindus the right to pray from a distance, from behind locked gates. Hindus and Muslims had been fighting several court cases on the issue for decades. There had also been a quarrel on the archaeological and historical findings from the site of the Babri masjid, where countering historians such as Romila Thapar, Bipan Chandra and Irfan Habib criticized the demand for the Ram temple at the site of the Babri masjid. The Ayodhya movement put up arguments from archaeologists who had worked on excavation at the site including B.B. Lal, K.K. Muhammed (the only Muslim who had done excavation work there), and, at that time, one of India's most celebrated investigative journalists, Arun Shourie.

To Habib's argument that 'There's no acceptable proof that the Babri Masjid had been built at the site of a Hindu temple, none of the fourteen inscribed Persian verses of the time of the original construction (1528[29], published in the official *Epigraphia Indica, Arabic and Persian Supplement 1965*, pages 58 to 62) even remotely mentioned this.'[28] K.K. Muhammed responded:

> 'When we went inside, I saw 12 pillars of the mosque which were made from temple remains. In almost all the temples of the 12th and 13th Centuries, you get "Purna Kalasha" at the base. It is in the structure of a "ghada" (water pitcher) from which foliage would be coming out. It is the symbol of prosperity in Hinduism and is known as "Ashtamangala Chinha"—one of the eight auspicious symbols. When you go inside, you can see a number of "Purna Kalashas" and a number of gods and goddesses. Similar things were there in Babri mosque also. There were no gods and goddesses but "Ashtamangala Chinha" was there.'[29]

Some of the early support for the cause of rebuilding a Ram temple at the site where the Babri Masjid stood, along with two other sites where the Mughal Emperor Aurangzeb and his lieutenants had destroyed temples to build mosques—at Varanasi, where the Kashi Vishwanath temple had been razed to build the Gyanvapi mosque, and at Mathura, where the old Keshavadeva temple, which stood in a place considered to be the birthplace of the Hindu god Krishna, had been torn down and a mosque constructed on the plinth of the original temple during the reign of Aurangzeb—had come from Congress politicians. A former Congress prime minister Gulzarilal Nanda had been one of the most important guests in an initial VHP rally for mobilizing Hindus for this cause in 1983.[30]

But the initial phase of what came to be known as the 'Ayodhya movement', in which Atal Bihari Vajpayee did not participate at all, but which Lal Krishna Advani, through party experience and an innate gut feeling did, would be transformative. In his biography, Advani explains that he had read the history of Somnath and how it was reconstructed under the orders of Sardar Patel. Even though the BJP was hesitant to participate in the early phases of the Ayodhya movement, Advani, who was always keener on being part of this as he instinctively felt the public eagerness, later explained it as, 'Everything that Mahatma Gandhi, Sardar Patel, Rajendra Prasad and K.M. Munshi said and did in transforming the dream of reconstruction of the Somnath temple into reality echoed loudly in my mind when the Ayodhya issue rose to the centre stage of national politics . . . indeed, in many ways, the Ayodhya movement was the continuation of the spirit of Somnath.'[31]

But before the movement could take off, Indira Gandhi sent in the Indian Army, following a long stand-off, to flush out heavily armed separatists hiding inside the Golden Temple, the holiest shrine of the Sikhs in Amritsar in Punjab in the summer of 1984.

The insurgents were flushed out and many killed, but the shrine was also greatly damaged and at the end of October of the same year, Indira Gandhi's Sikh bodyguards rained bullets into her as she came down the garden path of her home. The Ayodhya movement had been stalled by the assassination of one of the most powerful prime ministers in Indian history. In the following election, turbocharged by a massive sympathy wave, and the BJP's lacklustre connection to the only cause that could unite its parent base, the Ayodhya movement, the party won only two seats in Parliament and Atal Bihari Vajpayee lost his own seat from Gwalior. Rajiv Gandhi, the forty-year-old elder son of Indira Gandhi, came to power with a complete majority of the kind that has never been matched, 403 out of 515 seats for the Congress. This, even though following Indira Gandhi's death, violent riots, often led by Congressmen, broke out around the country and especially in Delhi where nearly 3000 Sikhs were murdered and many more made homeless in the violence that continued for four days. This started a decade of insurgency in Punjab, which was strongly fuelled by Pakistani infiltration and money. But, for the time being, there was euphoria about a young prime minister, who, it seemed to the RSS, was not averse to supporting Hindu causes.

In the BJP, Vajpayee was replaced as president by a man who had been anxiously listening to the cadre, Advani. While he had lost even his own seat, at least his closest compatriot was party president. The new BJP president was keen to bring in a young team of his own, quite like the young prime minister the country had chosen. Among the people Advani selected was Narendra Modi, then only thirty-six years old. Among other notables who were starting to get noticed around this time and who would play a critical role in this story were Jaswant Singh, a former army man who had served in the 1965 war; Murli Manohar Joshi, another lifelong recruit of the RSS, a professor of physics and deeply concerned with pedagogy and its ideologies and another name, which at that time was not connected with the BJP but was steadily making a name as an incorruptible newspaper journalist, Arun Shourie.

Despite his early promises, Rajiv Gandhi was soon mired in the pulls and pressures of politics and religion with the Shah Bano case in 1985 where, even after a Supreme Court judgment granting alimony to a Muslim woman (sixty-two-year-old Bano), the Rajiv Gandhi government quickly passed a law shifting the responsibility of maintaining the divorce to herself and her relatives or the Muslim Waqf Board. Arif Mohammad Khan was minister of state (home affairs) in Rajiv Gandhi's government and was asked to speak in Parliament to defend the Supreme Court's judgment. Khan later said on record that Gandhi supported the court judgment on Shah Bano but fell prey to Muslim fundamentalist opinion. Khan said later in an interview:

> 'Shah Bano wasn't a test case for secularism. The cry of secularism was raised by Maulana Sayyed Abul Hasan Ali, who was popularly known as Ali Miyan. He was then the chairman of the Muslim Personal Law Board. In the books he wrote, he denounced secularism as anti-Islam, praised former President Zia-ul-Haq for doing away with secularism in Pakistan and was a great supporter of the Saudi regime. But when the Supreme Court judgment on Shah Bano came, he said secularism was in danger in India. It was ridiculous of him to say that. In fact, Shah Bano was a test case of our collective sensitivity.'[32]

Rajiv Gandhi's government was also the first national government to ban Salman Rushdie's *The Satanic Verses* as soon as a fatwa was announced by the mullahs in Iran.[33] This kind of thing has a notorious history in India. In the 1920s, a book on the Prophet detailing his personal life and published by a member of the Arya Samaj led to three assassination attempts on the publisher's life, the last of which, by a twenty-year-old Muslim carpenter, succeeded.

The government's U-turn on the Shah Bano case created an uproar, with critics pointing out the discriminatory behaviour of an ostensibly secular state. For many, especially within the BJP and the RSS, this was exactly what Syama Prasad Mookerjee had warned would happen if reformist personal law was pushed through only for one community and not for all.

The blowback on the Shah Bano case caused a ripple effect that went all the way to Ayodhya. When a group of sadhus and other Hindu groups pledged to break open the locks to access the idols in the Babri Masjid, the Rajiv Gandhi government acted post haste (despite a local court refusing to allow immediate opening). This was widely seen as a balancing act for a decision in the Shah Bano case; the government trying to 'give something' to the Hindus as well.

The Ayodhya movement was back on track and not only was it accommodating religious anxieties and desires, it was also countering new mobilizations, for instance, among the so-called lower castes through new political parties such as the Bahujan Samaj Party (BSP), started by Kanshi Ram, an employee of the Explosive Research and Development Laboratory of the India's Defence Research and Development Organization (DRDO). Ram's explosive idea was to bring together the 'real majority' of India, the lower castes, into one unified voting bloc. The movement and mobilization towards the Ram temple in a sense was the reverse mobilization of what Ram was attempting to do— it hoped to unite Hindus, no matter the caste, or class, or creed into one goal, the construction of the temple.

Rajiv Gandhi's government was soon further derailed by a major accusation in 1987 of corruption in buying arms from a Swiss company, Bofors, and an ill-fated decision to intervene between 1987 and 1990 in the Sri Lankan civil war, between the Sinhalese government and Tamil rebels, which resulted in numerous deaths of Indian soldiers.

In between all this, what Advani had once suggested to filmwallahs in Bombay and elsewhere, the state-run Doordarshan began to broadcast a mega-serialized version of the Ramayana. This was no TV event; for tens of millions around India, this was darshan, the equivalent of going to a temple, of seeing Lord Ram in the flesh, moving, talking, fighting for dharma in front of them. The show became the most-watched TV show on earth. Work stopped, streets emptied, TV sets were garlanded during the show and incense burned before them, just as deities would be treated with submission in a temple. Ministers failed to show up for meetings, power cuts were scheduled around the show, and if the power failed during the show broadcast on Sunday mornings, mobs threatened mass action. To understand the power of the show broadcast three decades ago, note that in October 2022, a woman who bumped into Arun Govil, the lead actor who played the character of Ram in the TV show, at an airport wept tears of joy and touched his feet in devotion.[34] The show had been broadcast again during the Covid-19 lockdown in India. The broadcast of *Ramayana* was followed by another mega broadcast, of the other Indian epic, the Mahabharata, with exactly similar reactions across India.

What politics, regionalism and caste had divided was united by the power of India's eternal epics and the magic of television.

In the 1989 elections, a beleaguered Rajiv Gandhi lost to a coalition put together by Vishwanath Pratap Singh, his former defence minister who quit once the Bofors scandal broke. The same year, 'Advani decided to force the party's hand. At the Palampur national executive meeting in 1989, he moved a resolution, a rare exercise of presidential power, adopting Ayodhya as a core political cause of the BJP. Since a resolution moved by the president is passed without debate or vote, the naysayers had to bite their tongues and keep quiet. Thus was Ram Mandir added to what was till then a single-issue (abrogation of Article 370) core agenda; the demand for a Uniform Civil Code followed.'[35]

In coming to power, V.P. Singh recreated a Janata Dal using many of the old partners of the erstwhile Janata Party and the support of the BJP, whose seats' tally rose from two in the previous election to eighty-five. Singh would soon unleash a force that the BJP would match by going all-in with the Ayodhya agitation, in a battle that would be described as 'mandal-versus-kamandal[36]'. Mandal stood for the Mandal Commission, which had, in 1980, recommended greater reservations for backward castes in government jobs, especially the bureaucracy. The commission that suggested this be called the Mandal Commission after its head, a politician called Babu Bindheshwari Prasad Mandal, a rich backward ('Yadav') caste landlord-turned-politician from Bihar. Singh's announcement in August 1990 of the acceptance of the Mandal Commission's recommendations caused violent protests across the country, including deaths and a notorious case of self-immolation.[37]

Only a little over a month later, on 25 September 1990, Advani began what would become the most important event of his life and a turning point in both the histories of political Hinduism and India. Advani had thought of travelling around 10,000 kilometres in an air-conditioned Tempo Traveller van from Gujarat to Uttar Pradesh, from the Somnath temple to the proposed temple site in Ayodhya to perform *kar seva* or contribute to the construction of the Ram temple.

Thus, the dots join in the world of political Hinduism. Somnath, that emblem that worried everyone from Savarkar to Patel to Munshi to Prasad, was reimagined at a site of pledging renewal to another temple at Ayodhya. That morning in Gujarat, as Advani paid obeisance to the statue of Sardar Vallabhbhai Patel outside Somnath temple, he was joined by a forty-year-old leader from Gujarat, Narendra Modi, who would accompany him and help plan the Gujarat leg of Advani's travels. Advani has written that in his mind, at that moment, he 'thanked and drew inspiration from all the great men who had toiled for the reconstruction of the temple'.[38] The air rang with what would become a familiar cry in those days, '*Saugandh Ram ki khate hain, mandir wahin banayenge*' (We swear in the name of Ram, we shall build the temple right there).

As Advani headed out, the yatra played a song sung by India's greatest living singer, Lata Mangeshkar, which said, '. . . the Ayodhya in my mind remains empty and silent until Ram enters it'[39].

The rath yatra, as it wound through the country, received support that exceeded the wildest expectations, with tens of thousands of people cheering it, praying before it and even worshipping the Tempo-Traveller-turned-chariot. But it also received trenchant criticism, describing it as violently communal and, along with the Mandal agitation, economically crippling for the country. One critic wrote:

'A nation is, above all, an "imagined community"—a community of emotional bonds and perceived historical links. The invocation of a shared nationhood implicitly invites its citizens to submerge other differences, such as those arising from the distribution of property, or from received social status and class. The justification of the nation-state in turn, is economic growth—the continuing growth of the national income, from which different sections are entitled to their respective shares. The relative entitlements of different classes to the necessities, luxuries and privileges of life, are clearly encoded in the constitution of the nation-state. However, when the justification of the nation-state fails in periods of economic stagnation, disputes over material entitlements become endemic. Differences of class and status, submerged in the task of national development, come to the surface. Incapable of sustaining the politics of consensus, the nation-state begins to seek increasing recourse to the politics of coercion.'[40]

There were several cases of Hindu-Muslim clashes during the time period of the yatra and even clashes between Mandal and mandir agitators. Advani argued that in his speeches through the yatra, he had never said anything incendiary or against any religion or community. And the Belgian scholar Koenraad Elst would argue after researching the numbers, 'Whether Advani with his Rath Yatra was at 500 miles distance from a riot . . . or under arrest, or back home after the high tide of the Ayodhya agitation, every riot in the second half of 1990 was blamed on him.'[41]

On his yatra, Advani 'refused to denounce Muslims, he refused to advocate violence'[42]. Advani was arrested while travelling through Bihar by the Janata Dal chief minister Lalu Yadav, and his rath yatra came to an end. But the Ayodhya movement had only truly begun. As soon as Advani was arrested, the BJP withdrew support from the V.P. Singh government.

On 30 October, the day Advani was supposed to join the kar seva in Ayodhya, around 75,000 activists and kar sevaks faced off against the police force of another Janata Dal chief minister, Mulayam Singh Yadav. As the kar sevaks reached the mosque, Yadav ordered the police to open fire. Several died; it would be an incident that would also be remembered in the annals of political Hinduism, blood was shed to win the Ram temple.

The BJP started campaigning for the elections in 1991 with every hope to form a government, and they had a fighting chance, but for another ghastly tragedy. During campaigning, a suicide

bomber at Sriperumbudur in Tamil Nadu, from the Liberation
Tigers of Tamil Elam (LTTE) of Sri Lanka, killed Rajiv Gandhi
by detonating a bomb as she seemingly tried to touch his feet.
The Congress won the election and put forward the scholarly P.V.
Narasimha Rao with the Oxbridge economist Manmohan Singh
as his finance minister.

Faced with the worst economic crisis in its history and having
to pledge gold to service its debt, Rao and Singh decided to open
the Indian economy, dramatically cutting old socialist red tape,
inviting in foreign capital and liberalizing the economy. No doubt
aware of the opposition liberalization faced, Singh said in his
budget speech of 1991–92:

'The massive social and economic reforms needed to remove
the scourge of poverty, ignorance and disease can succeed
only if backed by a spirit of high idealism, self sacrifice and
dedication . . . I do not minimise the difficulties that lie ahead
on the long and arduous journey on which we have embarked.
But as Victor Hugo once said, "No power on earth can stop
an idea whose time has come." I suggest to this august House
that the emergence of India as a major economic power in the
world happens to be one such idea. Let the whole world hear it
loud and clear. India is now wide awake. We shall prevail. We
shall overcome.'[43]

First, though, the Opposition had to be overcome. In the
Opposition, most of the BJP protested such a move—after all,
they were a party of Gandhian socialism. But Advani argued for
the opening, and as party president, his word carried the day. The
RSS, though, started the Swadeshi Jagran Manch (SJM) in response
to liberalization to ensure that the self-reliance that they were

committed to had its own platform to monitor the economy. Was
the BJP, then, socialist, or free markets-leaning? What is Right or
Left? This confusion would persist for some time.

What was indisputable was that the Ayodhya movement was
coming to a boil. A kar seva was allowed by the Supreme Court
and the Narasimha Rao administration on 6 December 1992, with
the promise from Advani and others that it would be peaceful and
the structure of the mosque would not be touched.

But on that fateful day, as Advani, Joshi and others watched
(Vajpayee was in Delhi), the thousands who had gathered there,
from a motley group of organizations, climbed on to the mosque
and tore it down with pickaxes and their bare hands. Advani
and others, including Vijayaraje Scindia, would make repeated
appeals on the public address system for the kar sevaks to stop
and climb down from the mosque. But that was not to be. From
Nagpur, the RSS sent out a message saying that it was happy
that what it saw as a symbol of oppression had been removed but
said that it was not part of the agitation. That would not help.
The RSS was banned swiftly, chief ministers of BJP states were
removed and Advani himself resigned and was briefly arrested.
Advani called it 'the saddest day of my life' and spoke about the
'sudden loss of control and discipline' which had been key to his
RSS upbringing.[44] Vajpayee was distraught and restless too but
ready to return to play the role of the moderate face, a unifier to
calm waters that had become very choppy. Others in the larger
universe of political Hinduism were more euphoric; in Bombay,
the Shiv Sena supremo Bal Thackeray congratulated the men
who brought down the mosque and indicated that Shiv Sainiks
(as members of the Sena are referred to) were involved—and
whether Shiv Sainiks were or were not involved remains a matter
of debate even today.[45]

It was a strange moment for political Hinduism. One of its key ideological goals had been met, even though in circumstances that had hurt its credibility and attempt to become mainstream immensely. The tussle between focusing on core ideological issues or expanding/diverting attention to caste and reservations, price rise, jobs and other such topics would become more intense. There was one more thing that happened during this period which would haunt India, and political Hinduism, for a long time. In Kashmir, armed militants started to kill members of the long-standing Hindu minority, the Pandits, in the Valley, and mosques warned that the Hindus in Kashmir had to either convert, leave or die. The flight of the Kashmiri Pandits would cast a long shadow in Indian politics, one that has still not been entirely closed.

There were also more immediate concerns. The bringing down of the Babri masjid caused riots to break out across India. Especially in the city of Bombay, at the end of 1992, Hindu-Muslim riots killed more than 900. This was followed by the Bombay mafia, spearheaded by the infamous Dawood Ibrahim, triggering a series of twelve bomb blasts in March 1993, killing more than 250.

With court cases unfolding, not only on the demolition of the Babri masjid, but also on a black money issue where Advani was named[46], and the outbreak of violence, the baton of the BJP passed to Vajpayee, who became the face of the BJP for the next election. With the 'moderate face' of the BJP back in the driving seat, the party became the single largest political party in terms of seats won (161) in the 1996 elections. While they scrambled to make the numbers to get to 272 seats needed for a government to be formed, the BJP took the chance to form its first government, with Vajpayee as prime minister—and Advani sitting out, as he had promised not to take up an electoral position until his name was cleared in the black money (also known as 'hawala') case.

The Vajpayee government would last for only thirteen days, to be replaced by a 'third front' grouping of various political parties, including the communists, and with Congress support. But what was happening in the BJP held the key to India's future. One incident best illustrates these undercurrents—the RSS ideologue Govindacharya, considered close to Advani, referred to Vajpayee as a *mukhota* or a mask and noted that the real power in the party was Advani.[47] A hurt Vajpayee insisted on, and got, Govindacharya's distancing from the party, even though Govindacharya was considered one of the sharpest minds of the time in the RSS and the BJP. Later, Govindacharya would insist that he was misunderstood[48], but the incident and the removal of Govindacharya from the mainstream, front-facing work of the RSS threw up a larger question.

How could the BJP achieve, and retain, political power by erasing what it saw as core values? If indeed a projection of such erasure had to be consistently done—which is the implication of the 'mukhota' statement—would it be worth it, or transformational, for the country (which was the final aim of the BJP and the RSS)?

From the perspective of Advani, while the success of his rath yatra and the emotional reception of the van-turned-chariot wherever it went showed the depth of feeling and public uptake, subsequent events suggested that these emotions could not be addressed in a disciplined manner especially because many other groups, and not just RSS men, were involved in the movement. Advani argued that the BJP had wanted to 'respectfully shift the mosque to a different location'[49], either through a legal solution or through an amicable settlement between Hindus and Muslims, and not destroy it. But that hadn't happened, and now, with Vajpayee as the leader, issues like Ayodhya were being pushed to the back burner, even though it was Ayodhya that had revived and brought the BJP so close to power.

After a short-lived third front government again, Vajpayee led the BJP to the polls, emphasizing a governance-led, rather than ideology-led, position. This time the BJP and its allies mustered up the numbers. Vajpayee was prime minister again, and, since Advani had been cleared of the hawala charges in 1997 and contested the election and won, he became deputy prime minister and minister for home affairs—exactly the same posts held by the man he idolized, Sardar Vallabhbhai Patel.

One of the decisions this, the first real BJP government would take, would be to make India an explicit nuclear state. After the Chinese nuclear tests, India conducted what it termed a 'peaceful nuclear test' in 1974 under Prime Minister Indira Gandhi.[50] Now, this one would be at a bigger scale made up of five detonations— four of fission bombs and one, a fusion bomb.

Stringent economic and developmental sanctions were immediately placed in India. A strong international rejoinder was needed, especially after Pakistan conducted its tests only weeks later. This was provided by Jaswant Singh, whom the RSS chief K.S. Sudarshan had vetoed as finance minister because of Singh's previous mocking remarks about the RSS[51] but who had been brought back later as foreign minister by Vajpayee. It was Singh who wrote the definitive defence of the Indian nuclear tests in *Foreign Affairs* called 'Against Nuclear Apartheid'. Singh argued vociferously that India's security needs had not been understood and that the country was committed both to no-first-use and non-proliferation. Singh said that there was:

'. . . the need in this nuclearized world for a balance between the rights and obligations of all nations; restraint in acquisition of nuclear weaponry; of ending today's unequal division between nuclear haves and have-nots . . . India's nuclear policy has been marked by restraint and openness. It has not violated any international agreements, either in 1974 or 1998. This restraint is a unique example. Restraint, however, has to arise from strength. It cannot be based upon indecision or hesitancy. Restraint is valid only when it removes doubts, which is precisely what India's tests did . . . We have not entered a unipolar order. India still lives in a rough neighbourhood. It would be a great error to assume that simply advocating the new mantras of globalization and the market makes national security subservient to global trade. The 21st century will not be the century of trade. The world still has to address the unfinished agenda of the centuries . . .[52]'

Vajpayee and Advani agreed on another momentous decision—a bus ride for peace to Pakistan. In February 1999, Atal Bihari Vajpayee travelled in a bus to meet his Pakistani counterpart Nawaz Sharif, a historic move. This was one of the grandest peace gestures India had ever made to Pakistan. In this visit, Vajpayee, a lifelong RSS man, attempted to go beyond even the most bitter memory in the world of political Hinduism, the creation of Pakistan, by visiting the Minar-e-Pakistan or the monument in Lahore, which commemorates the Muslim League's declaration for the creation of Pakistan in March 1940.

But despite a much-vaunted Lahore Declaration between the two prime ministers where Pakistan joined India in condemning terrorism, months later—almost as if to ensure that the apprehensions of political Hinduism were fulfilled, in the middle of political chaos in Delhi when Vajpayee's second government had been brought down by one single vote in thirteen months—

Pakistani infiltrators attacked the Himalayan heights of Kargil, starting India's 'first televised war'. Vajpayee and Advani were dismayed because the man they had only recently embraced, Nawaz Sharif, didn't seem to know what was going on. The strings were being pulled by the Pakistan army, as usual, and its sitting general Pervez Musharraf.

To win the war, the first after the two acrimonious neighbours had become nuclear states, Vajpayee allowed the aerial bombings of the Himalayan heights. But, in keeping with the nuclear threat, he made sure that Indian fighter jets did not cross the Line of Control between India and Pakistan. This rule would be broken within two decades.

Vajpayee would go into the 1999 election as the hero of the Kargil War victory and as the one who announced a Kargil War Diwas or day to commemorate the Kargil War.

But the history of political Hinduism also made an appearance. In 1999, an Australian missionary, Graham Staines, and his two young sons died in Orissa after a mob led by a man associated with the Bajrang Dal—one of the strident Hindu groups that had emerged out of the Ayodhya agitation—called Dara Singh set fire to the Staines jeep while they were sleeping inside. Police would later say that the idea had been to scare Staines who was accused in the minds of his assailants of predatory religious conversions. Amidst widespread global outrage, Vajpayee severely condemned the attack, and after his arrest, Singh was sent in for life imprisonment. The Supreme Court made strong remarks about the adverse impact of conversion in secular societies in its judgment, then expunged those comments a few days later after widespread criticism in the media. An independent commission, called the Wadhwa Commission, after inquiry, ruled out any institutional involvement of the Bajrang Dal. The head of the

Bajrang Dal at that time was a man called Pratap Sarangi, who shall make an appearance in our story again two decades later.

Even as Vajpayee took the oath for the third time, the man who triggered the Kargil War, Pervez Musharraf, came to power in Pakistan after one more military coup in the country.

Vajpayee's last term as prime minister had a few critical ingredients—an attempt to revise what political Hinduism had always seen as biased, Marxist-leaning (or colonial) history for a more indigenous narrative; efforts by two men, neither from RSS stock, to further open the economy; a massive thrust on infrastructure building and a reconciliation with the United States.

As education minister, Murli Manohar Joshi applied ideas that he had earlier charted out. Simply, Joshi hoped to decolonize India's education system. Joshi argued, quoting researchers like William Adam and G.L. Prendergast in the early 1800s, G.W. Leitner in the second half of the nineteenth century and the Indian scholar Dharmpal, that India had its own detailed network of schools in almost every village in local languages until colonial rule destroyed this network.

'When the British took hold of India, they decided to impose Western education through the English language and thus destroyed the indigenous system. No single decision has done more to cut off the vast majority of Indians from their great national heritage and values and also deprive poor villagers from access to the most prestigious jobs in government and industry . . . The education system, therefore, needs a drastic reconstruction.'[53]

But what did that reconstruction look like?

Joshi argued:

'The sixteen aphorisms of Vedic mathematics are not related to any ritual, they have been termed Vedic because the seer who discovered them did so in the same manner in which the Vedic sages perceived the Vedic rishis. In a sense its introduction could motivate the students to think about the holistic approach of ancient Rishis and compare it with the reductionist approach of the Newtonian science. It may be recalled that the work of scientists like David Bohm, Bell, Capra and others have pointed out the limitations of the Cartesian approach and have pointed out that in many respects the eastern holistic approach provides a deeper understanding of the universe. Sanskrit language is the repository of ancient Indian contributions to the field of science, philosophy, literature, architecture and various performing arts. Kautilya wrote his famous treatise in Sanskrit and works of Arya Bhata, Varahmihira, Brahmagupta, Bhaskaracharya and a host of mathematicians cannot be properly understood without Sanskrit. The vast literature of Kalidasa, Bhavabhuti, Magh and others along with the Indian contributions to the field of technology, chemistry, astronomy, horticulture and agriculture cannot be appreciated without knowing Sanskrit. The moment a student comes to know about the rich Indian heritage in these fields a sense of self-confidence is generated in his own capacities. This releases immense psychological energy for the development of his own capabilities to take up any challenge. The story of India's independence movement will remain incomplete without mentioning the contribution of Ambedkar, Mahatma Phule, Veer Savarkar, Chandra Shekhar Azad, Sardar Bhagat Singh, K.B. Hegdewar and others who were not given their due place in the history of the freedom struggle. Without deleting anything from the textbooks, brief contributions by these great sons of mother India were incorporated. The coming generation should know about all those who had a burning passion for freedom but did not agree in full with the policies of the Congress.'[54]

Joshi would begin work on many of these issues, especially the rewriting of history books, but they would remain at a nascent stage for nearly two decades.

The disappointment that Vajpayee and Advani had felt with Pakistan would get accentuated after a plane hijack by Islamist terrorists forced the government—especially after the terrorists killed one hostage[55]—to free three Kashmiri terrorists in exchange for the plane full of people. It was a lesson the Indian state, the world of the BJP and the RSS would remember, as would one of the men sent to negotiate with the hijackers, a hardened Intelligence Bureau (IB) officer called Ajit Doval.

But India won diplomatically when US President Bill Clinton came to visit in 2000 for an unprecedented five days—and went only for a few hours to Pakistan—and began a process of 'de-hyphenation' that is complete today. No longer would the West, especially America, see the two countries together—their trajectories were clearly very different, their paths and destinies vastly different, and this was acknowledged. One year later, 9/11 would cement the difference between India and Pakistan, especially after Osama bin Laden was found eventually hiding in Pakistan.

But in the summer of 2001, Vajpayee and Advani would make one more attempt at making peace with Pakistan with a summit in Agra with General Pervez Musharraf. Right before the summit, in a meeting, Advani records that he asked Musharraf to hand over

Dawood Ibrahim, the mastermind of the 1993 Bombay bomb blasts but Musharraf insisted that Dawood was not in Pakistan.[56]

The summit failed and so did attempts to thrash out a lasting deal on a 'four-point formula' by Musharraf which, in essence, spoke of turning the two parts of Kashmir into autonomous zones with full freedom of travel between them, and monitoring of administration involving locals.

On 13 December 2001, terrorists attacked the Indian Parliament. The Indian state was being tested with a strike at its very heart. This led to the biggest mobilization of troops at the borders between India and Pakistan since 1971 but war was narrowly averted.

Something else would happen in 2001 which would transform the course of political Hinduism and the history of India. In the autumn of that year, the BJP was looking for a replacement for the ailing Keshubhai Patel, its chief minister in Gujarat. They zeroed in on a man who had been instrumental in many campaign victories and who had been part of the RSS from his childhood, since he was a boy helping at his father's tea stall at a railway station in Gujarat: Narendra Damodardas Modi.

Only weeks later, after Modi won a by-election to formalize his stature as a member of the state legislative assembly as required by electoral law after becoming chief minister, a train halted at Godhra station carrying kar sevaks from Ayodhya. The area, with a majority of Muslims, had had a history of Hindu-Muslim tension. That day, assailants who remain unidentified till today, shut the doors of the compartments and set the bogies of the train on fire. Fifty-nine kar sevaks, all Hindus, were burnt alive.

The riots that followed would be debated in India and around the world for more than a decade, and they still reverberate in polemical discussions. Critics argue that the Modi government did not do enough to stop the bloodletting for three days where mostly Muslims were killed. Modi and his supporters have always maintained that, as a new chief minister, he did everything he could in an extremely volatile situation. Gujarat had had a long history of Hindu-Muslim violence, but again, this was India's first 'televised riot', broadcast live to living rooms around the country and around the world. It made headlines in India and abroad. The Gujarat riots became independent India's most discussed, deliberated and argued-upon case of communal violence.

Despite trepidations, the BJP backed Modi and kept him as chief minister, and amidst the cacophony, Modi started rallies across Gujarat talking about Gujarati pride. In state elections a few months later, the BJP under Modi won two-thirds of the seats and so began his steady rise to the forefront of Indian politics.

In 2004, despite a powerful campaign of 'India Shining', a record of having built some of the finest highways ever made in India and opening the telecommunications sector to private capital in the country, ushering in the age of mobile phones and information technology, and of businesses such as Infosys and Wipro in Bengaluru that would make India the world's call centre, Atal Bihari Vajpayee failed to carry his party to power again. The shock of that loss effectively ended the political career of the man who first brought the BJP to government.

But some of the ideas of his key people would have a much longer shelf life. For instance, Vajpayee's disinvestment minister was Arun Shourie, a determined champion of the private sector and a fierce critic of China and Pakistan. It is Shourie who would argue in 2001 that India's security policy ought to be 'two eyes for an eye, and a jaw for a tooth'[57].

It is Shourie who would argue in 2003 that India had to close its growth gap with China, for economics' sake, and to ensure its safety.

'If the rates of growth of India and China continue to differ by the margins of the past 15 years, within the next 15 years the Chinese economy will be six times that of India. And the consequences will be worse than we can imagine . . . Economic strength is itself power. To take one instance, because China has been able to attract so many more to invest than we have, China today is able to mobilise so many more—American firms, for instance—as lobbyists—to advance its interests. Moreover, economic strength gives China the wherewithal to go in for comprehensive modernisation of its armed forces. Indeed, that there is so much talk of China's economic transformation obscures what China is already doing, what its economic modernisation already enables it to in the military sphere. Will a China six times stronger than India not administer another slap at us? Indeed, will it have to administer a slap? Will an India dwarfed to that extent not learn to pay heed to China's interests subliminally?'[58]

It is Shourie who was among the first to argue in Indian politics that China was overextending itself in infrastructure building, that China's controlled economy might run out of entrepreneurial steam, and that there were issues with Chinese data.

'. . . The achievements—the incredible infrastructure built in Shanghai, for instance, themselves remind us of problems it may be storing up: this infrastructure has been built by getting the country's banks to lend money to the special purpose vehicles that were created for building the projects. But everything has to be paid for in economics: what is the rate of return of these projects today, and how does it compare with what is needed to repay the investments? There is moreover a fundamental issue. The twenty-first century is going to be the century of knowledge—of its continuous unraveling and of its continuous application. One of the central lessons of the twentieth century is that where the state is pervasive, creativity does not flourish. The Chinese have indeed transformed their state. But it remains pervasive. How will they ensure creativity—of the kind, say, youngsters in our IT [information technology] firms have displayed? So we have many things working for us. In many ways, this is India's moment, even vis-à-vis China. For the first time, observers have begun to voice questions in public about China—its statistics; the fact, for instance, as a German investor said recently at a conference I was deputed to attend, that, "If you want your factory to come up quickly, go to China; if you want to make money, go to India." So it is the moment for India. It is a moment. But it is only a moment. What should we do to ensure we grasp it?'[59]

S. Gurumurthy, a chartered accountant, and one of the most cerebral minds in the RSS and leading light of the SJM, with a personal pledge never to enter politics, had other ideas. He pitched:

'Any long term analysis of the present-day world trade regime would indicate not its durability and stability but its instability and transitional nature. So globalisation and global trade regimes are unstable in their very conception and structure. The issue is whether a nation should restructure itself to suit the unstable global structure and ever-changing global institutions? That is, should a nation be largely directed by global perspectives and institutions or be mainly guided by factors inherent to itself? In other words, should an ever-changing global agenda lead a nation to marginalise its national ideas, beliefs and institutions, or should it be directed by its own national agenda based on its own ideas, in which the global situation plays a marginal role? If the answer is yes—then it is a return to swadeshi . . . That is where the civilisational assertion of India commenced in the pre-independence days. Swadeshi and nationalism were the foundation of the Indian freedom movement. They should have been the foundation of a free India. But the Anglo-Saxon domination of the Indian polity and establishment virtually defeated the very objective of the Indian struggle for freedom. The result was the fallacious attempt to westernise India on the socialist model. When socialism could not scratch the skin of the Indian psyche and collapsed with the demise of global communism, they swung to another Anglo-Saxon view, westernisation through globalisation. This too has become a transition, rather than the destination. We started the 20th century with swadeshi and nationalism; we are nearing the end of the century with the very same concepts—swadeshi and nationalism. The long interlude with socialism and the current interlude with globalisation are mere flirtations of the Indian elite establishment lacking in self-confidence. Ultimately, Indian society's unwillingness to disown its age-old values and traditions is manifest in the realisation that globalisation cannot be the core thought of India; it is India which will be the core of India, with the world as a marginal influence.[60']

Gurumurthy, as early as 1998, spoke of an 'India-first' approach (this is how he defined swadeshi) in the manner, according to him, America defined 'America-first'.

All of Shourie's anxieties and highlighting of opportunities, and Gurumurthy's insights and unconventional wisdom were being noticed, but more in Gujarat, than in Delhi.[61]

Vajpayee, already infirm, would never fight another election. But the lotus would bloom in a different way.

6

The Mouse Charmer

Narendra Modi is fond of telling a story, an anecdote he has repeated several times in India and outside before he became prime minister and after. In the story, Modi is travelling abroad when someone asks him, 'Does India still have snake charmers?' An amused Modi responds, 'No, not really, our ancestors had great abilities, we can't match them. But we have mouse charmers these days.'[1] His reference is to the computer mouse and India's prowess as a global technology hub, producing one of the largest numbers of engineers, including software engineers, each year.

There is one more. The year before he ran for prime minister, Modi spoke to students of the Shri Ram College of Commerce, mostly known by its popular acronym SRCC, where, during his speech, he paused to lift a glass of water on his lectern, half-full with water. Lifting the glass, Modi said that optimists would say this glass is half full, pessimists would say that it's half empty, but he had a different, third approach. He thought of the glass as full—half with water and half with air.

These two anecdotes perhaps give an indication of why Modi was able to capture, and continues to retain, immense popularity in India. At the end of 2022, seven years after he first became prime minister, and twenty-two years after he took charge as chief minister of the state of Gujarat, Modi topped the charts as the world's most popular head of government, with an approval rating of 77 per cent.[2] As we will see in this chapter, Modi's politics and its success derive a great deal from focusing on people who had traditionally not been a large part of the mainstream of India's political discourse—the less privileged among every community, the world of software and technology[3] and women. We will see in this chapter how these groups have contributed overwhelmingly to his election victories and his popularity.

Voluminous documentation is available about the Modi phenomenon and the broad highlights of its history. The Gujarat riots triggered an endless debate that continues even today about culpability even though a Special Investigation Team (SIT) set up by the Congress government presented a report in 2012 that cleared Modi of any personal blame, and a decade later, the Supreme Court of India came to the same conclusion[4] after further analysing the report. During this time, Modi won an uninterrupted series of elections that expanded his popularity across the state of Gujarat and then around the country. The rapid growth that Gujarat saw under his leadership came to be called 'the Gujarat model', which he pitched to win national elections with a historical full majority mandate in 2014 and then repeated the feat with an even bigger majority in 2019. There is wide speculation that he is likely to complete a hat-trick in 2024. Meanwhile, those riots are continuing to offer varying responses even in 2023 when the BBC broadcast a film suggesting, based on the opinion given by former British foreign secretary Jack Straw, that the Gujarat government didn't do enough to stop the riots, compelling even commentators who largely stay away from the hardened Modi critics to ask 'why the voices of retired diplomats from twenty years ago should be the voice of God and whether it is not a case of arrogance on the part of the BBC'[5], and a respected business leader to note:

'My Leftist NRI[6] friends were so happy when the former Central Bureau of Investigation (CBI) chief, R.K. Raghavan, was appointed to head the Special Investigation Team (SIT) in 2008—specifically set up to "fix" then Gujarat Chief Minister Narendra Modi. When I gingerly tried to tell them that there had been communal riots in India for hundreds of years and that in independent India, despite some ghastly riots, never had a chief minister been interrogated, they brushed me off. They never acknowledged that Modi had cooperated and testified. When Raghavan gave Modi a clean chit, suddenly, the honest cop became a bad guy! Again, in a low-key manner, when I mentioned to my "friends" that the Army General deputed to "suppress" the 2002 Gujarat riots, General Zameer Uddin Shah[7]—who, for the uninitiated, is a Muslim—had gone on record to praise Modi, they just brushed it off. When I mentioned that Shah was complimentary about Modi but not so much about our bureaucracy, even that did not register.'[8]

This chapter seeks to go beyond such enduring binaries of opinion and seeks to understand Modi and his work from the perspective of political Hinduism ideology and its evolution, development and future.

From a historical perspective, the challenge in analysing Modi's impact is that it is still very much an ongoing process and therefore it is tough to achieve the requisite distance to objectively study it. This chapter therefore seeks not so much to understand the impact of Modi on India and its history as much as it takes forward the story of political Hinduism and how the coming of Narendra Modi has taken the story of political Hinduism further than what any of the stalwarts of the movement could have imagined when it all began.

One of the most important things about Narendra Modi is that both his ardent supporters and his most fervent detractors have usually got him wrong. Many of his diehard supporters have seen him often through a unidimensional lens, as a rightwing pro-capitalist and/or religious partisan, seeking to favour only Hindus. His opponents say the reverse: they see partisanship against Muslims and other minorities, and the promotion of Big Capital instead of common-man economics.

This chapter argues that Modi is a much more complex phenomenon than either his supporters or detractors allow. Consider the following: Modi began and is about to complete the construction of the Ram temple following a Supreme Court judgment[9] that allowed Hindus to build on the site while allocating separate land nearby for Muslims to rebuild the mosque, and a majority of educational scholarships given to minority communities have been given to Muslims under the Modi government, benefitting more than 20 million students[10]. In Modi's first term, more Muslim students got scholarships than they ever did in the five years previous to the Modi government.[11]

While there was controversy about cattle smuggling-related violence and vigilante attacks on Muslims in the first term of the Modi-led BJP government, Muslim preference for Modi and the BJP has actually risen in the last seven years[12], as has the party's Muslim vote share[13]. Some of the reasons that have been offered for this seeming dichotomy is the spread of grassroots developmental policies such as 'electrifying villages and subsidising LPG connections generated Muslim support for the BJP from all sects'[14].

Modi's removal by the law of the triple *talaq*, a process under *sharia*, where a man can divorce a woman merely by saying the word 'talaq' three times, won support from many Muslim women groups[15]—though some Muslim men are still managing to find a loophole to avoid post-divorce responsibilities[16]. Curiously, the triple talaq has continued in India even though it is banned and considered un-Islamic in many Muslim countries, including Egypt, Pakistan, Bangladesh and Malaysia. Cases of triple talaq dropped by 82 per cent after its removal by law in August 2019.[17]

During Modi's time in office, the conversation between Hindus and minorities, especially Muslims, has become more acerbic in India's usually cacophonous public square—but outreach between the RSS and Muslims has never been as prominent. In 2018, RSS chief Mohan Bhagwat argued, 'Hindu Rashtra doesn't mean there's no place for Muslims. The day it becomes so, it won't be Hindutva. Hindutva talks about one world family.'[18] In 2021, Bhagwat said, 'Anyone who says Muslims should not live in India is not Hindu.'[19]

In the summer of 2022, and then again in January 2023, Mohan Bhagwat had detailed meetings with prominent civil society members from the Muslim community, including a former lieutenant governor of Delhi, a former election commissioner of India and a former member of Parliament (MP). These interactions have been analysed in India's biggest news magazine, *India Today*, as, 'The Muslim outreach of the BJP and the RSS is part of the wider Hindutva doctrine wherein both organisations—while being firmly against appeasement—profess that the government should extend benefits to all citizens without discriminating on the basis of caste or religion.'[20]

Shahid Siddiqui, the former MP, explained this as, 'We are concerned that whatever is happening in the country is weakening the religious unity in the country. So, we all had discussions on how to sustain and strengthen peace and brotherhood in the country.'[21] Bhagwat has also had detailed meetings with Muslim clergymen in recent years.

According to Delhi's former lieutenant governor, Najeeb Jung, Bhagwat emphasized three things:

1. Hindutva is an inclusive concept in which all communities have equal room;
2. The country can progress only when all communities are united;
3. The Indian Constitution is sacrosanct, and the entire country has to abide by it.

Bhagwat, according to Jung, sought to dispel the fear that RSS is seeking to abandon the Constitution at the first opportunity and that Muslims will be disenfranchised.[22]

Soon afterwards, Modi told a key gathering of top BJP leaders that they should reach out to different sub-sections of Muslims, the Pasmandas, the Bohras, educated and professional Muslims and, of course, women.[23] He had made a similar appeal in July 2022.

So, what's really going on? On one hand, Modi's India had been accused of having 'no space for Muslims', on the other, the prime minister was being quoted telling his party colleagues that '. . . no one, including Muslims, should be left out [and that] we follow the principle that every citizen is equal and should be treated as such.'[24]

There was a history to this. It is not well-known outside Gujarat that one of the communities Narendra Modi was closest to in his years as Gujarat chief minister was the Bohras, a tightly-knit mercantile community of Shia Muslims of about a million people, half of whom live in India, mostly in Gujarat. The Bohras, like other subsects of Muslims such as the Ahmadias and even the Shias, are considered apostates by mainstream Sunni Muslims. The Bohras usually have a spiritual head, titled Syedna, and the late Syedna Mohammed Burhanuddin was a close personal friend of Narendra Modi from the time the latter was a political worker in Gujarat. The community continued to be close to Modi through his years as chief minister, a relationship that has stayed the course even after he became prime minister.

Apart from the Bohras, Modi has instructed his party members to reach out to the Pasmandas, a less privileged section of Muslims. Indian Muslims are dominated by the *Ashraafs* or *Ashraafis*, who tend to be wealthier, educated and privileged (even though numerically they are a minority of Muslims).

The majority of Muslims are the less privileged Pasmandas (as many as 85 per cent of Indian Muslims fall under the Pasmanda category[25]) though they have traditionally had less access to power and resources. The vice chancellor of the Aligarh Muslim University has written that the BJP's outreach to Pasmanda Muslims under Modi,

'signals a political recognition of the unaddressed social justice issues within the Indian Muslim community. Since colonial times, tensions have simmered among Muslims between Ashraafs (elite or dominant Muslims who are in a minority) and Pasmandas (most backward Muslims who form the majority). The main grievance of the Pasmandas is their exclusion from power structures by the Ashraafs. The latter have been accused of prioritising religious and sentimental issues of the community—such as personal law, Babri Masjid—over the developmental concerns of the underprivileged Pasmandas. The propensity of the Ashraafs to galvanise Muslims around sentimental issues attracted favour with major political parties except the BJP. This explains why the minority Ashraafs have cornered the majority of the "Muslim political representation" in various political parties. The Muslim intelligentsia and civil society should also shoulder some responsibility for letting this anomaly perpetuate by failing to effectively bring Muslim identity differentials to the political fore.'[26]

This outreach by Modi follows a similar effort that has borne a rich electoral dividend for the BJP. Modi, himself from the Other Backward Castes (OBC) grouping, has made the BJP a party and political movement not of upper castes, as is traditionally understood and analysed, but a party that gets most of its votes in the biggest and electorally the most advanced states from the 'lower castes', the underprivileged, women and other groups, which have been traditionally less researched in their contribution to Indian electoral politics.

In this sense, Modi's politics draws directly from the Savarkarite roots of political Hinduism and pulls away from the classical understanding of academics like Jaffrelot and others[27], that political Hinduism is mainly upper-caste dominated because of the number of Brahmins who shared ideas of political Hinduism within the RSS leadership. In 2014, the BJP led by Modi 'succeeded in forming an unprecedented coalition of social groups' voting for it, including major chunks of OBCs and Dalits[28]. This has been repeated ever since.

How has this happened? How did a party that was always criticized for representing upper-caste business community interests make this transition? One theory offered by some researchers is the efforts of the Sangh to consistently push the narrative of a 'caste-less Hindu society' by organizing interdining and other events where there are no caste divides (this, of course, is an idea that goes all the way back to Savarkar, but years of efforts by other leaders in the political Hinduism universe are finally bearing fruit). Some researchers have noted that, in Uttar Pradesh, for instance, the home state of the upcoming Ram temple, the RSS and affiliate bodies 'in recent years have focused on massive inter-dining events and integrating subaltern heroes into broader Hindu mythology. Its campaign among the Valmikis, among the most impoverished SC castes forced to do sanitation work, has centred around imagining the writer of the Ramayana as a member of the caste and huge Ram katha *satsangs*[29] have become the site for political and electoral consolidation for the Sangh'[30].

But there is a policy angle in this. Before we come to that, it is worth noting that even though there was a lot of debate on whether Modi was pro-capitalist or not before his ascension to prime ministership, this stems from a larger historical debate about the economics of the BJP.

Throughout its four-decade-long history, the BJP has always been divided between two viewpoints on economics: the free-market model that embraces globalization and is private capital-oriented, or the more indigenous, protectionist system with a significant welfare component. In the years the BJP ruled India in the late 1990s, and beginning in 2014, the party has been wrestling with whether it should make the role of the state more prominent, or mainly champion enterprise. Even within the world of business, should the focus be domestic industry or bringing in foreign capital?

Understanding the history and context of such a dichotomy explains many aspects of the BJP's history and its stints in power as India's ruling party. Most importantly, it sheds light on the seemingly contradictory policies of the incumbent government led by Prime Minister Narendra Modi.

From the time Modi rose to prominence in the early 2000s as chief minister of Gujarat, he has been noted for his affinity towards promoting business and entrepreneurship; he himself has reiterated such inclinations on different occasions. Indeed, under his leadership, the western state's economy grew at a faster pace than the national average for more than a decade. During that time, Gujarat also transformed from a power-deficit to a power-surplus state and managed the difficult task of achieving growth in agriculture while reducing its share in the state's gross domestic product. This is particularly significant because Indian agriculture has long been plagued with low productivity, and while it employs vast numbers of people, often such participation in farm labour is due to the lack of alternative better-paying professional opportunities. The movement of excess farm labour to manufacturing and services remains one of India's key challenges. Gujarat became a model for 'freeing up space for private initiative and enterprise and the creation of an enabling environment by the State.'[31] Shortly before Modi became prime minister in 2014, the Ministry of Commerce and Industry under the Congress regime noted in a report that Gujarat's land acquisition system for business under the then chief minister Modi was the best in the country.[32]

Modi's rise to power as prime minister in 2014 came with great expectations of a slew of economic reforms. The government has brought several significant changes in the economic environment—including introducing a transformational bankruptcy law and pushing through the long-awaited Goods and Services Tax (GST). Certain key reforms, however, remain pending including, critically, a game-changing land reform law. Some early signs of building consensus for land reform were stalled early in his first term as prime minister following criticisms by the opposition that the government's proposal was anti-poor.[33] The other critical, and long-pending, task of labour reform is also impeded, as was a major initiative to enforce long-awaited reforms in the agriculture sector after protests mainly from farmers in Punjab. The government has been hesitant to address issues of land acquisition or labour, especially those involving wages and retrenchments because they often become mired in political protest and carry the risk of being used against the party during elections.

While India under Modi has removed thousands of archaic laws and implemented a historic reduction in corporate taxes, and most recently also reduced personal income tax and heavily promoted start-ups, which has made India the third biggest start-up ecosystem in the country, its key focus has to be to create a sort of tech-enabled welfare system focused on getting last-mile delivery right.

This was infamously contentious and corrupt in India, so much so that one prime minister, Rajiv Gandhi, was on record saying that 15 paise of every rupee spent by the government actually reaches the beneficiary. The BJP had traditionally complained about rent-seeking scandals and government schemes for local politicians and political parties in charge of distributing state funds.

When he became prime minister, Modi first sought to create a policy trinity called JAM which stood for Jan Dhan (a name given to basic bank accounts for everyone especially the hitherto unbanked), Aadhaar (the unique identity number programme, started by his predecessor Manmohan Singh, which Modi made the cornerstone of his welfarism to ensure the right beneficiaries get the goods of governance), and the Mobile phone (which became the one-stop-shop for all information, bypassing local administrators, some of whom might be rent-seeking).

This system was then put to use to reform India's public delivery system or what is known as direct benefit transfer (DBT). Since its inception in Modi's first term, more than Rs 25 trillion[34] has been distributed using this system eliminating, among other things, around one million fake or non-existent beneficiaries under rural development schemes, eradicating another around 50 million spurious beneficiaries of subsidized cooking gas cylinders, 40 million false beneficiaries of government rations and nearly 3 million false awardees of government scholarships.[35] This elimination not only saved the government a lot of money, it could instead be redirected to millions who need support.

Modi made the construction of toilets and the elimination of open defecation a priority, and to date, more than 110 million toilets have been built—a process that even resulted in a Bollywood hit film called *Toilet: A Love Story*! It has also helped create more than 470 million basic Jan Dhan bank accounts, insurance cover for more than 440 million, more than 90 million LPG cylinder connections and sent out cash assistance transfers directly via mobile phone and bank accounts worth more than two trillion rupees to more than 110 million farmers.[36] A housing scheme has built more than 30 million homes for the underprivileged since 2014.[37]

Throughout this entire process, what Modi has strived to create is a direct benefit interface with the Indian citizen—and of course, the voter—with an unspoken promise that retaining him in power would result in tangible benefits in their day-to-day lives. Philosophically, the strategy is the public policy equivalent of his regular radio show, *Mann ki Baat*, where he shares his thoughts with citizens. It could also be compared to the artful use of his Twitter account, which he has used to have a direct conversation with citizens. Indeed, it would appear that every delivery of a good or service has the imprint of Modi on it.

Contrary to the expectations of some libertarians, Modi as prime minister has not sought to dramatically reduce the role of the state. Rather, what he has done is a reinterpretation of the promise of small government—by reducing the government-to-citizen interface via technology with local bureaucracy, which is often a point of corruption. What the prime minister has done is to attempt to smoothen the strife at the touchpoint of delivery, for instance, petty corruption while delivering a service given by the state to the citizens. However, the overall role of the government has widened in scope. One of the early realizations of the first-term Modi government seems to have been that the Indian citizen may, in fact, not be seeking *less* government in a society where few other institutions offer even a nominal guarantee of monetary security; it wants *better* government, with a clear path of transactional delivery. People want to know what exactly they will receive from the government, and how.

In the case of the Modi government, the strategy veers towards streamlining the delivery of specific benefits (such as cooking gas cylinders or toilets) to the financially impoverished sections of the population. Instead of taking an open-for-all-citizens approach, the Modi government has preferred to sharply target the beneficiaries using identification technology to ensure minimum leakage. (This was one of the critical problems of the welfare schemes of its predecessor, the United Progressive Alliance or UPA government.[38])

This kind of targeting has had the electoral benefit of changing Modi's image from being a markets-and-entrepreneur-friendly politician to someone who is much more focused on delivering governance to the bottom of the pyramid.

The question then remains as to whether Modi is growth-and-free-market-oriented, or he is transitioning to the welfare state model. Researchers like Krzysztof Iwanek have pointed out some of the early contradictions in economic thinking with the RSS, the ideological parent of the BJP and the mentoring ground of Modi. The second head of the RSS, M.S. Golwalkar, for instance, denounced both communism and capitalism for confining man's experience of life merely to the material. But Golwalkar also argued that 'the success of any government or any particular theory of government is to be measured in terms of its capacity to give every citizen two square meals, a place to rest in, sufficient clothing, treatment in case of illness and education. That is the acid test.'[39] Iwanek has argued that 'Golwalkar probably really favoured capitalism, but he chose to hide it under the garb of some old Indian tradition of political economy which was somehow more ethical than modern capitalism.'[40]

This contradictory theme recurs throughout the history of the BJP. Consider the views of another economic stalwart of the RSS and its affiliate organization, the Sangh Parivar, Dattopant Thengadi. For example, Thengadi's 1995 book, *The Third Way*, promotes what its title says: a 'third way', between capitalism and communism both of whose demise it foresees. It advocates instead an indigenous, sustainable path with a special focus on environmental upkeep. 'The world of communism has virtually collapsed. But this need not generate euphoria. Apart from the weight of its own internal self-contradictions, a number of contributory factors have been responsible for its downfall. These have not yet been properly evaluated. Capitalism is on the decline. But its demise is being delayed. Knowledgeable circles have started their search for a third alternative.'[41]

The Thengadi model, which could now be said to be the Modi model, while not entirely dismissing the impact of globalization, argues for a domestic-first model with strong elements of protectionism. In this, they are joined by the stalwart of the Hindutva worldview, V.D. Savarkar, a great believer in swadeshi or self-manufacture, arguing, 'every step must be taken by the State to protect national industries against foreign competition.'[42]

However, another leading light of the Parivar pantheon, Syama Prasad Mookerjee, 'judged every scheme and policy by the criterion of its practicability and usefulness to the people and was not wedded to any dogma or concept.'[43] He was India's first industries minister who laid the foundation for major industrial projects after independence in 1947, including the Chittaranjan Locomotive Works. The political party Mookerjee started, the Bharatiya Jana Sangh, the predecessor of the BJP, occasionally defended village enterprises in a Gandhian way, while also promising to let in foreign capital, promote enterprise and reduce taxes.[44] For his part, Deendayal Upadhyaya, another key ideologue in the 1960s, gave the Hindutva movement its *Integral Humanism* text and argued for similar swadeshi ideas. When the Bharatiya Janata Party was created in 1980, however, it committed itself to Gandhian socialism. The BJP's current constitution document has a clause that talks about the party's commitment to the 'Gandhian approach to socio-economic issues leading to the establishment of an egalitarian society free from exploitation.'[45]

All of this is to be compared with the BJP's record of disinvestment under Prime Minister Atal Bihari Vajpayee between 1999 and 2004, including the setting up of a separate ministry for disinvestment and selling Videsh Sanchar Nigam Limited (VSNL), Hindustan Zinc, Balco, Indian Petrochemicals Corporation Limited, several state-run hotels and Modern Food Industries. It should be noted, however, that Yashwant Sinha, a finance minister of that period, lamented about economic reforms that the 'national highway project is regarded as the high point of the NDA government's achievement, yet in 2004 general elections the NDA lost all the 14 seats it had won in 1998 along NH-2 (the key highway).'[46] Sinha argued that economic reforms must be seen to be touching the lives of people.

Modi seems to have learnt from these experiences and teachings that the path to electoral success is to continuously balance welfarism and growth. Modi's breakthrough realization seems to have been that most of India is at a stage where globalization has critically sharpened cultural and economic inequities—and mass-scale delivery of public goods by the state can assuage grievances. While the focus on growth is critical for India, unless the benefits of that growth are felt at the grassroots through the delivery of goods and services directly from the state, it might be impossible to contain the anxieties and restlessness unleashed by globalization. At the same time, Modi is signalling that giving up on growth would lead to a downward spiral that would make it impossible for the state to deliver goods and services. The flight of global capital from India could cripple and even imperil his government.

Faced with the upcoming challenge of mass automation, there is an understanding that the state must step in to assist in crucial ways while ensuring that it is seen to be doing so. The benefit of this endeavour is already clear—unlike Vajpayee who pitched 'India Shining' but was rejected by a large number of India's poorest voters who perhaps felt that their lives were not directly touched by the 'shine'—Narendra Modi's model is to ensure that there are direct touchpoints of benefit that are embedded in the minds of the voters. That it has helped the BJP win successive elections with a full majority speaks of the potency of such a model. In the around eight years of Modi rule, India's GDP, despite the Covid-19 pandemic, continues to be among the fastest-growing in the world[47], inflation has risen but is still under relative control, unemployment has crashed from the highs during the pandemic, exports crossed $400 billion for the first time in financial year 2022[48], and foreign direct investment has touched a new record every year during the Modi government and was last at more than $83.5 billion[49]. It has since dipped due to a global slowdown but there is increasing consensus that rarely has the Indian economy looked as attractive. In July 2023, a report that included views from 142 chief investment officers, heads of asset classes along with senior portfolio strategists from eighty-five sovereign wealth funds and fifty-seven central banks, said, 'India has now overtaken China as the most attractive emerging market for investing in emerging market debt.[50]' The report by the asset management company Invesco noted, 'India is increasingly viewed positively for its improved business and political stability, favourable demographics, regulatory initiatives, and a friendly environment for sovereign investors.[51]'

This has given Modi the leeway to expand the grassroots welfare net and due to the sheer logic of demographics, the majority of the beneficiaries have been underprivileged groups. In Uttar Pradesh, for instance, estimates suggest that while the state has just about 20 per cent Muslims, almost 40 per cent of the homes built by the government[52] have gone to Muslims, as has

22 per cent of the toilets constructed, 37 per cent of the LPG
cylinders distributed[53] and 30 per cent of small loans for
businesses given by the government[54]. Around half of the homes
built are estimated to have gone to Pasmanda Muslims[55], and
the community, traditionally makers of many handmade local
artisanal products, has benefited from schemes such as the one
that promotes unique products from each district of the country[56].

Data also shows that in the state of Uttar Pradesh, India's
largest and most politically important state with more than 200
million people, OBCs and other lower castes who are classified
under Scheduled Castes or SCs accounted for:

- 57.5 per cent of the BJP's Uttar Pradesh Lok Sabha candidates
  in the 2019 general election
- 52.8 per cent of its candidates in the 2017 assembly poll that
  it won handsomely
- 50 per cent of its office-bearers in the state in 2020
- 48.1 per cent of Uttar Pradesh Chief Minister Yogi
  Adityanath's council of ministers (Yogi Adityanath is from
  the BJP)
- 35.6 per cent of the BJP's district-level presidents[57]

This kind of new data crunching by political scientists like Nalin
Mehta[58] has gone beyond the old analysis of theorists, such as
Christophe Jaffrelot, who have often argued that the BJP is 'anti-
poor' and against the interests of underprivileged castes.[59]

In fact, the BJP, in 2021, underlined its pro-poor and lower
caste push by announcing a 27 per cent reservation for OBCs and
10 per cent for economically weaker sections or what is known as
the EWS category, in the national quota system for undergraduate
and postgraduate medical and dental courses. All this has borne

electoral fruit—one-third of Dalit voters opted for the BJP in 2019 compared to one-fourth in 2014, and the party has mopped up more support from OBC voters than ever.[60]

This is more than clever resource distribution for economic gain. It is, in fact, the culmination of a process that began with Advani's Ram Janmabhoomi movement. It is rarely ever recognized in traditional discourse about political Hinduism that the movement that really gave it countrywide popularity was fronted not by Brahmins but by firebrand 'lower-caste' leaders. Not only did it have organizers like Modi, who were not Brahmin, but in Uttar Pradesh and Madhya Pradesh, the heartland of the campaign for the Ram temple, it was led by non-Brahmin, lower-caste firebrand leaders like the then chief minister of Uttar Pradesh Kalyan Singh, the ascetic Uma Bharti and Vinay Katiyar[61]. The man[62] who laid the foundation stone of the Ram Janmabhoomi temple was a Dalit, and the first *prasadam* or offering after the ground-breaking ceremony of the new temple in 2020 was sent to a Dalit family. Even the face of the Ram Janmabhoomi movement was not the Brahmin leader of the BJP, Atal Bihari Vajpayee, but Lal Krishna Advani, who is from a subsection of the *vaishya* or trader caste called Lohana.

What happened with the Ram temple movement with the BJP is that what used to be primarily an upper-caste Hindu movement broadened its base and Modi's victory sealed the subaltern rise not only in India but also within political Hinduism. Modi had been mocked by his rivals from the Congress for his humble origins as someone who once worked as a tea-bearer at a relative's roadside tea stall, but Modi changed the game, pitching himself as the authentic representative of those who had been left behind by the elite capture of India's institutions.[63]

As one Dalit scholar has written:

'Contrary to clichéd liberal discourse, Hindutva and the
promise of a common Hindu identity always appealed to a
[section of the] large Dalit and OBC castes as it promises
to liberate them from the narrow identity of a weaker caste,
and induct them into a powerful Hindu community. The
appeal is especially strong among the non-dominant Dalit
and OBC castes, which are numerically smaller and weaker
in terms of socio-economic and cultural capital. For them,
only the Hindu identity promises social mobility, inclusion
and political power. It is far easier for them to appeal to
Hindu unity to push back against caste discrimination,
and exclusion, than to form an independent outfit like the
dominant subaltern castes . . . the pivotal moment was the
Ram Janambhoomi movement, when almost all the Hindu
castes were mobilised. For several subaltern castes, it was the
first time they entered mainstream political mobilisation and
imagination. Trapped in the echo-chamber of radicals and
firebrand activists, one would think that Ram and Ramayan
are reviled among the Dalit and OBC communities. But it
misses the simple point that Ram was a main deity in the
Bhakti movement in both *sagun* and *nirgun* strains[64], with
widespread popularity among the subaltern for its challenge
to social exclusion. There are numerous sects of Ram *bhakti*
rooted in these subaltern castes. The Ayodhya movement
was complemented by the conscious effort of the Hindutva
organisations to adopt a more local and caste-specific
narrative, rather than the old homogenous language derived
from the upper-caste cultural milieu. The caste narrative
of Dalit and OBC castes, their icons, histories and desire
to be 'visible' in the historical narrative has finally found
mainstream expression within the Hindutva fold.'[65]

This explains partly why the Modi-led BJP continues to find unprecedented electoral success. There are other equally important reasons for his success. One concerns the nature of the debate on secularism—after all, the main accusation Modi's critics always offer is the lack of secular values in Modi and the BJP. And yet, as Modi was rising up the popularity rungs as chief minister of Gujarat, a familiar subversion of the principles of secularism, quite like in the time of Rajiv Gandhi before the Ram Janmabhoomi movement, was unfolding in India. In 2009, a new education policy created by the Congress-led government exempted only 'minority schools' or all Muslim, Christian and other faith-based schools, but made no such exemption for Hindu schools. In 2011, the same government tried to bring in a law that recognized 'communal violence' as only violence committed on Muslims, Christians and others, but not on Hindus. In 2013, again the same government pushed for special fast-track courts to examine matters where only Muslims arrested on terror charges would be given a swifter hearing. One state government, in Uttar Pradesh, attempted to unilaterally drop terror charges against Muslim accused until the local high court stopped the plan.[66] In the same state, the government tried to make special reservations in all government schemes of up to 20 per cent only for Muslims, even though religion-based quotas are not legal in India. In the state of Bengal, special government funds were announced only for *maulvis* (cleric-teachers in Islamic madrassas). Manmohan Singh, the Oxbridge-educated prime minister, said that minorities, especially Muslims, had the 'first right' to the developmental resources of the country. Singh said, 'We will have to devise innovative plans to ensure that minorities, particularly the Muslim minority, are empowered to share equitably the fruits of development. These must have the first claim on resources.'[67]

All of this created a climate in which Modi in 2014, unapologetic about his Hindu identity, but speaking only a language of development and with the slogan 'Sabka saath, sabka vikas' (with everyone, and development for everyone), found a large audience willing to listen to his alternative, especially since for a decade his Gujarat model of governance had made news around the country. When Modi won, a prominent liberal theorist wrote a piece called 'How Modi Defeated Liberals like Me' where he said:

'What secularism did was it enforced oppositions in a way that the middle class felt apologetic and unconfident about its beliefs, its perspectives. Secularism was portrayed as an upwardly mobile, drawing room discourse they were inept at . . . With Mr. Modi around, the message claimed, "We don't need to be ashamed of our religion. This could not have happened earlier." At first the message irritated me and then made me thoughtful. A colleague of mine added, "You English speaking secularists have been utterly coercive, making the majority feel ashamed of what was natural." The comment, though brutal and devastating, was fair.[68]'

With his message of unapologetic traditionalism and positivism, Modi also appeared at a critical juncture of Indian history—after about two decades (when he made his bid for prime ministership) of economic liberalization and growth that had pushed India towards never-before levels of wealth and prosperity. Between 1991 and 2014, per capita GDP rose from around $300 to $1500 per annum. Even on Maslow's terms, many Indians had enough material satisfaction to start thinking about and asking deeper questions about identity. It is worth adding here that India's per capita income has doubled since Modi took office about a decade ago[69], and during the same time, India has risen from being the tenth-biggest to the fifth-largest economy in the world.

It has been argued that Modi rode at the intersection of several propelling forces, some of which we have seen earlier in this chapter, but there were other compelling reasons which facilitated his rise.

The first is the sheer volume of young people seeking change (and jobs), which is likely to top off at around 485 million aged between fifteen and thirty-four of a population of 1.5 billion in 2030. These young people grew up, many of them, with the story of Gujarat's development and, in parallel, by the time it was 2014, were plagued by corruption, scams, internal Maoist violence and 'policy paralysis', which threatened to crash the Indian economy.[70]

These young people, often from non-metropolis but fast-growing urban and semi-urban centres, sought a different narrative about themselves and about the country, and Modi provided it.

The *Guardian* newspaper in England wrote a prescient editorial that captured the mood accurately on the day Modi won his first national election:

'Today, 18 May 2014, may well go down in history as the day when Britain finally left India. Narendra Modi's victory in the elections marks the end of a long era in which the structures of power did not differ greatly from those through which Britain ruled the subcontinent. India under the Congress party was in many ways a continuation of the British Raj by other means. The last of midnight's children[71] are now a dwindling handful of almost 70-year-olds, but it is not the passing of the independence generation that makes the difference.

'The India those men and women lived in was one that, like its predecessor, was centralised, garrisoned, culturally constricted, and ruled by a relatively small English-speaking elite whose attitude toward the masses was alternately benevolent and exploitative but never inclusive. Universal suffrage gave Indians a vote but not, at least for much of the time, a voice. When that voice was occasionally heard, as it was in 1977 in the elections that followed the disastrously unpopular Emergency declared by prime minister Indira Gandhi, there could be a sudden sense of its almost volcanic capacity to remake the political landscape, but such moments were rare. Now that voice has been heard again. It has endorsed a new kind of leader in the shape of Mr. Modi. He is from the lower castes. He is not a natural English speaker. He has no truck with the secular and socialist traditions that shaped Congress. But, more important, that voice has announced a new kind of India. In the old India the poor were there to be helped, when the elite remembered to do so or when they needed to seek or, in effect, to buy votes. The middling classes were taken for granted and sometimes snubbed. The new India, most observers agree, is not interested in handouts, and refuses to be snubbed.

'Instead it wants the obstacles it sees as impeding its aspirations swept away. It has discarded the deference it displayed toward the Gandhi family and toward the Anglicised or, these days, Americanised top levels of society. Whether in its older and purer socialist guise or in its later embrace of the market, Congress has lost its magic, even though the party includes some profoundly decent and well-intentioned people. The core constituency of the Bharatiya Janata party, meanwhile, never shared the non-sectarian values that Congress imperfectly upheld and wants an India where its version of Hinduism has unchallenged primacy.

'It should be obvious that these underlying changes in Indian society have brought us Mr. Modi and not the other way round. He sensed a great shift in mood and played to it.'[72]

It is worth underlining that 2014 was the first election when Indians born after 1991, the year the economic liberalization process began, were entitled to vote. It was the first election where a new demographic, children of the liberalization, got a chance to emphasize their political preferences. Modi went into 2014 urging his campaign to target young and first-time voters.[73] And this bore fruit—the 2014 election saw the highest-ever voter turnout in the history of national polls in India; it also saw the highest number of youth voters casting their vote. In 2009, the election before 2014, the all-India voter turnout was 58 per cent compared to 66 per cent five years later, and among voters aged between eighteen and twenty-five, the voting percentage jumped from 54 per cent in 2009 to 68 per cent in 2014.[74] In 2019, a similarly high level of young voters participated in polling, and in both 2014 and 2019, an all-time high of 66 per cent of eligible women voters made their choice at the ballot box.

Second, Narendra Modi made women voters a special target group in his policymaking and his speeches. The LPG scheme was pitched as a major relief measure for women who were the worst sufferers of indoor air pollution caused by wood-burning stoves[75], making it a major campaign point. In 2019, the BJP received more votes from women than it ever had, and in February–March 2022, in four of the five state elections that the BJP won[76] including in the most important state electorally, Uttar Pradesh, more women turned out to vote than men.[77]

So, the Modi phenomenon has benefited not only from a surge in youth and women voters but it also must be remembered that these were voters who were empowered in a sense by the decade of high growth India had seen between 2003 and 2011, and were impatient for a repeat performance especially when growth and policymaking stuttered from around 2012 onwards.

Modi's politics, coming as it does from one of the most industrialized and urbanized states in the country, Gujarat, also benefited from the fact that the entire country had been moving in that direction.

'Officially, 32 percent of India's population are full-time residents and voters in urban areas (by 2011 census figures). However, some 60 percent of the GDP is linked to cities, constituting the urban economy. By 2030, this figure will rise to 70 percent.[78] The discrepancy between the GDP and population numbers is glaring. It masks the fact that a larger section of people—more than 32 percent—are associated with or dependent on the urban economy. It fails to factor in migrant workers or recipients of remittances, for instance, whose household income and family prosperity is tied to the city, even if they vote in the village. This means, and there is empirical evidence to support it, that voters are learning to distinguish between provincial and national elections, and realising that jobs in the big city cannot be fixed by a local politician. India is therefore seeing the beginnings of a broader middle class with a heightened sense of macroeconomic issues.[79]'

The third undeniable element of the Modi pitch has been his embrace of technology, not just via policy, but as a constant vocal championing of the adoption of deep digitization as a key to better governance. From the early use of Twitter, where he is among the most followed people on Earth[80], to the use of 3D holograms to ensure that he could be giving speeches at multiple locations simultaneously, Modi has made technology an integral part of his world view. One of his most prized achievements is the roll-out of the United Payments Interface (UPI), a baseline digital tech architecture upon which all fintech solutions sit in the country, and digital transactions account for about half of all financial transactions in India. India is now exporting the UPI technology and the RuPay card as an alternative payment mechanism (apart from the SWIFT system) to countries such as Singapore, Malaysia, Bhutan, the UAE, France and others.[81]

Modi has sought to use technology to create a vision of what I call 'Indofuturism', which promotes a celebration of old Indian culture empowered with technology. After the success of UPI, Modi has announced plans to launch a countrywide digital health programme that has been touted as the game changer in delivering healthcare solutions at the grassroots level.[82] Under Modi's watch, some of the largest Hindu statues have been commissioned and built, including a 221-metre statue of Ram at Ayodhya alongside the Ram temple, a Shivaji statue off the shores of Mumbai, a statue of the philosopher-saint Shankara at Kedarnath in the Himalayas and a 66-metre Ramanuja statue in Hyderabad. Of course, there is the grand statue of the saviour of the Somnath temple in the political Hinduism pantheon, the 182-metre Sardar Vallabhbhai Patel statue in Gujarat, with the reconstruction of the Kashi Vishwanath temple pathway as a corridor separating it from the rest of Benaras as a neatly designed space connected straight from the ghats or river banks of the Ganga and free of the urban sprawl and clutter that used to crowd it. In each of these projects, the ambition, the dimensions and the technical skills needed to deliver them have helped Modi pitch his version of what India's rise should look like.

Modi's journey, in fact, could be seen as delivering on all the things that have been core issues in the world of political Hinduism. The removal of Article 370 or the special, relatively autonomous, status of Kashmir, the banning of triple talaq and the building of the Ram temple fulfils some of the most integral aims of political Hinduism.

Even through the controversies, for instance, violence related to cow slaughter, in which Modi had to make an appeal, 'Today, when I hear that someone is killed in the name of a cow—whether he is innocent or guilty is something the law will decide—no person has the right to take the law into his own hands. I appeal to the people of the country: Violence is not a solution to the problems'[83], some fundamental issues that had been highlighted in the discourse of political Hinduism came to be more widely tackled. In this case, it was the problem of cattle being smuggled from India to Bangladesh causing significant local agrarian distress and unrest. Due to stricter policing at the India-Bangladesh border, cattle confiscated during illegal transit reduced from around 1,68,000 to 46,000 between 2016 and 2020.[84] The introduction of the Citizenship (Amendment) Act (CAA), which offers sanctuary and citizenship to minorities facing persecution in other South Asian countries, triggered controversy when coupled with a National Register of Citizens (NRC) for fears of being discriminatory towards Muslims. But the CAA on its own has long been an agenda of political Hinduism, especially as the numbers of persecution and ostracism of Hindu minorities in Pakistan and Bangladesh have grown. On Pakistan, Modi crossed a psychological barrier that no Indian prime minister, including Vajpayee, had touched, when he sent fighter jets across the Line of Control after a deadly terror attack killed forty soldiers in the Pulwama region of Kashmir in 2019 and risking escalation between nuclear-armed countries. In India, it was widely seen as calling Pakistan's bluff of threatening nuclear escalation and showed that the restraint that held back Vajpayee after the attack on the Indian Parliament was no longer available and India was prepared to up the ante if attacked. No major terror attack has happened since then in India. Under Modi, India's nuclear triad has been completed with the successful testing of the country's indigenous ballistic missile nuclear submarine, INS Arihant, in October 2022, the successful testing of an anti-satellite weapon (only the fourth country to do so after the US, Russia and China)[85], and we are in the process of acquiring a hypersonic missile[86].

Some of these issues will not go away any time soon. The Indian Army has been locked in its deadliest face-off ever, after the 1962 war, with Chinese forces in the high Himalayas since 2020, with no sign of any resolution. The clash between India and China ought to get as much attention as China's contest with the US. It is certainly as dangerous. But by taking a tough stance of confrontation at the border (even though India-China trade exceeded $135 billion in 2022) in line with the role America wants India to play, but at the same time refusing to toe the American line on the war in Ukraine where India has refused to outright condemn Russia, Modi is demonstrating that political Hinduism as a strategic ideology can face the heat of hard diplomacy—practising continuity with an adequate vocabulary of change. Russia is an old, tested Indian ally, and non-alignment or independence in foreign policymaking is a Nehruvian holy grail. But Modi has given all this his very own twist, encouraging far more aggressive language (including Foreign Minister S. Jaishankar calling out American F-16 fighter jet sales to Pakistan in the middle of the Ukraine war and pressure to condemn Russia, while sitting in Washington[87]) and a hard realpolitik edge—all the while talking about India's redefinition of itself as a civilizational state (incidentally what China calls itself, too) rather than a mere constitutional democracy. In doing so, Modi is negating the old idea that Hindutva is a 'minor school'[88] of Indian strategy making—he is arguing that political Hinduism is right up there as a major school that only lacked its own prime ministers to push its case. That, despite differences of approach on the war in Ukraine and on Russia, Modi was given a red carpet welcome[89] in the US in June 2023 has strengthened the idea that India was finally pulling its weight in geopolitics.

Beyond these military measures, Modi has achieved one immeasurable thing—he made political Hinduism mainstream. Today, the powerful chief ministers of the Congress party in states such as Chhattisgarh[90] and Rajasthan[91] are united with their BJP predecessors in promoting the idea that cow slaughter must invoke the strictest punishment and significant state resources must be spent on ensuring the welfare of the cow. In India's largest state, Uttar Pradesh, the BJP now has a two-time chief minister who is a Hindu saffron-robe-wearing monk, Yogi Adityanath, with a reputation of being a tough-talking, no-nonsense administrator who is as, if not more, committed to the ideals of political Hinduism as Modi himself. And Pratap Sarangi won an election in 2019 to become a minister.

If Modi goes to Hindu temples, Delhi Chief Minister Arvind Kejriwal has become famous for his annual Diwali puja[92], and even Rahul Gandhi of the Congress, a party once famous for organizing fast-breaking *iftar* parties during Ramzan, is now seen in elaborate rituals at ancient temples, in full traditional temple attire[93]. Public consensus on the cruelty of the Islamic invasions and some Mughal rulers, such as Aurangzeb, has developed, and while his name once adorned a key road in the heart of Delhi, it has been replaced with the name of the much-loved Muslim president, the scientist A.P.J. Abdul Kalam. There has been a sort of decolonization impact of Modi's rule in everything from the promotion of yoga to Ayurveda, to the mass use of India-made goods. Modi's personal promotion of Gandhi's khadi and handmade products has made the country's Khadi and Village Industries Commission clock in more than Rs 1 trillion in revenue[94]—making it India's biggest FMCG brand. Even the 'Khan Market consensus'[95], the name was once given to a sort of Left-leaning elite groupthink about India lies demolished, mocked by Modi himself when he said in an interview in 2019, 'Modi's image has not been created by the Khan Market gang, or Lutyens Delhi, but forty-five years of his toil . . . good or bad. You cannot dismantle it.'[96]

In foreign policy, the Modi impact is not only seen in the emphasis on India as 'a civilizational state'[97] but also in the debates on control of the Indian Ocean where the history of the Indian Cholas competes with China's assertion of its own naval hero Zheng Xe, and the incumbent Indian foreign minister's assertion that the Mahabharata should be studied to understand Indian diplomacy.[98] The Cholas were a maritime power devoted to spreading their influence through military and cultural expeditions across the Indian Ocean region and planting the flag of their Hindu religious beliefs around South-east Asia.

This is the backdrop against which India has always considered the Indian Ocean as its own, its backyard as it were, and firmly under its influence. It takes the 'Indo' in the Indo-Pacific very seriously.

Not without increasing contest, though. China, which the Indo-Pacific strategy including the Quad, or the quadrilateral security dialogue, made up of the US, India, Australia and Japan, seeks to contain, has its own historical reading.

China's history teaches it about Zheng He. Recently, Zhou Bo, a retired senior colonel from China, associated with the Tsinghua University's Center for International Security and Strategy, gave a lecture at King's College, London. Bo said, 'It's only a matter of time before a Chinese carrier strike group appears in the Indian Ocean' and that India should get accustomed to China's presence in South Asia.

'I do not think it's necessary to remind everyone that during the Ming Dynasty, Zheng He's fleet, the most powerful fleet in the world, went to the Indian Ocean seven times. Therefore, China is not a newcomer to the Indian Ocean. To safeguard China's growing interests in the Indian Ocean and maintain the security of strategic sea lanes, the Chinese navy must maintain or even strengthen its presence in the Indian Ocean,' Bo said.

'Since the end of 2008, the Chinese navy has been sending naval formations to patrol the Gulf of Aden and the Somali Basin in the Indian Ocean,' he added.

Zheng He is one of the most famous maritime voyagers and generals in Chinese history. Commandeering some of the biggest ships of his time in the early fifteenth century, He led seven great voyages across the Indian Ocean from South-east Asia to West Africa to bring back treasures for the Chinese emperors.

Chinese President Xi Jinping has invoked the legacy of Zheng He to promote his dream Belt and Road project in 2017. 'In the early 15th century, Zheng He, the famous Chinese navigator in the Ming Dynasty, made seven voyages to the Western Seas, a feat which still is remembered today,' Xi Jinping had said.

In pitching these legacies, each country emphasizes the long history, the cultural depth and how this country could be a bedrock of future collaboration. This, of course, also means that these histories form the basis of the two Asian giants butting heads in the Indian Ocean.

Not just Modi or the BJP, but the RSS too has become a global network with branches in every major country and affiliated units in every major university around the world, including most prominently, the Hindu Swayamsevak Sangh (HSS) in the United States. The organizational work done by such bodies has helped local Indian Hindu communities, the best-educated and wealthiest minority group in America, organize and protest against negative representations of Hindus in all walks of life including in the media. One prominent example of such community organization was the protest against harmful misrepresentations in the CNN show *Believer* fronted by the Iranian-American academic Reza Aslan, whose episode on Hinduism was criticized by the United States India Political Action Committee saying, '[w]ith multiple reports of hate-fueled attacks against people of Indian origin from across the U.S., the show characterizes Hinduism as cannibalistic, which is a bizarre way of looking at the third largest religion in the world[99]' and by the fellow academic Vamsee Juluri, among many others, as 'reckless, racist, and anti-immigrant[100]'. US Congresswoman Tulsi Gabbard, who identifies as Hindu, joined the protest calling the show akin to 'touring a zoo[101]'. The show was not renewed for a second season, though the final decision came after Aslan tweeted abuse at then-US President Donald Trump, but this kind of organized protest would have been unheard of a decade ago.

The only major agenda of political Hinduism that remains unfulfilled is that of introducing a uniform civil code but that is widely understood to be a work in progress.

In all this, the underbelly of political Hinduism has not disappeared. One of the stark examples of this is a recent legal case filed by a Youtuber espousing extreme political Hindu beliefs[102] (and supported by a former director of the Central Bureau of Investigation)[103] against the head of the RSS, Mohan Bhagwat, for his open-minded, plural views on homosexuality and LGBTQ issues (these have never been an issue in Hinduism, and Bhagwat was only reiterating long-standing consensus). Bhagwat's views were particularly logical because it was under the Modi government that India finally decriminalized its old colonial law against homosexuality[104] (after all, it was only with the coming of the British that such a law had been introduced in India). However, some newly radicalized political Hinduism activists don't want to listen to this accommodative historical lesson. Other incidents such as the murder of journalist Gauri Lankesh and those of rationalists Narendra Dhabolkar and M.M. Kalburgi, have been traced to shadowy hardline groups espousing political Hinduism like the Sanatan Sanstha established in the sun-and-sand holiday destination of Goa in 1990. Indian social media, especially Twitter, is a minefield of competing hatreds where extreme political Hinduism views often trend, creating a climate, along with raucous news channels, of prejudice and discrimination along religious lines. One recent target of this has been Hindi cinema with calls for boycotts against films whose storyline or characterization is seen to be offensive to Hindus. Hindi cinema has traditionally been seen as the most powerful symbol of Indian secularism where the biggest stars in recent years have been Muslim but often fully embracing of Hindu cultural values and even participating in Hindu festivities and rituals. But some of the criticism has teeth. According to a report published in 2015 by a professor of India's elite Institute of Management in Ahmedabad, conducted on data across six decades and fifty films (all from Hindi cinema or Bollywood):

'In nearly 78 per cent of the movies promiscuous women had a Christian name; 58 per cent of the corrupt politicians in films had a Hindu brahmin last name; and, 62 per cent of the corrupt businessman had a vaishya[105] last name . . . Eighty-four of the Muslims in films were shown as strongly religious and honest (even when they are shown in the film as engaged in crime) and 88 per cent of the films presented kshatriya last-name individuals to be courageous. Nearly 74 per cent of the films presented Sikhs as laughable . . . In addition, we examined 20 Bollywood movies that had Pakistan as the setting. In 18 of those films, Pakistanis were projected as welcoming, courteous, open-minded and courageous . . . However, in the same movie, Indians were largely projected as narrow-minded, unwelcoming, and conservative.'[106]

But there are limits to raucous 'boycott Bollywood' hashtags and especially the participation of political leaders in such protests when, in January 2023, Modi told his party colleagues that unnecessary comments on films were overshadowing the government's hard work.[107] This came after threatened protests for India's biggest Hindi film star Shah Rukh Khan and his new film, *Pathaan*. As it transpired, fuelled by the star's umpteen fan clubs in India and around the world, the action-filled spy thriller, Khan's first film in four years, swiftly became the biggest Hindi film of all time in terms of revenue at the box office (it had crossed $100 million at the time of writing[108]).

It is an old Indian, and Hindu, adage that the fundamental rule of the universe is balance. And no extreme point of view can last for too long. In India, contradictions are what makes the country unique. Note that one of the most prominent and strident gay rights activists, Ashok Row Kavi, who is himself gay, in India, is strikingly to the right of the RSS and was once banned from TV for abusing Gandhi.[109] In such a kaleidoscope, what then is the future of political Hinduism? In the next, which is also the last, chapter of this book, I shall argue that the future of political Hinduism is a considered, and watchful (of extremism from those it considers its foes) embrace of the inherent liberal values of Hinduism.

Conclusion

The Age of Ram

The famous Indian journalist and prolific writer, Khushwant Singh, himself a turbaned Sikh, and as fond of Nehruvian secularist identity as he was of his nightly whisky, interviewed M.S. Golwalkar in the 1970s. Singh had read *Bunch of Thoughts* and had some predetermined opinions about Guru Golwalkar and the RSS.

He remembered Golwalkar as a 'frail man in his mid-sixties, black hair curling to his shoulders, a moustache covering his mouth, a wispy grey beard dangling down his chin. An unerasable smile and dark eyes twinkling through his bifocals. He looks like an Indian Ho Chi Minh. For a man who had only recently undergone surgery for breast cancer, he looks remarkably fit and cheerful.'[1]

Singh asked Golwalkar about Christians and Muslims in India. On Christians, Golwalkar offered, 'We have nothing against the Christians except their methods of gaining converts. When they give medicines to the sick or bread to the hungry, they should not exploit the situation by propagating their religion to those people. I am glad there is a move to make the Indian churches autonomous and independent of Rome.'[2]

Asked about Muslims, Golwalkar offered, 'As a matter of fact I would say the only right policy towards Muslims is to win their loyalty by love . . . Muslims must forget that they ruled India. They should not look upon foreign Muslim countries as their homeland. They must join the mainstream of Indianism . . . Time is a great healer. I am an optimist and feel that Hinduism and Islam will learn to live with each other.'[3]

Singh, who was so close to the Congress and to Indira Gandhi that he even defended the Emergency and Gandhi's strongman younger son, Sanjay, responsible for force-sterilizing thousands during the Emergency, exited the meeting feeling 'impressed'. 'He did not try to persuade me to his point of view. He made me feel that he was open to persuasion.'[4]

But this story is important not because of Singh's change of perception after meeting Golwalkar, it is important because it records Golwalkar's views only months before his death in the summer of 1973. Because Singh was a die-hard critic of the RSS, there is no possible reason why he would downplay or soften any of Golwalkar's views.

Golwalkar's idea that time would heal differences between Hindus and Muslims is an idea worth underlying because the question, then, to ask is—how does one know when that time will come?

It is my educated speculation at the conclusion of this book that that time is already coming or has come in the assessment of the people who lead the RSS and the BJP. The spate of conciliatory moves that have been detailed in the previous chapter adds up to such an assessment. The most bitter critics of the BJP and the RSS always suggested that a long-term BJP government would lead to uncontrollable violence and rioting between religious groups in India triggered by a massive religious divide between communities and that religious minorities would feel irretrievably threatened under BJP rule.

Yet, in 2021, a comprehensive survey conducted by America's Pew Research Centre found that 'Indians value religious tolerance, though they also live religiously segregated lives. Across the country, most people (84 per cent) say that to be "truly Indian", it is very important to respect all religions. Indians also are united in the view that respecting *other* religions is a very important part of what it means to be a member of *their own* religious community (8 per cent). People in all six major religious groups overwhelmingly say they are very free to practice their faiths, and most say that people of other faiths also are very free to practice their own religion.'[5]

Among the BJP's and the RSS's core constituency, the Hindus, this survey showed that the ideals of political Hinduism had become well-entrenched.

'For many Hindus, national identity, religion and language are closely connected. Nearly two-thirds of Hindus (64 per cent) say it is very important to be Hindu to be truly Indian. Among Hindus who say it is very important to *be Hindu* to be truly Indian, 80 per cent also say it is very important to *speak Hindi* to be truly Indian', and, 'Among Hindus, views of national identity go hand-in-hand with politics. Support for the ruling Bharatiya Janata Party (BJP) is greater among Hindus who closely associate their religious identity and the Hindi language with being truly Indian. In the 2019 national elections, 60 per cent of Hindu voters who think it is very important to be Hindu *and* to speak Hindi to be truly Indian cast their vote for the BJP, compared with 33 per cent among Hindu voters who feel less strongly about both these aspects of national identity.'[6]

In short, the broad framework of Hindi, Hindu, Hindustan has already come true.

Having achieved this, there is also a growing sense that the agenda being pushed by radical political Hindu groups— for instance, the ones who 'worship' Godse or defend caste discrimination (Bhagwat made some of his strongest statements against caste discrimination in February 2023[7]) are not only electorally harmful, they also create incessantly divisive headlines, keeping away, as Modi noted, information about 'good work being done by the government'. Having achieved all its major goals, incessant anger in society and collisions derail the conversation about a rising India or as Modi puts it, the dream to make India a *vishwa guru* or world teacher.

There is another possible deeper reason for embracing the more plural outlook. The RSS has always considered deep into the future planning decades in advance. It might be clear that the young people who helped bring the BJP to power, both men and women, are now in their mid-thirties to early forties. Deep in their professional life, they seek an India that continues to give rapid growth and opportunities for economic success—otherwise many of the most talented people would just choose to build a life elsewhere. Few would wish to approach middle age in a turbulent country. And retaining talent and capital for the next three decades would be one of the most critical tasks for India to ensure its growth and rise.

There is also a new generation in their late teens and approaching voter age. These are people who have only seen a BJP government and while nationalistic, they are, thanks to technology, the most global-minded generation in India's history, the first digital-native generation. This is the generation that is readying to vote.

This is the 'woke' generation that is connected to a broader global movement of the young who seek a better life for themselves and their ecosystems—an ecosystem of constant conflict. A narrative of injury, retribution and aggression would be much less appealing to them than the message of sustainable growth, cultural confidence and the lived experience of pluralism.

The future of political Hinduism lies in being able to incessantly highlight such values and demonstrate them in everyday policy and activity. Political Hinduism has fought and won, for now, all its major battles. What lies ahead is the question of being able to create a purposeful programme that brings hope and opportunity— which are the values Modi sought to embody and promise, and the reasons that brought him unprecedented success.

The increasing focus on bridging the caste divide comes from an assessment of mainstream political Hinduism organizations, that future challenges could arise from this constituency even as some political parties in southern India attempt to use the caste question to formulate a north-south divide. This is accentuated by the fact that the South is increasingly wealthier and more progressive than the North, or indeed any part of India.

Therefore, retaining power and retaining peace—critical for at least twenty years when India plays catch-up to China on economic growth and moves towards becoming the third-largest economy in the world—is absolutely urgent.

In its own growth too, as the RSS prepares to celebrate its centenary in 2025, its motto for itself is to reach out to the world and become front-facing in a manner that it has never been before. Khushwant Singh in his interview with Golwalkar had begun by telling the RSS leader, 'I am told you shun publicity and your organisation is secret.'[8] To which Golwalkar replied, 'It is true we do not seek publicity but there is nothing secret about us. Ask me anything you want to.'

And yet, the perception has persisted, especially outside India. Now the RSS believes that for too long interlocutors have defined what it is, and the time might be ripe when it should speak for itself in public, not only in India but around the world. This outreach, which is likely to be its biggest in history, would naturally hope to win friends and influence rather than present any divisive points. While this does not mean that either the RSS or the BJP would compromise on any core political Hinduism talking points—why would they jettison what brought them to power?—it also means that the mainstream of political Hinduism is entering a new age of reframing its contours and the dynamics of its arguments for a global, not just a local or national, audience. One of the groups that the RSS and its affiliates are engaging, for instance, are neo-pagan movements in the West to explore commonalities in formulating a different language and grammar of civilization that is non-Abrahamic. Deeper cooperation between political Hindu groups and those of political Buddhism, and moderate Muslim groups especially from Indonesia and Saudi Arabia, in efforts led by Modi's National Security Adviser Ajit Doval, are also emerging.

Therefore, while this is not in popular discourse at the moment, the future of political Hinduism is likely to be more 'liberal', even though adherents would not like that word necessarily, than has been traditionally imagined.

In this journey, of course, there is much that the world of political Hinduism could learn from one of its most influential heroes, Swami Vivekananda, whose key disciples were not only from the West but were, in fact, Western women.

Vivekananda could be a particularly potent teacher because, in a sense, he makes all the arguments for political Hinduism—in the most universal sense. Vivekananda, in his voluminous speeches and writings, noted the possibility that caste was originally a method of work distribution with seamless mobility from one subdivision to the other, and did not fail to recognize that, already in his time, 'Modern caste distinction is a barrier to India's progress. It narrows, restricts, separates. It will crumble before the advance of ideas.'[9]

It was Vivekananda who engendered that India was a supplier, and not merely a receiver, of knowledge in the world, and the intellectual material that it had to bring to the table was among the foremost, if not the best, in the world. Said Vivekananda,

'As Western ideas of organization and external civilisation are penetrating and pouring into our country, whether we will have them or not, so Indian spirituality and philosophy are deluging the lands of the West. None can resist it, and no more can we resist some sort of material civilization from the West. A little of it, perhaps, is good for us, and a little spiritualisation is good for the West; thus the balance will be preserved. It is not that we ought to learn everything from the West, or that they have to learn everything from us, but each will have to supply and hand down to future generations what it has for the future accomplishment of that dream of ages — the harmony of nations, an ideal world[10] . . . Give and take is the law; and if India wants to raise herself once more, it is absolutely necessary that she brings out her treasures and throws them broadcast among the nations of the earth, and in return be ready to receive what others have to give her.[11]'

This is a most important lesson as India revisits its past and seeks to unearth its forgotten glories—in the course of this, it should not paper over or neglect to weed out the flaws that Vivekananda so ably demonstrated. Not everything about India's past is necessarily glorious and reinvigoration of national culture should not, in some minds, descend to trying to roll back much-needed reform that has happened over hundreds of years or valorize obscurantism in the name of tradition. There is hardly a better teacher to explain this than Vivekananda.

As India rises, it will have to negotiate new terms of engagement with the world and especially the West. This negotiation must come neither from a place of supplication, nor unnecessary arrogance—and Vivekananda is a worthy guide in meeting the West midway with a steady, even-footed gaze.

As India enters an age of embracing technology, Vivekananda, who inspired the creation of the famed Indian Institute of Science, is relevant, in the age of artificial intelligence to teach the idea of embracing a 'wide empiricism' or the view that 'while experience is the primary source of knowledge, the category of experience encompasses both the sensory and the supersensuous. While sensory experience is the basis of the natural sciences, supersensuous experience is the basis of the science of religion.'[12]

The greatest lesson of Vivekananda is perhaps bringing an unmistakable sense of the modern to the most ancient— he is a modernist, determined to explain that the age-old and the contemporary are not forces that need to collide; they can coexist. This is the most important lesson India must learn if it has to reinforce and grow its self-assertion as a civilizational state. Underlying tensions especially about caste (and not just religion) remain in pockets of India and some of these have resurfaced via social media as a vocal 'trad' (short for traditional community), which seeks to justify old prejudices as traditional and erase or dismiss reformist concerns as merely 'woke'. In this process, in this societal churn, Vivekananda's wisdom would prove invaluable for political Hinduism as a lighthouse in the tempest.

It is Vivekananda who said:

'Give up all those old discussions, old fights about things which are meaningless, which are nonsensical in their very nature. Think of the last six hundred or seven hundred years of degradation when grown-up men by hundreds have been discussing for years whether we should drink a glass of water with the right hand or the left, whether the hand should be washed three times or four times, whether we should gargle five or six times. What can you expect from men who pass their lives in discussing such momentous questions as these and writing most learned philosophies on them! There is a danger of our religion getting into the kitchen. We are neither Vedantists, most of us now, nor Paurânics, nor Tântrics[13]. We are just "Don't-touchists". Our religion is in the kitchen. Our God is the cooking-pot, and our religion is, "Don't touch me, I am holy." If this goes on for another century, every one of us will be in a lunatic asylum. It is a sure sign of softening of the brain when the mind cannot grasp the higher problems of life; all originality is lost, the mind has lost all its strength, its activity, and its power of thought, and just tries to go round and round the smallest curve it can find. This state of things has first to be thrown overboard, and then we must stand up, be active and strong; and then we shall recognise our heritage to that infinite treasure, the treasure our forefathers have left for us, a treasure that the whole world requires today. The world will die if this treasure is not distributed. Bring it out, distribute it broadcast. Says Vyasa: Giving alone is the one work in this Kali Yuga; and of all the gifts, giving spiritual life is the highest gift possible; the next gift is secular knowledge; the next, saving the life of man; and the last, giving food to the needy. Of food we have given enough; no nation is more charitable than we. So long as there is a piece of bread in the home of the beggar, he will give half of it. Such a phenomenon can be observed only in India. We have enough of that, let us go for the other two, the gifts of spiritual and secular knowledge. And if we were all brave and had stout hearts, and with absolute sincerity put our shoulders to the wheel, in twenty-five years the whole problem would be solved, and there would be nothing left here to fight about . . .'[14]

In a world plagued by conflict, this would be sane advice to heed, both for the future of political Hinduism and in turn, the future of India.

As far as the tribute to Ram is concerned, apart from the grand Ram temple, which will be built by the end of 2023, and the annual festival of lights that is now organized on the river Sarayu that flows through the town and creating records in the Guinness Book[15] by replicating the celebrations that welcomed Ram after his return from exile, there is perhaps another lesson to learn from Ram for the future of political Hinduism.

Kabir Das, more popularly Kabir, was a fifteenth-century mystic, part of the *Bhakti* movement that sought to speak of a love for God that was beyond organized religion and its myriad frictions and differences.

It is said that Kabir preached that there is one Ram who is the son of Dashrath[16], there is another Ram who is sitting at every nook and corner, yet another Ram who suffuses the whole of creation and then, there is a fourth Ram whose description is impossible to give.

Having won its temporal battles, at least for now for its next phase, political Hinduism could focus on the transcendental message of the 'fourth Ram'. That might take it more swiftly to the final goal, which was idealized both by Gandhi and the world of political Hinduism, that of 'Ram Rajya', or the ideal, just, prosperous, corruption-free, morally upright and invincible society, the kingdom or the age of Ram.

References

Anderson, Benedict (2006), *Imagined Communities* (London: Verso Books).

Eck, Diana, *India: A Sacred Geography* (New York: Three Rivers Press, 2012).

Gandhi, Mohandas Karamchand (Pune: Harijan, 1938),

Gopal, Sarvepalli, 'The Formative Ideology of Jawaharlal Nehru', Bombay: *Economic and Political Weekly*, Vol. 11, No. 21, 1976.

Gupta, Charu, *Anxious Hindu Masculinities in North India: Shuddhi and Sangathan Movements*, New York, CrossCurrents, Vol. 61, No. 4, 2011.

Guttman, Anna, *Compromise and Contradiction in Jawaharlal Nehru's Multicultural Nation-State: Constructing National History in The Discovery of India* (Purdue: Clio, 2003).

Husain, Arif, 'The Educated Elite: Collaborators, Assailants, Nationalists, *Journal of the Historical Society of Nigeria*, Lagos, 1974.

Huntington, C.C., 'Geography as a Social Science', *London: Social Science*, Vol. 3, No. 3, 1928.

Kis, Danilo, 'On Nationalism', *Massachusetts: Performing Arts Journal* Vol. 18, No. 2, 1996.

Krishnamurti, Sailaja, 'Uncles of the Nation: Avuncular Masculinity in Partition-era Politics', *South Asian History and Culture*, Volume 5, Issue 4, 2014.

References

Nehru, Jawaharlal, *The Discovery of India* (New Delhi: Oxford University Press, 1985).

Oomen, T.K., 'Conceptualising Nation and Nationality in India', Bombay: *Sociological Bulletin*, Indian Sociological Society, Vol. 48, No. ½, 1985.

Plamenatz, John, 'Two Types of Nationalism' in Eugene Kamenka, ed., *Nationalism: The Nature and Evolution of an Idea* (London: Edward Arnold, 1976).

Ruddiman, John A., *Becoming Men of Some Consequence: Youth and Military Service in the Revolutionary War* (Charlottesville: University of Virginia Press, 2014).

Savarkar, Vinayak Damodar (1969, fifth ed.), *Hindutva* (Bombay: Veer Savarkar Prakashan).

Schama, Simon (1995), *Landscape and Memory* (Toronto: Random House Canada, 1969).

Notes

Introduction

1. Smriti Kak Ramachandran, 'Quietly, Relentlessly, RSS Worked Behind the Scenes to Power BJP Win', *Hindustan Times*, 24 May 2019, https://www.hindustantimes.com/lok-sabha-elections/how-sangh-shaped-bjp-s-victory-march/story-ze26WjD949AakvJphY9O8O.html.
2. Nehru was prime minister for seventeen years between August 1947 and May 1964.
3. In further references, 'the Congress', as it is popularly known. It is also the party of Mahatma Gandhi.
4. Chetan Ahya, 'India's Coming Decade of Outperformance', 8 November 2022, the *Financial Times*, https://www.ft.com/content/489cc92c-c950-47de-ad5f-586b9da33b70.
5. Press Trust of India (PTI), 'India on Way to Become "Vishwa Guru" under PM Narendra Modi: Amit Shah', *Indian Express*, 19 August 2017, https://indianexpress.com/article/india/india-on-way-to-become-vishwa-guru-under-modi-amit-shah-4804375/.
6. Ibid.
7. Ibid.

8. "'Constitution Is Government's Only 'Holy Book'", PM Modi Says', the *Times of India*, 27 November 2015, https://timesofindia. indiatimes.com/india/constitution-is-governments-only-holy-book-pm-modi-says/articleshow/49950277.cms.

9. The biggest-selling English language newspaper of India.

10. Meaning 'unbeliever'. Aurangzeb brought back the *jiziya*, a tax paid by non-Muslims living under Muslim rule. This had been removed by Akbar.

11. William L. Jackson, *Vijayanagara Voices: Exploring South Indian History and Hindu Literature*, 2005.

12. Contrary to popular belief, Savarkar is not the first person who used the word 'Hindutva'. The word was born in Bengal where nineteenth-century educationist and litterateur Chandranath Basu first mentioned the term in *Hindutva: Hindur Prakrita Itihas* (Hindutva, the Authentic History of the Hindus) in 1892. It is important to note that both Basu and Savarkar were concerned with 'the essence' or 'essentials' of Hindutva. This kind of trying to reach a sublime core that describes or holds the key to social and political resurgence was a common feature of a lot of rhetoric in the nationalist period.

13. This is something that connected him to Babasaheb Ambedkar, India's great anti-caste reformer, who wrote the country's Constitution.

14. Vikram Sampath, *Savarkar: Echoes From a Forgotten Past* (Viking/ Penguin, 2019), p. 481–82

15. Meaning, the degenerate.

16. M.S. Golwalkar, *We Or Our Nationhood Defined* (Nagpur: Bharat Publications, 1939), p. 12.

17. Pratap Bhanu Mehta, 'Congress, Secularism and Freedom", *Seminar*, June 2003, https://india-seminar.com/2003/526/526%20pratap%20 bhanu%20mehta.htm#top.

18. Kanchan Chandra, 'How Hindu Nationalism Went Mainstream', *Foreign Policy*, 13 June 2019, https://foreignpolicy.com/2019/06/13/ how-hindu-nationalism-went-mainstream/#cookie_message_ anchor.

19. Amy Kazmin, 'How Hindu Nationalism Went Mainstream in Modi's India', *FT Magazine*, 9 May 2019, https://www.ft.com/ content/4b68c89c-711c-11e9-bf5c-6eeb837566c5.

20. Lauren Frayer, 'Hindu Nationalism: The Growing Trend in India', *NPR*, 22 April 2019, https://www.npr.org/2019/04/22/715875298/hindu-nationalism-the-growing-trend-in-india.

21. Tejasvi Surya vs Supriya Shrinate: 'Does "New India" Have A Place for Dissent?', *India Today*, Conclave South 2021, 12 March 2021, https://youtu.be/F4iqtD3DR6g?si=Z7VzBZxqJLJP7lkY; Vasudha Venugopal, 'Neither Sinicisation nor Nehru's Secularism the Way Forward: Book by RSS Leader J. Nandakumar', *Economic Times*, 6 January 2020, https://economictimes.indiatimes.com/news/politics-and-nation/neither-sinicisation-nor-nehrus-secularism-the-way-forward-book-by-rss-leader-j-nandakumar/articleshow/73124947.cms?from=mdr

22. Considered a thing of the past in Indian politics until Modi's win in 2014.

23. Ramadan.

24. Soutik Biswas, 'Nathuram Godse: the Mystery Surrounding Mahatma Gandhi's Killer', *BBC*, 24 January 2022, https://www.bbc.com/news/world-asia-india-60013807.

25. From Rashtriya Swayamsevak Sangh.

26. Hindol Sengupta, 'From Ram to Rupee: The New Hindutva', *Fortune*, 5 June 2014, https://www.fortuneindia.com/macro/from-ram-to-rupee-the-new-hindutva/100519.

27. Hindol Sengupta, 'The Economic Mind of Narendra Modi', *ORF Online*, 1 October 2019, https://www.orfonline.org/research/economic-mind-narendra-modi-56004/.

28. Hindol Sengupta, 'An Obscure Book Holds the Key to the RSS View of the Economy', *Fortune*, 6 October 2018, https://www.fortuneindia.com/polemicist/an-obscure-book-holds-the-key-to-the-rss-view-of-the-economy/102555.

29. Hindol Sengupta, 'Jawaharlal Nehru and Vinayak Damodar Savarkar: Ideological Intersection in the Origins of the Idea of India', India Foundation, 5 January 2021, https://indiafoundation.in/articles-and-commentaries/jawaharlal-nehru-and-vinayak-damodar-savarkar-ideological-intersection-in-the-origins-of-the-idea-of-india/.

30. Hindol Sengupta, 'Changing Hindutva by Technology', from *Religion and Technology in India*, ed. Knut A. Jacobsen and Kristina

Myrvold (London: Taylor and Francis/Routledge, 2018), https://
www.taylorfrancis.com/chapters/edit/10.4324/9781351204798-9/
changing-hindutva-technology-hindol-sengupta.

Chapter 1: The Age of Fire

1. Now called Kolkata.
2. Sudipta Sen, *Empire of Free Trade: The East India Company and the Making of the Colonial Marketplace* (Philadelphia: University of Pennsylvania Press, 1998), p. 2.
3. Peter Watson, *The French Mind* (London: Simon & Schuster, 2022), p. 25.
4. Thomas Babington Macaulay, 'Minute on Indian Education', 2 February 1835, https://archive.org/details/dli.csl.5518/mode/2up.
5. Bankim Chandra Chattopadhyay, *Bankim Rachanabali, Ananda Math* (Kolkata: Sahitya Sansad, p. 617.
6. A seminal figure in the Bengal Renaissance, Ram Mohan Roy (1772–1883) was an aristocrat and a social reformer who founded the Brahmo Samaj that wished to return Hinduism to its core philosophies and texts, namely the Vedas and the Upanishads, and away from what he saw as degraded superstitions and ritualism.
7. People who practice philosophies of the Vedas and the Upanishads.
8. Hitendra Anupam and Amardeep Yadav, 'How Swami Vivekananda Viewed the Historical Civilizations of His Motherland', the *Pioneer*, 12 January 2023, https://www.dailypioneer.com/2023/state-editions/how-swami-vivekananda-viewed-the-historical-civilizations-of-his-motherland.html.
9. Julius J. Lipner, 'Re-translating Bankim Chatterji's Ananda Math', *India International Centre Quarterly*, Vol. 30, No. 1, Summer 2003, p. 69.
10. Chetan Bhatt, *Hindu Nationalism: Origins, Ideologies and Modern Myths* (Oxford: Berg, 2001), p. 23.
11. Ibid., p. 25.
12. The quotation is the English translation of a line from the Bhagavad Gita.
13. Karl Baier, 'Swami Vivekananda: Reform Hinduism, Nationalism and Scientist Yoga', *Interdisciplinary Journal for Religion and Transformation in Contemporary Society*, 2019.

14. Tanika Sarkar, 'Imagining a Hindu Nation: Hindu and Muslim in Bankimchandra's Later Writings', *Economic and Political Weekly*, Vol. 29, No. 39, 24 September 1994, pp. 2555.
15. Julius J. Lipner, 'Re-translating Bankim Chatterji's Ananda Math'.
16. Ibid.
17. Chandranath Basu, *Hindutva: Hindur Prakrita Itihas*, 1892, https://archive.org/details/in.ernet.dli.2015.352815.
18. Amiya P. Sen, 'A Hindu Conservative Negotiates Modernity. Chandranath Basu (1844–1910)' and 'Reflections on the Self and Culture in Colonial Bengal', https://hasp.ub.uni-heidelberg.de/reader/download/366/366-43-81620-1-10-20180704.pdf.
19. Ibid.
20. Julius J. Lipner, 'Re-translating Bankim Chatterji's Ananda Math', p. 62.
21. Swami Adiswarananda, 'Swami Vivekananda: His Message of Vedanta and the Western Way (Part 6)', Ramakrishna-Vivekananda Center of New York, https://ramakrishna.org/vedanta6.html.
22. Abdul Rasul (1874-1917), St John's College, Oxford, https://www.sjc.ox.ac.uk/discover/about-college/st-johns-and-colonial-past/exhibition/abdul-rasul/.
23. 'Independence Day Special: Evolution of the Indian Flag', *India Today*, 17 August 2015, https://www.indiatoday.in/fyi/story/evolution-indian-flag-independence-day-15th-august-288436-2015-08-15.
24. Srirupa Roy, 'A Symbol of Freedom: The Indian Flag and the Transformations of Nationalism, 1906-2002', the *Journal of Asian Studies*, Vol. 65, No. 3, August 2006, p. 500.
25. Alternative spelling of Vande Mataram.
26. Baljit Rai, *Muslim Fundamentalism in the Indian Subcontinent* (Delhi: B.S. Publishers, 1990), p. 368.
27. Muhammad Ali Jinnah, the leader of the Muslim League.
28. Deepak Pandey, 'Congress-Muslim League Relations 1937–39: The Parting of the Ways', *Modern Asian Studies*, Vol. 12, No. 4, 1978, p. 641.
29. Sabyasachi Bhattacharya, 'Vande Mataram: In Rewind Mode', *The Hindu*, 4 December 2009, https://frontline.thehindu.com/the-nation/article30185996.ece.

30. Ibid.
31. Suggested replacements from Pant included 'Hindustan Hamara' and 'Jai He'.
32. Agencies, 'Fatwa against "Vande Mataram" Cannot Be Withdrawn: Darul Uloom', the *Indian Express*, 9 November 2009, https://indianexpress.com/article/india/latest-news/fatwa-against-vande-mataram-cannot-be-withdrawn-darul-uloom/.
33. Khan was once a prominent Congress politician and is now part of the BJP.
34. Outlook Web Desk, 'Unnecessary and Irrelevant', *Outlook*, 3 February 2022, https://www.outlookindia.com/website/story/unnecessary-and-irrelevant/232420.
35. Special Correspondent, 'Congress Divided Vande Mataram, India: Amit Shah', *The Hindu*, 27 June 2018, https://www.thehindu.com/news/national/cong-decision-on-vande-mataram-cause-for-partition/article24272610.ece.
36. TNI, 'Stopping Vande Mataram Recital Is like Treason: Amit Shah', the *Times of India*, 3 January 2019, https://timesofindia.indiatimes.com/india/stopping-vande-mataram-recital-is-like-treason-amit-shah/articleshow/67357900.cms
37. PTI, 'Citizens Must Show Equal Respect to Jana Gana Mana, Vande Mataram', *The Hindu*, 5 November 2022, https://www.thehindu.com/news/national/citizens-must-show-equal-respect-to-jana-gana-mana-vande-mataram-centre-to-delhi-high-court/article66099732.ece.
38. National Symbols, india.gov.in, https://www.india.gov.in/india-glance/national-symbols.
39. Modi is part of what is known as other backward castes (OBC) in India. The OBC population is numerically the largest among various sub-groups—around 35 per cent.

Chapter 2: The Victory Seekers

1. V.D. Savarkar, *Essentials of Hindutva*, https://library.bjp.org/jspui/bitstream/123456789/284/1/Essentials%20of%20Hindutva.pdf.
2. HT Correspondent, 'No One Can Stop India from Rewriting Its History: Amit Shah', *Hindustan Times*, 25 November 2022, https://

www.hindustantimes.com/india-news/no-one-can-stop-india-from-rewriting-its-history-amit-shah-101669315613971.html.

3. Ibid.

4. *Hindustan Times*, 'PM Modi's Message to World: "India Rewriting History of Slavery, Conspiracy during British Era"', YouTube video, 25 November 2022, https://www.youtube.com/watch?v=io29NTeC67g.

5. Now in modern-day Pakistan.

6. In present-day Rajasthan in western India.

7. Founder of the Lohara dynasty and ruled Kashmir between 1003 and 1028 CE.

8. HT Entertainment Desk, 'Kangana Ranaut Announces Manikarnika Returns: The Legend of Didda, To Play Kashmiri Warrior Queen', *Hindustan Times*, 14 January 2021, https://www.hindustantimes.com/entertainment/kangana-ranaut-announces-manikarnika-returns-the-legend-of-didda-to-play-kashmiri-warrior-queen-101610616611739.html.

9. Saurav Anand, 'PM Modi Pays Tribute to Celebrated Assamese Warrior Lachit Borphukan', Mint, 24 November 2022, https://www.livemint.com/news/india/pm-modi-pays-tribute-to-celebrated-assamese-warrior-lachit-borphukan-11669274914910.html#:~:text=This%20Lachit%20Diwas%20is%20special,visionary%20leader%2C%22%20he%20added; Swati Bhasin, 'PM Remembers General Who Fought Mughals: "Defeated Oppressors, Got no Credit"', *Hindustan Times*, 25 November 2022, https://www.hindustantimes.com/india-news/our-history-was-distorted-deliberately-pm-while-paying-tribute-to-assam-hero-101669359205308.html.

10. In present-day Rajasthan in western India.

11. Historians have dated this text to have been written and revised between the thirteenth and sixteenth centuries CE, and is credited to Chand Bardai, a court poet of Prithviraj.

12. India Today Web Desk, 'History from India's Perspective: Mohan Bhagwat Lauds Akshay Kumar's Samrat Prithviraj', *India Today*, 4 June 2022, https://www.indiatoday.in/movies/celebrities/story/history-from-india-s-perspective-mohan-bhagwat-lauds-akshay-s-samrat-prithviraj-1958323-2022-06-04.

13. 'When Lord Shri Ram & Maharana Pratap Shunned Casteism, Who Are We to Follow It: RSS', Daijiworld.com, 10 October 2022, https://www.daijiworld.com/news/newsDisplay?newsID=1008360.

14. FE Online, 'Yogi Adityanath at RSS Event: "Only Maharana Pratap Was Great, Akbar Was Not"', *Financial Express*, 15 June 2018, https://www.financialexpress.com/india-news/yogi-adityanath-at-rss-event-only-maharana-pratap-was-great-akbar-was-not/1207063/.

15. Modern-day Jaipur, capital of the state of Rajasthan.

16. Originally from Fergana in present-day Afghanistan, Babur originally wanted to conquer and control Samarkand. But after losing repeatedly, he turned his forces towards India and established the Mughal dynasty after defeating Ibrahim Lodi, the sultan of Delhi, in the First Battle of Panipat in 1526 CE.

17. Organiser Bureau, 'How the British Enslaved Bharat', *Organiser*, 9 August 2022, https://organiser.org/2022/08/09/90910/bharat/how-the-british-enslaved-us/.

18. Narendra Modi, 'Photograph of Narendra Modi with the Late Maharaja Marthanda Varma of Travancore', Facebook photo, 16 December 2013, https://m.facebook.com/narendramodi/photos/a.10150164299700165.421791.177526890164/10153622399960165/?type=1&p=30.

19. Dr Ankita Kumar, 'Kerala Varma Pazhassi Raja Martyrdom Day: Lion of Kerala, Who Beat Arthur Wellesley, the Vanquisher of Napoleon', *Organiser*, 30 November 2022, https://organiser.org/2022/11/30/85334/opinion/pazhassi-raja-lion-of-kerala/.

20. Text of the PM's remarks on the commissioning of Coast Ship Barracuda (pib.gov.in).

21. 'DefExpo 2018: PM Modi Hails TN by Remembering Chola Dynasty', Tamil Nadu News, YouTube, 12 April 2018, https://www.youtube.com/watch?v=dQyxZ168FZQ.

22. Atiq Khan, Srutisagar Yamunan, 'RSS to Mark Millennium of Rajendra Chola', *The Hindu*, 21 October 2014, https://www.thehindu.com/news/national/tamil-nadu/rss-to-mark-millennium-of-rajendra-chola/article6520437.ece.

23. John M. Fritz, George Michell and M.S. Nagaraja Rao, 'Vijayanagara: The City of Victory', *Archaeology*, Vol. 39, No. 2, March 1986, p. 22.

24. Pavan Varma, *Adi Shankaracharya: Hinduism's Greatest Thinker* (New Delhi: Tranquebar, 2018).
25. William Dalrymple, *The Untold Story of Hampi* (Open, 27 July 2018).
26. Michael Rugnetta, 'Phantom Limb Syndrome', Britannica.com, https://www.britannica.com/science/phantom-limb-syndrome.
27. William Dalrymple, *The Untold Story of Hampi*.
28. Ibid.
29. Ibid.
30. Robert Sewell, *A Forgotten Empire: Vijayanagar* (New Delhi: Asian Educational Services, 2000), p. 400.
31. John M. Fritz, George Michell and M.S. Nagaraja Rao, 'Vijayanagara: The City of Victory', *Archaeology*, p. 25.
32. Philip B. Wagoner, 'Sultan Among Hindu Kings: Dress, Titles and the Islamacization of Hindu Culture at Vijayanagara', *The Journal of Asian Studies*, Vol. 55, No. 4, 1996.
33. Kenneth Warren Chase, *Firearms: A Global History to 1700* (Cambridge: Cambridge University Press), p. 130.
34. Manu Pillai, 'The Sultan Who Painted His Nails', Mint, 16 June 2018.
35. Anila Verghese, 'Deities, Cults and Kings at Vijayanagara', *World Archaeology*, Vol. 36, No. 3, The Archaeology of Hinduism.
36. John M. Fritz, George Michell and M.S. Nagaraja Rao, 'Vijayanagara: The City of Victory', *Archaeology*.
37. Burton Stein, *The New Cambridge History of India* (Cambridge: Cambridge University Press, 2008), p. 37.
38. V.S. Naipaul, *India: A Wounded Civilisation* (London: Penguin Books, 1979), p. 17.
39. Staff Reporter, 'Vijayanagar Empire's Superior Knowledge in Science and Architecture Thrills Nadda', *The Hindu*, 18 April 2022, https://www.thehindu.com/news/national/karnataka/vijayanagara-empires-superior-knowledge-in-science-and-architecture-thrills-nadda/article65332063.ece.
40. William Dalrymple, *The Untold Story of Hampi*.
41. Ibid.
42. Vamsee Juluri, *Rearming Hinduism* (New Delhi: Westland, 2015).
43. Mark T. Lycett and Kathleen D. Morrison, 'The "Fall" of Vijayanagara Reconsidered: Political Destruction and Historical Construction in

South Indian History', *Journal of the Economic and Social History of the Orient*, Vol. 56, No. 3, p. 438.

44. Ibid.

45. Sirisena Amarasekara, 'Sinhalese: A Nation Comfortable in Isolation—Part 2', *Sri Lanka Guardian*, 12 December 2022, http://slguardian.org/sinhalese-a-nation-comfortable-in-isolation-part-2/.

46. Earlier Bombay.

47. PTI, 'Shivaji Statue in Sea to Cost Maharashtra Rs 3643.78 Crore', *India Today*, 24 December 2018, https://www.indiatoday.in/india/story/shivaji-statue-to-cost-maharashtra-rs-3643-78-crore-1416064-2018-12-24.

48. Arjun Sengupta, 'Shivaji's Great Escape: What Happened in Agra during Aurangzeb's Rule?' the *Indian Express*, 2 December 2022, https://indianexpress.com/article/explained/shivajis-great-escape-what-happened-in-agra-during-aurangzeb-rule-8300476/.

49. Pradeep Barua, *The State at War in South Asia* (University of Nebraska Press, 2005), p. 42.

50. Satish Chandra, *Medieval India: Society, the Jagirdari Crisis, and the Village* (Macmillan, 1982), p. 140.

51. Sheldon Pollock, *Forms of Knowledge in Early Modern Asia: Explorations in the Intellectual History of India and Tibet, 1500–1800* (Duke University Press, 2011), p. 60.

52. Following Gandhi's return from South Africa in 1915. Gandhi had not joined active politics when Tilak returned from his deportation to Mandalay (Myanmar) and rejoined the Congress.

53. The reference is to the Hindu deity Krishna who annihilates the evil Kamsa to enforce dharma.

54. Foreigner/outsider.

55. Mughals.

56. Devotee.

57. Shivaji.

58. Maratha.

59. Swami Vivekananda's evening talk on Shivaji published under the title 'The Echoes of the Teachings of Vivekananda' by M.C. Nanjunda Rao in *Vedanta Kesari* during 1914–16 in six parts, https://archive.org/details/Swami_Vivekananda_On_Sivaji_by_MC_Nanjunda_Rao_1916_Vedanta_Kesari/page/n1/mode/2up.

60. Ibid.

61. He was dissuaded by a senior monk and told that.

62. They were called Shivaji Utsav (the Festival of Shivaji) and Pratinidhi (the Representative)

63. Practice or perseverance.

64. Some of the influences and inspirations that the Anusilan Samiti and others like it drew from included Italian nationalist groups like the Carbonari, the writings of Giuseppe Mazzini and the history of the Risorgimento or Italian unification.

65. Now Puducherry in southern India near the city of Chennai (Madras).

66. The guru of Shivaji.

67. The goddess Durga who was worshipped by Shivaji and the Maratha kings before battle.

68. Aurangzeb.

69. Mughal.

70. Sri Aurobindo, 'Sivaji-Jai Singh', The Incarnate World, https://incarnateword.in/sabcl/03/shivaji-jai-singh.

71. Jadunath Sarkar, *Shivaji and His Times* (London: Longmans, Green and Co., 1919), pp. 442–43.

72. Jadunath Sarkar was knighted in 1929 as Companion of the Order of the Indian Empire.

73. Imperial Gazetteer, Oxford: Clarendon Press, 1908–31, Vol. 2, p. 440.

74. Jawaharlal Nehru, *The Discovery of India*, https://library.bjp.org/jspui/bitstream/123456789/277/1/The-Discovery-Of-India-Jawaharlal-Nehru.pdf.

75. V. D. Savarkar, 'Hindunrusimha', savarkar.org, http://savarkar.org/en/Encyc/2017/5/23/Hindunrusimha.html.

76. Ibid.

Chapter 3: Freedom, with Hindu Characteristics

1. Then Burma.

2. Proposals for putting an end to the revolutionary activity in Bengal. Proposed deportation under Bengal Regulation III of 1818 of 53 persons, File No. 33-40, 1910-13, National Archives, India.

3. The Ramayana and the Mahabharata are India's epics, both Hindu, and the Gita is part of the Mahabharata.

4. Bal Gangadhar Tilak: His Writings and Speeches, Appreciation by Babu Aurobindo Ghosh (Madras: Ganesh & Co., July 1922), https://www.vifindia.org/sites/default/files/139221794-Tilak-Speeches-Writings-With-Foreword-3rd-Ed-1922.pdf.

5. Aurobindo was one of the prime accused in what came to be known as the Alipore Bombing Case but was acquitted due to lack of evidence.

6. Eternal law or moral code, a core principle in Hinduism.

7. Sri Aurobindo, 'Uttarapara Speech', 30 May 1909, http://www.sriaurobindoinstitute.org/saioc/Sri_Aurobindo/uttarpara_speech#uttarpara_speech.

8. The Encyclopedia Britannica notes: 'In Hinduism, the most-revered body of sacred literature, considered to be the product of divine revelation. Shruti works are considered to have been heard and transmitted by earthly sages, as contrasted to Smriti, or that which is remembered by ordinary human beings. Though Shruti is considered to be the more authoritative, in practice the Smriti texts are more influential in modern Hinduism. The revealed texts encompass the four Vedas—Rigveda, Yajurveda, Samaveda and Atharvaveda—and the Brahmanas (ritual treatises), the Aranyakas ('Forest Books'), and the Upanishads (philosophical elaborations on the Vedas that form the basis of much of later Hindu philosophy and theology). The Smriti texts include the important religious manuals known as the *Kalpa-sutra*s; the compilations of ancient myth, legends and history, the Puranas; and the two great epics of India, the *Ramayana* and the *Mahabharata*. The latter contains within it probably the single most influential text in Hinduism, the *Bhagavadgita*. In time the term Smriti came to refer particularly to the texts relating to law and social conduct, such as the *Manu-smriti* (*Laws of Manu*).'

9. The reference to varnashrama dharma is to Hinduism's old societal division through what came to be known as 'castes' (from the Portuguese 'casta') but was originally known as 'varnas'. Some Hindu scriptures, including the Manu-smriti, described a society where everyone was placed in different subdivisions—the Brahmins

as priests and scholars, the Kshatriyas as warriors and kings, the Vaishyas as merchants and tradespeople, and the Shudras as workers and labourers. In the views of Gandhi, this system was originally based on merit or capability with complete mobility between the subdivisions—the Ramayana and the Mahabharata were both written, for instance, by non-Brahmins, but in time, these morphed into a rigid, birth-based discriminatory system where some were even considered 'untouchables'. Gandhi argued that that the discrimination was a manipulation of the original system that had been good but had been deeply compromised and sullied.

10. M.K. Gandhi, '39. What I Value in Hinduism', https://www.mkgandhi.org/my_religion/39hinduism.htm.
11. Eck 2011.
12. Schama 1995:56.
13. Plamenatz 1973.
14. (Nehru 1946: 51).
15. (Savarkar 1969: 12).
16. Ibid.
17. (Anderson 2006: 4).
18. (Nehru 1946: 51).
19. (Savarkar 1969: 5).
20. (Huntington 1928).
21. (Anderson 2006).
22. (Nehru 1946: 191).
23. Used here synonymously to India but charting a territory covering most of modern South Asia.
24. (Nehru 1946: 59).
25. (Savarkar 1969: 101).
26. (Nehru: 1946: 235).
27. (Savarkar 1969: 44).
28. (Plamenatz 1973).
29. (Plamenatz 1973: 25).
30. (Nehru 1946: 152).
31. (Savarkar 1969: 21).
32. Matthew Arnold, 'Obermann Once Again', PoetryFoundation.org.
33. (Nehru 1946: 142).

34. (Savarkar 1969: 19).
35. The Anarchical and Revolutionary Crimes Act of 1919. It was called the Rowlatt Act after Sidney Rowlatt, head of the committee that decided on these laws linking sedition and political terrorism to political activism against colonial rule.
36. (Oomen 1999).
37. (Ruddiman 2014).
38. (Nehru 1946: 15).
39. (Nehru 1946: 15).
40. (Nehru 1946: 47).
41. (Savarkar 1969: 3).
42. (Nehru 1946: 444).
43. Gupta 2011.
44. (Savarkar 1969: 134).
45. (Savarkar 1969: 59).
46. Ibid.
47. (Nehru 1946: 216).
48. (Savarkar 1969: 129).
49. Collected Works of Mahatma Gandhi, Vol 5, pp. 429–30.
50. Gandhi was born in 1869, while Savarkar was born in 1883.
51. Vikram Sampath, 'Gandhi, Savarkar Two Irreconcilable Poles in Indian History', *The Week*, 22 June 2019, https://www.theweek.in/theweek/cover/2019/06/21/gandhi-savarkar-two-irreconcilable-poles-in-indian-history.html
52. The Indian Councils Act 1909, commonly known as the Minto–Morley Reforms, was an act of the Parliament of the United Kingdom that brought about a limited increase in the involvement of Indians in the governance of British India. Named after Viceroy Lord Minto and Secretary of State John Morley, the act introduced elections to legislative councils and admitted Indians to councils of the Secretary of State for India, the viceroy, and to the executive councils of Bombay and Madras states. Muslims were granted separate electorates according to the demands of the Muslim League.
53. M.K. Gandhi, '12 The Condition of India (Continued): Doctors', *Hind Swaraj*, https://www.mkgandhi.org/hindswaraj/chap12_indiadoctors.htm.

54. M.K. Gandhi, '13 What Is True Civilization?', *Hind Swaraj*, https://www.mkgandhi.org/hindswaraj/chap13_truecivilization.htm.

55. V.D. Savarkar, *Essentials of Hindutva*, https://library.bjp.org/jspui/bitstream/123456789/284/1/Essentials%20of%20Hindutva.pdf.

56. Muslims.

57. Ibid.

58. Ibid.

59. Jinnah lost the first case, and Tilak was deported to prison in Mandalay in Myanmar (then Burma) for six years. However, the second time around, Jinnah won and Tilak was acquitted.

60. M.K. Gandhi, '10 The Hindus and Mahomedans', *Hind Swaraj*, https://www.mkgandhi.org/hindswaraj/chap10_hindumahomedans.htm.

61. Ibid.

62. V.D. Savarkar, 'Cow-Protection and Cow-Worship', https://savarkar.org/en/encyc/2017/5/23/Cow-protection-and-cow-worship.html.

63. V.D. Savarkar, *Essentials of Hindutva*, https://library.bjp.org/jspui/bitstream/123456789/284/1/

64. Essentials%20of%20Hindutva.pdf.

65. Bohra and Khoja are sub-sects among Muslims.

66. Islam.

67. In the Hindu faith, Vishnu, the Preserver, has ten avatars or incarnations over the ages.

68. Culture.

69. V.D. Savarkar, *Essentials of Hindutva*, https://library.bjp.org/jspui/bitstream/123456789/284/1/

70. Essentials%20of%20Hindutva.pdf.

71. British Secretary of State for India between December 1905 and November 1910.

72. M.K. Gandhi, '10 The Hindus and Mahomedans', *Hind Swaraj*, https://www.mkgandhi.org/hindswaraj/chap10_hindumahomedans.htm.

73. Durga Das, *India: From Curzon to Nehru* (Delhi: Rupa Publications, 2002), p. 76.

74. Ibid.

75. Trained at the London School of Economics and Columbia University, the lawyer-economist Ambedkar was born 'lower caste'

and would become the foremost antagonist of Gandhi on this issue. He considered Gandhi an insidious defender of the discriminatory caste system. He was the key author of independent India's Constitution.

76. Muslim.

77. https://mea.gov.in/Images/attach/amb/Volume_08.pdf, p. 155.

78. Also spelt as Moplah.

79. The 'land of the infidels'—Islamic teaching divides territories as *dar-ul-harb* and *dar-ul-Islam*, or land of unbelievers and believers, and the idea of jihad is to convert one to the other.

80. Ernad and Wallurana were regions in the Malabar area.

81. B.R. Ambedkar, 'Hindu Alternative to Pakistan: The Riot-Torn History of Hindu-Muslim Relations (1920–1940)', *Pakistan or the Partition of India*, http://www.columbia.edu/itc/mealac/pritchett/00ambedkar/ambedkar_partition/307c.html#n01.

82. Mahatma Gandhi, *Collected Works*, Vol. 26, http://www.gandhiashramsevagram.org/gandhi-literature/mahatma-gandhi-collected-works-volume-26.pdf, Young India, Vol. 26: 24 January 1922–12 November 1923, p. 27.

83. Mahatma Gandhi, *Collected Works*, Vol. 25, http://www.gandhiashramsevagram.org/gandhi-literature/mahatma-gandhi-collected-works-volume-25.pdf, Young India, Vol. 25: 27 October 1921–22 January 1922, p. 451.

84. One hundred thousand.

85. Annie Besant, *The Future of Indian Politics* (Theosophical Publishing House, 1922), p. 252.

86. Christophe Jaffrelot (ed.), *Hindu Nationalism: A Reader* (New Jersey: Princeton University Press), p. 41.

87. Prabhu Bapu, *Hindu Mahasabha in Colonial North India, 1915-1930: Constructing Nation and History*. Routledge, 2013.

88. Cleansing in Hindi.

89. *Dr. Babasaheb Ambedkar Writings & Speeches Vol. 9*, Dr. Ambedkar Foundation, 1991, pp. 23–24.

90. Mahatma Gandhi, *Collected Works*, Vol. 38, https://www.gandhiashramsevagram.org/gandhi-literature/mahatma-gandhi-collected-works-volume-38.pdf.

91. Ibid.

92. Shudra.
93. Christophe Jaffrelot (ed.), *Hindu Nationalism: A Reader*, p. 53.
94. Ibid., p. 54.
95. Ibid., p. 56.
96. Benoy Kumar Sarkar, 'Hindu Theory of International Relations', *The American Political Science Review*, Vol. 13, No. 3, August 1919, pp. 400–14.
97. Ibid.
98. Swaraj.
99. Freedom.
100. Ibid.
101. Martin J. Bayly, 'Imagining New Worlds: Forging "Non-western" International Relations in Late Colonial India', *British Academy Review*, 30, 2017. pp. 50–53.
102. Christophe Jaffrelot (ed.), *Hindu Nationalism: A Reader*, p. 64.
103. He mentions Sardar Mohammad Gul Khan who appeared before the Frontier Enquiry Committee in 1923 as a witness in the capacity of president of Islamia Anjuman, Dera Ismail Khan in the North-West Frontier Province.
104. Ibid., p. 73.
105. Speech of Sir Syed Ahmed at Meerut (1888), http://www.columbia.edu/itc/mealac/pritchett/00islamlinks/txt_sir_sayyid_meerut_1888.html.
106. Christophe Jaffrelot (ed.), *Hindu Nationalism: A Reader*, pg. 74
107. Arun Anand, '"Braveheart, Fanatic Anarchist": What Bhagat Singh Wrote of Savarkar and Their Common Cause', ThePrint, 23 March 2021, https://theprint.in/india/braveheart-fanatic-anarchist-what-bhagat-singh-wrote-of-savarkar-and-their-common-cause/626451/.
108. V.D. Savarkar, *Essentials of Hindutva*, https://library.bjp.org/jspui/bitstream/123456789/284/1/Essentials%20of%20Hindutva.pdf.
109. Balakrishna Shivaram Moonje disagreed with Gandhi on non-violence and the Gandhian version of secularism.
110. This has been altered to khaki full pants in recent years.
111. Marzia Casolari, 'Hindutva's Foreign Tie-Up in the 1930s: Archival Evidence', *Economic and Political Weekly*, Vol. 35, No. 4, January 22–28 2000), pp. 218–28.

112. Ibid.

113. Aravindan Neelakandan, *Hindutva: Origin, Evolution and Future* (Delhi: BlueOne Ink LLP, 2023), p. 195.

114. 'To Romain Rolland', Mani Bhavan Gandhi Sangrahalaya, 20 December 1931, https://www.gandhi-manibhavan.org/educational-resources/letter-to-romain-rolland.html.

115. The Salt March, also known as the Salt Satyagraha, Dandi March and the Dandi Satyagraha, was an act of non-violent civil disobedience led by Mahatma Gandhi. The twenty-four-day march lasted from 12 March to 6 April 1930 as a direct action campaign of tax resistance and non-violent protest against the British salt monopoly.

116. A series of conferences between the British government and Indian representatives on India's future.

117. Choudhary Rahmat Ali, 'Now or Never; Are We to Live or Perish Forever?', Wikisource, 28 January 1933, https://en.wikisource.org/wiki/Now_or_Never;_Are_We_to_Live_or_Perish_Forever%3F.

118. G. Allana, Two letters from Iqbal to Jinnah (1937), 28 May 1937, Pakistan Movement Historical Documents (Karachi: Department of International Relations, University of Karachi, nd [1969]), pp. 129–33, http://www.columbia.edu/itc/mealac/pritchett/00islamlinks/txt_iqbal_tojinnah_1937.html.

119. Ibid.

120. Ibid.

121. Q & A, savarkar.org, https://savarkar.org/en/encyc/2017/5/29/Q-A6.html.

122. Swatantryaveer Vinayak Damodar Savarkar, Lok Sabha Secretariat, New Delhi, February 2003, https://eparlib.nic.in/bitstream/123456789/56237/1/Swatantryaveer_VDSavarkar.English.pdf.

123. G. Allana, Presidential Address by Muhammad Ali Jinnah to the Muslim League, Lucknow, October 1937, *Pakistan Movement Historical Documents* (Karachi: Department of International Relations, University of Karachi, nd [1969]), pp. 140-151, http://www.columbia.edu/itc/mealac/pritchett/00islamlinks/txt_jinnah_lucknow_1937.html.

124. Hindu Rashtra Darshan, V.D. Savarkar, Maharashtra Prantik Hindusabha, Poona, https://savarkar.org/en/pdfs/hindu-rashtra-darshan-en-v002.pdf.

125. Ibid.

126. Vikram Sampath, *Savarkar: A Contested Legacy* (Delhi: Viking/Penguin), pp. 208–9.

127. Sancara Ramacandra Date, *Bhagnagar Struggle: A Brief History of the Movement Led by Hindu Mahasabha in Hyderabad State in 1938-39* (Poona: Loksangraha Press), p. 68.

128. Tathagata Roy, *Syama Prasad Mookerjee: Life and Times* (Delhi: Viking/Penguin), p. 80.

129. Hindu Rashtra Darshan, V.D. Savarkar, Maharashtra Prantik Hindusabha, Poona, https://savarkar.org/en/pdfs/hindu-rashtra-darshan-en-v002.pdf.

130. Madan Mohan Malviya.

131. Ibid., p. 82.

132. At Mohsana in Madhya Pradesh.

133. Prabha Chopra, *Quotes of Sardar Patel*, Publications Division, Ministry of Information and Broadcasting, Government of India, Internet Archive, 2005, https://archive.org/details/quotesofsardarpa00prab.

134. At the Congress session in Ahmedabad.

135. Ibid.

136. At a gathering in Delhi.

137. Muslims.

138. Parsis.

139. Ibid.

140. 'Text of the 1940 Lahore Resolution of the All-India Muslim League by Brian McMorrow'. *PBase*, https://pbase.com/bmcmorrow/image/140584822.

141. Presidential Address by Muhammad Ali Jinnah to the Muslim League, Lahore, 1940, *Address by Quaid-i-Azam Mohammad Ali Jinnah at Lahore Session of Muslim League, March, 1940* (Islamabad: Directorate of Films and Publishing, Ministry of Information and Broadcasting, Government of Pakistan, Islamabad, 1983), pp. 5–23, http://www.columbia.edu/itc/mealac/pritchett/00islamlinks/txt_jinnah_lahore_1940.html.

142. Writing from Sevagram on 1 March 1942.

143. M.K. Gandhi, *Letters to Sardar Vallabhbhai Patel* (Ahmedabad: Navajivan Publishing House, December 1957), https://www. mkgandhi.org/ebks/letters-to-Sardar-Patel.pdf.

144. Letter of 28.2.42 in Nandurkar (ed.), *Bapu, Sardar ane Mahadevbhai*, p. 301, as quoted in *Gandhi, Rajmohan, Patel: A Life* (Ahmedabad: Navjivan Publishing House, 2013), p. 303.

145. Jaywant Joglekar, *Veer Savarkar: Father of Hindu Nationalism* (Lulu. com [self-published], 2006), p. 158.

146. This was published in 1945.

147. B.R. Ambedkar, 'Chapter XII National Frustration', *Pakistan or the Partition of India* (Bombay: Thackers, 1945), http://www.columbia. edu/itc/mealac/pritchett/00ambedkar/ambedkar_partition/412d. html#part_5.

148. Syed Umar Hayat, 'The Direct Action Day (1946): Myth and Reality', *Pakistan Journal of History & Culture*, Vol. XXI/1 (2000), http:// www.nihcr.edu.pk/Latest_English_Journal/Pjhc%2021-1,%20 2000/2-Syed-Umar-Hayat.pdf.

149. Prabha Chopra, *Quotes of Sardar Patel*, Publications Division, Ministry of Information and Broadcasting, Government of India, Internet Archive, 2005, https://archive.org/stream/quotesofsardarpa00prab/ quotesofsardarpa00prab_djvu.txt.

150. Ibid.

151. H.M. Seervai, *Partition of India: Legend and Reality* (Oxford University Press, 1990), p. 78.

152. 'India: Written in Blood', *Time.* 28 October 1946, p. 42, https:// content.time.com/time/subscriber/article/0,33009,804007,00. html.

153. Dinesh Chandra Sinha and Ashok Dasgupta, *1946: The Great Calcutta Killings and Noakhali Genocide* (Kolkata: Himangshu Maity, 2011), pp. 278–80.

154. Prabha Chopra, *Quotes of Sardar Patel*, Internet Archive.

155. M.K. Gandhi, *Letters to Sardar Vallabhbhai Patel* (Ahmedabad: Navajivan Publishing House, December 1957), https://www. mkgandhi.org/ebks/letters-to-Sardar-Patel.pdf, p. 205.

156. Ibid., p. 206.

157. *Historic Statements by Savarkar,* https://savarkar.org/en/ encyc/2017/5/23/2_12_15_55_historic_statements_by_savarkar. v001.pdf_1.pdf.

158. Ibid.

159. One crore = 10 million.

160. Ibid.

161. *Historic Statements by Savarkar,* https://savarkar.org/en/ encyc/2017/5/23/2_12_15_55_historic_statements_by_savarkar. v001.pdf_1.pdf.

162. B.R. Ambedkar, 'Chapter V: Weakening of the Defences', *Pakistan or the Partition of India,* (Bombay: Thackers, 1945), http://www. columbia.edu/itc/mealac/pritchett/00ambedkar/ambedkar_ partition/205.html#part_3.

163. Dhananjay Keer, *Veer Savarkar* (Delhi: Popular Prakashan), p. 295.

164. B.R. Ambedkar, 'Chapter V: Weakening of the Defences', *Pakistan or the Partition of India.*

165. Ibid.

166. Stephanie Kramer, '1. Population Growth and Religious Composition', Pew Research Centre, 21 September 2021, https:// www.pewresearch.org/religion/2021/09/21/population-growth-and- religious-composition/#:~:text=A%20note%20on%20large%20 numbers&text=For%20example%2C%20Hindus%20increased%20 from,28%20million%20(2.8%20crore).

167. Elizabeth Roche, 'Slow Genocide of Minorities in Pakistan: Farahnaz Ispahani', Mint, 19 January 2016, https://www.livemint. com/Politics/F4r3Tmf51k8Sm6DGjPRaEN/Slow-genocide-of- minorities-in-Pakistan-Farahnaz-Ispahani.html.

168. Pinaki Chakraborty, 'In 30 Years There Would Be No Hindus in Bangladesh', the *Times of India,* 6 June 2022, https://timesofindia. indiatimes.com/india/in-30-years-there-would-be-no-hindus-in- bangladesh/articleshow/92017468.cms.

169. Balarao Savarkar, Hindu Mahasabha Parva, p. 53, quoted in Sampath, *Savarkar,* p. 192.

170. Explained Desk, 'Explained: The Revolutionaries Whom Modi Mentioned in His Independence Day Speech', the *Indian Express,* 16 August 2022, https://indianexpress.com/article/explained/

revolutionaries-whom-modi-mentioned-in-his-independence-day-speech-8091906/.

171. The other is the ancient strategist Kautilya (also known as Chanakya), often referred to as 'the Indian Machiavelli', though Shah would probably argue that being much older in historical provenance than Machiavelli, it was Machiavelli who was the Indian Kautilya. Shah has also suggested that India's highest civilian award, the Bharat Ratna, be given to Savarkar.

172. Now Mumbai.

173. Brahma Chellaney, 'The Non-violence Myth: India's Founding Story Bestows upon It a Quixotic National Philosophy and Enduring Costs', the *Times of India, 3* February 2019, https://timesofindia. indiatimes.com/blogs/toi-edit-page/the-non-violence-myth-indias-founding-story-bestows-upon-it-a-quixotic-national-philosophy-and-enduring-costs/.

174. Joseph McQuade, 'The Forgotten Violence That Helped India Break Free from Colonial Rule', The Conversation, 9 November 2016, https://theconversation.com/the-forgotten-violence-that-helped-india-break-free-from-colonial-rule-57904.

175. Yannick Lengkeek, 'Staged Glory: The Impact of Fascism on "Cooperative" Nationalist Circles in Late Colonial Indonesia, 1935–1942', Brill, 5 May 2018, https://brill.com/view/journals/fasc/7/1/article-p109_109.xml

176. 'Ji' is an honorific in Hindi, read 'Mr Jawaharlal'.

177. *Historic Statements by Savarkar*, https://savarkar.org/en/encyc/2017/5/23/2_12_15_55_historic_statements_by_savarkar. v001.pdf_1.pdf.

178. V.D. Savarkar, *Essentials of Hindutva*, https://library.bjp.org/jspui/bitstream/123456789/284/1/Essentials%20of%20Hindutva.pdf.

179. V.D. Savarkar, *Hindu Rashtra Darshan*, n.d., p. 81.

180. *Historic Statements by Savarkar*, https://savarkar.org/en/encyc/2017/5/23/2_12_15_55_historic_statements_by_savarkar. v001.pdf_1.pdf.

181. V.D. Savarkar, *Hindu Rashtra Darshan,* pg. 81.

182. 'Associates in Hindutva Movement', https://savarkar.org/en/encyc/2017/5/23/Associates-in-Hindutva-Movement.html.

183. Ibid.
184. Ibid.
185. Ibid.
186. M.S. Golwalkar, *We Or Our Nationhood Defined* (Nagpur: Bharat Publications, 1939), p. 87.
187. Ibid., p. 79.
188. Akshaya Mukul, 'RSS Officially Disowns Golwalkar's Book', the *Times of India,* 9 Mar 2006, https://timesofindia.indiatimes.com/india/rss-officially-disowns-golwalkars-book/articleshow/1443606.cms.
189. Rakesh Sinha, *Shri Guruji and Indian Muslims*, https://www.archivesofrss.org/Encyc/2014/1/21/23_07_02_19_muslim.pdf.
190. M.S. Golwalkar, *Bunch of Thoughts*, https://www.thehinducentre.com/multimedia/archive/02486/Bunch_of_Thoughts_2486072a.pdf.
191. Ibid.
192. The reference here is to Rostam or Rustam, a legendary hero in Persian mythology, the son of Zāl and Rudaba, whose life and work were immortalized by the tenth-century Persian poet Ferdowsi in the *Shahnameh*, or Epic of Kings, which contains pre-Islamic Iranian folklore and history.
193. Mustafa Kemal Ataturk, the founder of modern Turkey, which emerged after the fall of the old Ottoman Empire.
194. Ram, the god-king hero of the Ramayana, one of India's two great epics. The other is the Mahabharata.
195. Indonesia's national airlines is called Garuda, the Hindu divine creature who is the mount of Vishnu, the Preserver in the Hindu trinity.
196. Persians who fled during the Islamic invasion of Persia.
197. M.S. Golwalkar, *Bunch of Thoughts*.
198. Late in 1947, Patel wrote to an interlocutor, 'I quite agree with you that we have to turn the enthusiasm and the discipline of the Rashtriya Swayamsewak Sangh into right channels. In fact, I have been advising them accordingly.' (Chopra and Chopra, *The Collected Works of Sardar Vallabhbhai Patel*, p. 265).
199. J. Nehru, *Letters for a Nation: From Jawaharlal Nehru to his Chief Ministers (1947–1963)*, ed. Madhav Khosla (Delhi: Allen Lane, Penguin, 2014).

200. File Number: HOME_POLITICAL_I_1942_NA_F-28-8, Note on the organization, aims, etc., of the Rashtriya Swayam Sewak Sangh, National Archives, India.

201. Then called the United Nations Organization (UNO).

202. Chopra and Chopra, *The Collected Works of Sardar Vallabhbhai Patel*, Vol. 13, p. 219.

203. Nehru and Patel wrote to one another disagreeing with each other in December 1947. Nehru sent his note to Gandhi on 6 January 1948 and Patel on 12 January 1948.

204. As early as 1938, Godse wrote to Savarkar requesting him to take charge of the Hindu Mahasabha so that it could compete with the Congress and complaining that the Mahasabha 'completely lacks solidarity' (File No. 64, 02.08.38, Godse letter to Savarkar [in Marathi], Printed Record of Mahatma Gandhi Murder Case, Vol. V, National Archives, India).

205. By this time, Godse, who had wanted Savarkar to ensure solidarity among the Hindu Mahasabha, would have also seen that no matter the public protestations of the Hindu Mahasabha and Savarkar against the Muslim League, the Mahasabha joined the League to run local governments in Sindh, Bengal and the North-West Frontier Province between 1941 and 1943. Savarkar explained this as necessary for the defence of Hindus in those areas.

206. Chopra and Chopra, *The Collected Works of Sardar Vallabhbhai Patel*; Mahatma Gandhi Murder Case, Vol. V, National Archives, India.

207. Godse, N.V., *May It Please Your Honour: Nathuram Godse* (New Delhi: Surya Prakashan), p. 64.

208. Ibid., p. 65.

209. Ibid., p. 156.

210. Ibid., p. 156–57.

211. Ibid., p. 156.

Chapter 4: The Third Way

1. Around 2000 of them.

2. In Pakistan.

3. K.M. Munshi, *Pilgrimage to Freedom* (New Delhi: Bhavans, 2018), p. 560.

4.   Gandhi.

5.   *Sardar Patel's Correspondences (1945–50)*, ed. Durga Das (Ahmedabad: Navjivan Press, 1973), p. 55.

6.   Ibid., p. 56–57.

7.   A commission set up to re-examine the matter after Savarkar's death in 1966 held that some crucial evidence had not been studied and Savarkar was, in fact, connected to the murder. Later, around fifty years after the assassination of Gandhi, when the Supreme Court of India was asked to reopen the matter, it declined to do so.

8.   Ibid., p. 65.

9.   Roy, *Mookerjee,* p. 297.

10.   Ibid., p. 66.

11.   Gita Piramal, *Business Legends*, Penguin.

12.   Ibid.

13.   Ibid.

14.   Roy, *Mookerjee*, p. 245.

15.   Genteel folk in Bengali.

16.   Ibid., p. 258.

17.   140 million.

18.   *Constituent Assembly Debates, Book No. 4* (New Delhi: Lok Sabha Secretariat, Reprinted 2014), p. 1391.

19.   Roy, *Mookerjee,* p. 273.

20.   Sardar Vallabhbhai Patel Papers, File Identifier: PP_000000005559, National Archives, 1950.

21.   Ibid.

22.   Parliamentary Debates, Part II, Volume I to IV, 1950, 19 April, p. 3017–22; *Syama Prasad Mookerjee Papers*, New Delhi: Nehru Memorial Museum and Library, Instalment 1(c), Sl. No. 3, p. 1–13.

23.   Outlook Web Desk, '"Pakistan Should Take Care of Its Minorities . . ." MEA on Hindu Woman's Beheading', *Outlook*, 29 December 2022, https://www.outlookindia.com/international/-pakistan-should-take-care-of-its-minorities-mea-on-hindu-woman-s-beheading-news-249284.

24.   India Today Web Desk, 'Vandalisation of Durga Puja Pandals In Bangladesh "Disturbing", in Touch with Authorities: MEA', *India*

Today, 15 October 2021, https://www.indiatoday.in/india/story/vandalisation-durga-puja-pandals-bangladesh-authorities-mea-vhp-suvendu-adhikari-pm-modi-1864971-2021-10-14.

25. PTI, 'Home Minister Amit Shah Raises Issue of Attacks on Minorities, Temples in Bangladesh with Counterpart', the *Tribune*, 18 November 2022, https://www.tribuneindia.com/news/nation/home-minister-amit-shah-raises-issue-of-attacks-on-minorities-temples-in-bangladesh-with-counterpart-452234.

26. Bikash Singh, 'Muslims Constitute 35% of Assam's Population, They Cannot Be a Minority, Says CM Sarma', the *Economic Times*, 16 March 2022, https://economictimes.indiatimes.com/news/india/muslims-constitute-35-of-assams-population-they-cannot-be-a-minority-says-cm-sarma/articleshow/90245598.cms.

27. Prabin Kalita, 'Hindu-Muslim Population Growth Rate Difference Dangerous, Says Assam CM Himanta Biswa Sarma', the *Times of India*, 30 June 2021, https://timesofindia.indiatimes.com/city/guwahati/hindu-muslim-population-growth-rate-difference-dangerous-says-assam-cm-himanta-biswa-sarma/articleshow/83975805.cms.

28. Bharti Jain, 'Step up Border Vigilance to Check Infiltration: Amit Shah', the *Times of India*, 25 September 2022, https://timesofindia.indiatimes.com/india/step-up-border-vigilance-to-check-infiltration-amit-shah/articleshow/94425899.cms.

29. Kamaljit Kaur Sandhu, 'BSF DG: Demographic Change in Assam, Bengal Is a Key Reason for Jurisdiction Extension', *India Today*, 30 November 2021, https://www.indiatoday.in/india/story/bsf-jurisdiction-extended-bengal-assam-punjab-demographic-changes-dg-pankaj-singh-1882658-2021-11-30.

30. Roy, *Mookerjee*, p. 282.

31. 'Jaishankar Slams US Media for "Biased" India Coverage. Here's What He Said', Mint, 26 September 2022, https://www.livemint.com/news/india/jaishankar-slams-us-media-for-biased-india-coverage-here-s-what-he-said-11664168367767.html.

32. PTI, 'Minorities in India Being Targeted by Extremist Groups, Alleges Pak PM Imran Khan', the *Indian Express*, 10 January 2022, https://indianexpress.com/article/world/minorities-in-india-being-targeted-by-extremist-groups-alleges-pak-pm-imran-khan-7716129/.

33. 'Ironic That Pakistan Lectures on Minority Rights: India at UN', NDTV, 22 September 2022, https://www.ndtv.com/india-news/ironic-that-pakistan-lectures-on-minority-rights-india-at-un-3366278.

34. Chopra and Chopra, *The Collected Works of Sardar Vallabhbhai Patel*, Vol. 15, p. 27.

35. Ibid., p. 28.

36. Syama Prasad Mookerjee, *Eminent Parliamentarians Monograph Series*, Lok Sabha Secretariat, New Delhi 1990, https://eparlib.nic.in/bitstream/123456789/58670/1/Eminent_Parliamentarians_Series_Syama_Prasad_Mookerjee.pdf, p. 54.

37. *Kesari*, 1954, as quoted in Sampath, *Savarkar,* p. 530.

38. Roy, *Mookerjee*, p. 288.

39. Till 1965, when the posts of prime minister and head of state were separately appointed in Kashmir.

40. Two were from Bengal, and one from Rajasthan.

41. Ibid., p. 326.

42. The Hindu Code Bill was introduced in 1951, and then adopted in four parts between 1952 and 1956 as the Hindu Marriage Act, Hindu Succession Act, Hindu Minority and Guardianship Act and the Hindu Adoptions and Maintenance Act.

43. Syama Prasad Mookerjee, *Eminent Parliamentarians Monograph Series*, Lok Sabha Secretariat, New Delhi 1990, https://eparlib.nic.in/bitstream/123456789/58670/1/Eminent_Parliamentarians_Series_Syama_Prasad_Mookerjee.pdf.

44. Ibid., p. 384.

45. Dr Anirban Ganguly, 'The Final Battle,' Dr Syama Prasad Mookerji Research Foundation, https://www.spmrf.org/the-final-battle/.

46. Barring a few examples like RSS ideologue Ram Madhav's analysis from an insider's point of view in *The Hindutva Paradigm* in 2021.

47. Raghu Vira was one of the editors of the critical edition of the Mahabharata that was compiled at the Bhandarkar Oriental Research Institute, Pune.

48. Even though Deendayal Upadhyaya's own solitary attempt at fighting an election in 1963 from Jaunpur in Uttar Pradesh was not successful.

49. Deendayal Upadhyaya, 'Integral Humanism', BJP Philosophy print, http://avap.org.in/Uploads/Publication/Integral%20Humanism3.pdf.

50. HT Correspondent, 'Everyone Who Lives in India Is Hindu by Identity, Says RSS Chief Mohan Bhagwat', *Hindustan Times*, 19 September 2018, https://www.hindustantimes.com/india-news/everyone-who-lives-in-india-is-hindu-by-identity-says-rss-chief-mohan-bhagwat/story-AkrwvZutu2pR4T2v7RP45O.html.

51. Priest.

52. Deendayal Upadhyaya, 'Integral Humanism', BJP Philosophy print, http://avap.org.in/Uploads/Publication/Integral%20Humanism3.pdf.

53. Ibid.

54. RSS and Sangh are being used synonymously.

55. DNA Web Team, 'Nehru Died Due to Shock of India-China War, Says Mulayam Singh', DNA, 30 April 2016, https://www.dnaindia.com/india/report-nehru-died-due-to-shock-of-india-china-war-says-mulayam-singh-2207820.

56. Indians and Chinese are brothers.

57. The state of Nagaland within the Union of India was created in 1963 to stem the separatist movement which, after decades of talks, is still not fully resolved. Golwalkar mentions the connections between Naga rebels and a British Christian missionary, Michael Scott, and a report in the *New York Times* dated 16 April 1966 also states that the Indian government had strongly protested what it saw as partisan behaviour on the part of Scott who was acting as a middleman in the talks with the Naga rebels. https://www.nytimes.com/1966/04/13/archives/india-says-british-cleric-takes-side-of-naga-rebels-in-dispute-rev.html. 'Nagaland for Christ' is the motto of the biggest rebel group of Nagaland, the National Socialist Council of Nagaland (NSCN).

58. M.S. Golwalkar, *Bunch of Thoughts*, https://www.thehinducentre.com/multimedia/archive/02486/Bunch_of_Thoughts_2486072a.pdf.

59. Motherland.

60. Ibid.

61. Also spelt as Sharif.

62. Ibid.

63. S. Umadevi, 'Humanism in Indian Philosophy: Contributions of Swami Vivekananda and Deendayal Upadhyaya: An Analysis', *The Indian Journal of Political Science* 76, No. 3 (2015): p. 271–76, https://www.jstor.org/stable/26534828.

64. Deendayal Upadhyaya, 'Integral Humanism', BJP Philosophy print, http://avap.org.in/Uploads/Publication/Integral%20Humanism3.pdf.

65. S. Umadevi, 'Humanism in Indian Philosophy: Contributions of Swami Vivekananda and Deendayal Upadhyaya: An Analysis'.

66. Ibid.

67. Ram Madhav, *The Hindutva Paradigm* (New Delhi: Westland Publications, 2021), p. 202.

68. This, Upadhyaya described, as the soul or identity of a nation.

69. Which he called Bharatiya Technology.

70. Deendayal Upadhyaya, 'Integral Humanism', BJP Philosophy print, http://avap.org.in/Uploads/Publication/Integral%20Humanism3.pdf.

71. Constitution and Rules, Bharatiya Janata Party, September 2012, https://www.bjp.org/images/pdf_2012_h/constitution_eng_jan_10_2013.pdf.

72. Deendayal Upadhyaya, 'Integral Humanism', BJP Philosophy print, http://avap.org.in/Uploads/Publication/Integral%20Humanism3.pdf.

73. 'Sarva Dharma Sambhav' loosely translates to all faiths or religions are relevant or possible.

74. The family name was originally Thakre but Keshav was a fan of the writer William Makepeace Thackeray and changed the spelling accordingly.

75. Now Mumbai.

76. 'Congress Party of Natural Governance: Sonia', the *Times of India,* 18 May 2009, https://timesofindia.indiatimes.com/india/congress-party-of-natural-governance-sonia/articleshow/4543978.cms.

Chapter 5: The House of God

1. December 1924–August 2018.

2. Vajpayee had also travelled with Syama Prasad Mookerjee in his fateful journey to Kashmir and after Mookerjee was arrested, he was

sent back early with explicit instructions to continue Mookerjee's campaign.

3.   Prof. Pramod Kumar, 'Republic Day Parade: When Jawaharlal Nehru Recognised the Contribution of RSS Swayamsevaks', *Organiser*, 26 January 2023, https://organiser.org/2022/09/21/94570/bharat/ when-pt-nehru-recognised-the-contribution-of-rss-swayamsevaks/.

4.   'RSS in R-Day Parade: Highlight of Citizens' Group', *Organiser*, Vol. 16., No. 26, 4 February 1963, p. 1, Nehru Memorial Museum and Library archives.

5.   Prabhash K. Dutta, 'When Nehru Saw a PM in Atal Bihari Vajpayee Who Returned Favour as Foreign Minister', *India Today*, 16 August 2018, https://www.indiatoday.in/india/story/atal-bihari-vajpayee-jawaharlal-nehru-1261286-2018-06-15.

6.   Sourav Roy Barman, 'When Atal Bihari Vajpayee Was Called 'Nehruvian in Jan Sanghi Garb': New Book Traces Their Complex Relationship', the *Indian Express,* 12 May 2023, https://indianexpress. com/article/political-pulse/new-book-on-atal-bihari-vajpayee-nehruvian-8604343/.

7.   'When Atal Bihari Vajpayee Delivered Emotional Speech after Jawahar Lal Nehru's Death', the *Economic Times,* 17 August 2017, https://economictimes.indiatimes.com/news/politics-and-nation/ when-atal-bihari-vajpayee-delivered-emotional-speech-after-jawahar-lal-nehrus-death/articleshow/65445156.cms.

8.   Sourav Roy Barman, 'When Atal Bihari Vajpayee Was Called 'Nehruvian in Jan Sanghi Garb': New Book Traces Their Complex Relationship', the *Indian Express*.

9.   Paul McGarr, *The Cold War in South Asia: Britain, the United States and the Indian Subcontinent, 1945–1965* (Cambridge University Press, 2013), p. 331.

10. Devin Hagerty, *South Asia in World Politics* (Rowman & Littlefield, 2005), p. 26.

11. 'When Lal Bahadur Shastri Invited RSS' Shri Guru Ji to All-Party Meet during 1965 Indo-Pak War', MirrorNowNews, 7 June 2018, https://www.timesnownews.com/mirror-now/in-focus/article/ lal-bahadur-shastri-rss-shri-guru-ji-all-party-meet-1965-indo-pak-war/236863.

12. Mekhala Saran, 'Atal Bihari Vajpayee Had Refuted Calling Indira Gandhi "Durga"', The Quint, 17 August 2018, https://www.thequint.com/news/politics/vajpayee-said-he-never-called-indira-gandhi-durga.

13. Srishti Choudhary and Aakanksha Ahuja, 'How a PM and Opposition Took India along during 1971 Bangladesh War', 4 March 2019, https://www.livemint.com/news/india/how-indira-gandhi-and-atal-bihari-vajpayee-led-india-during-1971-bangladesh-war-1551643929931.html.

14. Christophe Jaffrelot, The Hindu Nationalist Movement in India (Columbia University Press, 1996), p. 257.

15. Balasaheb Deoras, Shri Balasaheb Deoras Answers Questions (rpnt, Bangalore: Sahitya Sindhu, 1984), pp. 36–7, in Jaffrelot, Hindu Nationalism: A Reader, p. 188.

16. Ibid.

17. Rakesh Ankit, 'Janata Party (1974-77): Creation of an All-India Opposition', History and Sociology of South Asia (11) (1) (2017): 39–54, p. 42

18. L.K. Advani, My Country, My Life (New Delhi: Rupa Books, 2009), p. 192.

19. Maseeh Rahman, 'Crawling through the Emergency', Outlook, 27 January 2022, https://www.outlookindia.com/website/story/crawling-through-the-emergency/294674.

20. Advani had spent the entire period in prison, while Vajpayee was mostly out being treated for various ailments.

21. Advani, My Country, p. 304.

22. Ibid., pp. 302–03.

23. At the end of the autumnal Hindu Durga Puja celebrations.

24. Ibid., p. 305.

25. Ibid., p. 313.

26. Vinay Sitapati, Jugalbandi: The BJP Before Modi, p. 114.

27. Meenakshi Jain, The Battle for Rama (New Delhi: Aryan Books, 2017, pg. 1-2

28. Humra Quraishi, 'BJP, Not Historical Facts Played Big Role in Babri Masjid Demolition Says Historian Irfan Habib,' National Herald, 15 March 2019, https://www.nationalheraldindia.com/opinion/bjp-

not-historical-facts-played-big-role-in-babri-masjid-demolition-says-historian-irfan-habib.

29. Times Now Digital, 'Did You Know Seven Evidences Unearthed by ASI Proved a Temple Existed at Ayodhya? Details Here', TimesNowNews, 4 August 2020, https://www.timesnownews. com/india/article/did-you-know-seven-evidences-unearthed-by-asi-proved-a-temple-existed-at-ayodhya-details-here/631910.

30. Christophe Jaffrelot, *The Hindu Nationalist Movement in India*, p. 365.

31. L.K. Advani, *My Country*, p. 351.

32. Ajaz Ashraf, 'Arif Muhammad Khan on Shah Bano case: "Najma Heptullah Was Key Influence on Rajiv Gandhi"', Scroll.in, 30 May 2015, https://scroll.in/article/730642/arif-mohammad-khan-on-shah-bano-case-najma-heptullah-was-key-influence-on-rajiv-gandhi.

33. In an open letter published in the *New York Times*, Rushdie wrote to Rajiv Gandhi, 'The book was banned after representations by two or three Muslim politicians, including Syed Shahabuddin and Khurshid Alam Khan, both members of Parliament. These persons, whom I do not hesitate to call extremists, even fundamentalists, have attacked me and my novel while stating that they had no need actually to read it. That the Government should have given in to such fires is profoundly disturbing.'

34. Anindita Mukherjee, 'Woman Touches Ramayan Actor Arun Govil's Feet at Airport. Watch', *India Today*, 2 October 2022, https://www.indiatoday.in/television/celebrity/story/woman-touches-ramayan-actor-arun-govil-s-feet-at-airport-watch-2007387-2022-10-02.

35. Kanchan Gupta, 'A Chariot in History', *Open the Magazine*, 15 November 2019, https://openthemagazine.com/cover-stories/a-chariot-in-history/.

36. Kamandal is a metal water pot usually carried by mendicants.

37. A son of a Brahmin clerk from Punjab set himself on fire after nine days of hunger strike.

38. Advani, *My Country*, p. 375.

39. Ibid., p. 375.

40. Sukumar Muralidharan, 'Mandal, Mandir aur Masjid: "Hindu" Communalism and the Crisis of the State', *Social Scientist*, Vol. 18, No. 10, October 1990, p. 27–49.

41. Koenraad Elst, *The Saffron Swastika* (New Delhi: Rupa Books, 2001).

42. Sitapati, *Jugalbandi*, p. 162.

43. Budget 1991-92 Speech of Shri Manmohan Singh, Minister of Finance, 24 July 1991, https://www.indiabudget.gov.in/budget2021-22/doc/bspeech/bs199192.pdf.

44. NDTV, 'What L.K. Advani said on Babri Masjid Demolition (Aired December 2000)', YouTube, https://www.youtube.com/watch?v=FFNSO7ho2DI&t=44s.

45. Mustafa Shaikh, 'Shiv Sena Ad on Babri Masjid Demolition Ahead of Ram Temple Ceremony Triggers Controversy', *India Today*, 5 August 2020, https://www.indiatoday.in/india/story/shiv-sena-s-ad-on-babri-masjid-demolition-ahead-of-ram-temple-ceremony-triggers-controversy-1707888-2020-08-05.

46. Later, this case would be seen as Narasimha Rao's revenge on Advani for failing to keep the promise of leaving the Babri mosque intact.

47. 'Govindacharya Calls Vajpayee "Mask", Lands BJP in Crisis', Rediff on the Net, http://www.rediff.com/news/oct/16bjp.htm.

48. K.N. Govindacharya, 'I Called Vajpayee "Face of BJP", Media Made It "Mukhota": Govindacharya', *Outlook*, 17 August 2018, https://www.outlookindia.com/website/story/i-called-vajpayee-face-of-bjp-media-made-it-mukhota-govindacharya/315135.

49. L.K. Advani, *My Country*, p. 408

50. This, apart from the 1971 war victory, is another reason why, despite the Emergency, both Vajpayee and the RSS had some fondness for Indira Gandhi.

51. Conversation with the late Shakti Sinha, who worked in the Vajpayee PMO, in February 2021.

52. Jaswant Singh, 'Nuclear Apartheid', *Foreign Affairs*, Vol. 77, No. 5, September–October 1998, pp. 41–52.

53. Murli Manohar Joshi, 'Reorienting Education', *Seminar*, Delhi, no. 417, May 1994, pp. 26–29.

54. Ibid.

55. Rupin Katyal, twenty-five, was killed when Zahoor Mistry, one of the hijackers, stabbed him using a sharp object.

56. L.K. Advani, *My Country*, p. 609.

57. 'Two Eyes for an Eye, a Jaw for a Tooth: Shourie', Rediff.com, https://www.rediff.com/news/2001/dec/24parl.htm.

58. A. Shourie, *Listen to the New India* (New Delhi: BJP, 2003).

59. Ibid.

60. S. Gurumurthy, 'Swadeshi and Nationalism', *Seminar*, no. 469, Delhi, September 1998.

61. Shourie and Gurumurthy had a connection. It was under Shourie's editorship of the *Indian Express* newspaper that Gurumurthy had published a series of path-breaking stories of corruption.

Chapter 6: The Mouse Charmer

1. NDTV, '"We Are a Nation of Mouse Charmers Now", Modi at SRCC', YouTube, 6 February 2013, https://www.youtube.com/watch?v=KeemGpCG_zc.

2. India News Desk, 'Modi Dominates List of Most Popular World Leaders with 77% Approval Rating: Survey', *Financial Express*, 25 November 2022, https://www.financialexpress.com/india-news/prime-minister-narendra-modi-top-world-leader-morning-consult-political-intelligence-survey/2892082/.

3. So much so that critics have even complained of 'tech populism' but supporters have lauded Modi's focus on trying to use tech not only in his campaigns but to solve some of India's hardest problems.

4. Aneesha Mathur, 'SC Confirms SIT Clean Chit to PM Modi, Rejects Zakia Jafri's Plea', *India Today*, 24 June 2022, https://www.indiatoday.in/india/story/gujarat-riots-sc-dismisses-plea-challenging-clean-cheat-to-pm-modi-2002-violence-1966192-2022-06-24.

5. Revati Laul, 'BBC Documentary on Narendra Modi Tries Too Hard to Balance "Both Sides"', The Wire, 31 January 2023, https://thewire.in/communalism/bbc-documentary-on-narendra-modi-tries-too-hard-to-balance-both-sides.

6. Non-resident Indian.

7. Shah is the brother of the Hindi cinema actor Naseeruddin Shah.

8.   Jaitirath Rao, 'BBC's Anti-Modi Stance Promotes Imagined Hindu Supremacy. Muslims in India Are Not at Risk', ThePrint, 1 February 2023, https://theprint.in/opinion/bbcs-anti-modi-stance-promotes-imagined-hindu-supremacy-muslims-in-india-are-not-at-risk/1344940/.

9.   HT Correspondent, 'Ayodhya Verdict: Understanding the Supreme Court Judgement', *Hindustan Times*, 28 July 2020, https://www.hindustantimes.com/india-news/ayodhya-verdict-understanding-the-supreme-court-judgment/story-G7mzXfBFEDJ88PmuLj8CpL.html.

10. '2.3 Crore Muslim Students Got Edu Aid in 5 Years', the *Times of India*, 15 March 2022, https://timesofindia.indiatimes.com/india/2-3-crore-muslim-students-got-edu-aid-in-5-years/articleshow/90211533.cms.

11. Fatima Khan, 'More Muslims Got Government Scholarships under Modi Government than under Congress-Led UPA-2', ThePrint, 21 October 2019, https://theprint.in/india/more-muslims-govt-scholarships-modi-govt-congress-upa/308154/.

12. Hilal Ahmed, 'BJP Is Emerging as Second-Most Preferred Political Choice for Voters in Modi's India', ThePrint, 24 April 2019, https://theprint.in/opinion/muslim-vote/bjp-is-emerging-as-second-most-preferred-political-choice-for-muslim-voters-in-india/225041/.

13. IANS, 'Uttar Pradesh Polls: Survey Shows 8% Muslims Voted for BJP', *Business Standard*, 13 March 2022, https://www.business-standard.com/article/elections/uttar-pradesh-polls-survey-shows-8-muslims-voted-for-bjp-122031300448_1.html.

14. Christopher Finnigan, 'Muslims and an Inclusive India under Modi 2.0', The London School of Economics and Political Science, 8 July 2019, https://blogs.lse.ac.uk/southasia/2019/07/08/long-read-muslims-and-an-inclusive-india-under-modi-2-0/.

15. PTI, 'Muslim Women Thank PM Modi on Passage of Triple Talaq Bill', the *Economic Times*, 31 July 2019, https://economictimes.indiatimes.com/news/politics-and-nation/muslim-women-thank-pm-modi-on-passage-of-triple-talaq-bill/articleshow/70465902.cms?from=mdr.

16. TNN, Himanshi Dhawan, 'How Husbands Are Evading Triple Talaq Ban', the *Times of India,* 28 August 2022, https://timesofindia.

indiatimes.com/india/how-husbands-are-evading-triple-talaq-ban/
articleshow/93833590.cms.

17. PTI, 'About 82% Decline in Triple Talaq Cases since Law Enacted
By Modi Government: Naqvi', *The Hindu*, 22 July 2020, https://
www.thehindu.com/news/national/about-82-decline-in-triple-talaq-
cases-since-law-enacted-by-modi-govt-naqvi/article32160348.ece.

18. Smriti Kak Ramachandran, 'No Hindu Rashtra without
Muslims, Hindutva Based on Unity in Diversity: Mohan
Bhagwat', *Hindustan Times*, 18 September 2018, https://www.
hindustantimes.com/india-news/no-hindu-rashtra-without-muslims-
hindutva-based-on-unity-in-diversity-mohan-bhagwat/story-
DRFWYkKTNfSVyDPQMVFV1I.html.

19. HT Correspondent, '"Anyone Who Says Muslims Should Not
Live in India Is Not Hindu", Mohan Bhagwat', *Hindustan Times*,
4 July 2021, https://www.hindustantimes.com/india-news/anyone-
who-says-muslims-should-not-live-in-india-is-not-hindu-mohan-
bhagwat-101625412723564.html.

20. Anilesh S. Mahajan, 'How Modi, Mohan Bhagwat's Muslim
Outreach Isn't Anti-Hindutva, Rather Part of Its Larger
Doctrine', *India Today*, 3 February 2023, https://www.indiatoday.
in/india-today-insight/story/how-modi-mohan-bhagwats-
muslim-outreach-isnt-anti-hindutva-rather-part-of-its-larger-
doctrine-2329203-2023-02-01.

21. 'RSS Chief, Muslim Intellectuals Discuss Religious Harmony in
Country', NDTV, 21 September 2022, https://www.ndtv.com/
india-news/rss-chief-meets-muslim-intellectuals-mohan-bhagwat-to-
discuss-religious-harmony-in-country-3362890.

22. Dr Prashant Prabhakar Deshpande, 'RSS Chief's Outreach to
Muslims—A Beginning of Hindu-Muslim Bonding?', the *Times of
India*, 6 October 2022, https://timesofindia.indiatimes.com/blogs/
truth-lies-and-politics/rss-chiefs-outreach-to-muslims-a-beginning-
of-hindu-muslim-bonding/.

23. Tariq Mansoor, 'BJP's Outreach to Pasmandas a First in India. The
3 Factors behind It: Amu VC', ThePrint, 30 January 2023, https://
theprint.in/opinion/bjp-olive-branch-pasmandas-momentous-first-
in-india-3-factors-behind-it-amu-vc/1341204/.

24. Eltaf Najafizada, 'India's Modi Urges His Hindu Nationalist Party to Not Discriminate Against Muslims', *Time*, 18 January 2023, https://time.com/6247963/indias-modi-urges-his-hindu-nationalist-party-to-not-discriminate-against-muslims/.

25. 'Explained: Who Are the Pasmanda Muslims, the Group That BJP Is Trying to Woo?', the *Times of India*, 9 July 2022, https://timesofindia.indiatimes.com/india/explained-who-are-the-pasmanda-muslims-the-group-that-bjp-is-trying-to-woo/articleshow/92766145.cms.

26. Tariq Mansoor, 'BJP's Outreach to Pasmandas a First in India. The 3 Factors behind It: Amu VC', ThePrint.

27. 'Christophe Jaffrelot on Narendra Modi and Hindu Nationalism', Democracy Paradox, 13 July 2021, https://democracyparadox.com/2021/07/13/christophe-jaffrelot-on-narendra-modi-and-hindu-nationalism/.

28. Jyoti Mishra, Vibha Atri and Nitin Mehta, 'The Bahujan Vote in 2014 Elections: Voting Patterns among Dalits, Adivasis, and Backward Castes', *Research Journal Social Sciences*, Vol. 22, No. 2, 2014, p. 73.

29. Gatherings where the primary aim is to collectively sing devotional songs.

30. Snigdha Poonam, Dhrubo Jyoti and Guru Prakash, 'Why Dalits Voted for the BJP', *Seminar*, August 2019, https://www.india-seminar.com/2019/720/720_snigdha_dhrubo_guru.htm.

31. Bibek Debroy, 'Politics Aside, Is Gujarat a Great Growth Story?', the *Economic Times*, 7 October 2012, https://economictimes.indiatimes.com/news/politics-and-nation/politics-aside-is-gujarat-a-great-growth-story/articleshow/msid-16701209,curpg-3.cms?from=mdr.

32. 'Centre Report Gujarat Government's Land 'Best''', *India Today*, 7 May 2014.

33. 'Suit-Boot-Ki-Sarkar Tag Trips PM Narendra Modi's Privatization', the *Financial Express*, 3 July 2018, https://www.financialexpress.com/opinion/suit-boot-ki-sarkar-tag-trips-pm-narendra-modis-privatisation/1229041/.

34. Direct Benefit Transfer, https://dbtbharat.gov.in/.

35. Ibid.

36. Speech of Nirmala Sitharaman, Minister of Finance, Budget 2023-2024, 1 February 2023, https://www.indiabudget.gov.in/doc/budget_speech.pdf.

37. '3 Crore Houses Built for Poor across India in Last 8 Years: PM Modi', 8 September 2022, https://www.livemint.com/news/india/3-crore-houses-built-for-poor-across-india-in-last-8-years-pm-modi-11662620904883.html.

38. Sarika Malhotra, 'MNREGA Still under the Scanner Due to Rampant Corruption', *Business Today*, 23 December 2014, https://www.businesstoday.in/latest/economy-politics/story/mgnrega-still-under-the-scanner-due-to-rampant-corruption-138586-2014-12-23.

39. M.S. Golwalkar, *Bunch of Thoughts*, p. 28.

40. Krzysztof Iwanek, 'The Political Economy of Hindu Nationalism: From V.D. Savarkar to Narendra Modi', Hankuk University of Foreign Studies, 2014, p. 4–5.

41. Dattopant Thengadi, *The Third Way* (New Delhi: Janaki Prakashan), p. 17.

42. Swatantryaveer Vinayak Damodar Savarkar, Lok Sabha Secretariat, New Delhi, February 2003, https://eparlib.nic.in/bitstream/123456789/56237/1/Swatantryaveer_VDSavarkar.English.pdf., p. 7.

43. Syama Prasad Mookerjee, *Eminent Parliamentarians Monograph Series*, Lok Sabha Secretariat, New Delhi 1990, https://eparlib.nic.in/bitstream/123456789/58670/1/Eminent_Parliamentarians_Series_Syama_Prasad_Mookerjee.pdf.

44. Shubh Mathur, *The Everyday Life of Hindu Nationalism* (New Delhi: Three Essays Collective, 2006); Jaffrelot, Christophe, *The Hindu Nationalist Movement and Indian Politics, 1925 to the 1990s: Strategies of Identity Building, Implementation and Mobilisation* (New Delhi: Penguin Books India (Viking), 1997).

45. BJP, 'Constitution and Rules', accessed from https://www.bjp.org/en/constitution.

46. Yashwant Sinha, 'ET Awards 2012: Economic Reforms in India Must Be Seen Touching Lives of People, Says Yashwant Sinha', the *Economic Times*, 25 October 2012, https://economictimes.indiatimes.com/et-awards-2012-economic-reforms-in-india-must-be-seen-touching-

lives-of-people-says-yashwant-sinha/articleshow/16946235.
cms?from=mdr

47. Kirtika Suneja, 'India Seen Fastest Growing among 7 Largest Emerging
     and Developing Economies: World Bank', the *Economic Times*,
     11 January 2023, https://economictimes.indiatimes.com/news/
     economy/indicators/india-seen-fastest-growing-among-7-largest-
     emerging-developing-economies-world-bank/articleshow/96890524.
     cms?from=mdr.

48. PIB, 'India Achieves $400 Billion Merchandise Exports Well
     Before Target Date—Shri Piyush Goyal', Press Information
     Bureau, 23 March 2022, https://pib.gov.in/PressReleaseIframePage.
     aspx?PRID=1808831#:~:text=The%20Union%20Minister
     %20of%20Commerce,every%20stakeholder%20in%20the%
     20nation.

49. PIB, 'India Gets the Highest Annual FDI Inflow of USD 83.57
     Billion in FY21-22', Press Information Bureau, 20 May 2022, https://
     pib.gov.in/PressReleasePage.aspx?PRID=1826946

50. 'India Overtakes China to Become the Most Attractive Emerging
     Market for Investing', Mint, 10 July 2023, https://www.livemint.
     com/economy/india-top-emerging-market-for-investing-in-em-debt-
     invesco-report-11688982338557.html.

51. Ibid.

52. Under the Pradhan Mantri Awas Yojana.

53. Under the Pradhan Mantri Ujjwala Yojana.

54. Ashutosh Bhardwaj, 'BJP's Pasmanda Move Pushes Muslim Politics
     to a New Moment', *Outlook*, 19 August 2022, https://www.
     outlookindia.com/national/bjp-s-pasmanda-move-pushes-muslim-
     politics-to-a-new-moment-news-217046.

55. Ibid.

56. Under the One District One Product Scheme.

57. Nalin Mehta, 'Nalin Mehta Writes: Three Reasons Why Experts Got
     it So Wrong on BJP in UP', News18, 14 March 2022, https://www.
     news18.com/news/opinion/nalin-mehta-writes-three-reasons-why-
     experts-got-it-so-wrong-on-bjp-in-up-4873370.html.

58. See Mehta's 2021 book *The New BJP* (New Delhi: Westland
     Publications).

59. Christophe Jaffrelot, 'Class and Caste in the 2019 Indian Election–Why Have So Many Poor Started Voting for Modi?', LOKNITI, Centre for the Study of Developing Societies, 12 November 2019, https://journals.sagepub.com/doi/abs/10.1177/2321023019874890?journalCode=inpa.

60. Sanjay Kumar and Pranav Gupta, 'Where Did the BJP Get Its Votes from in 2019?', Mint, 3 June 2019, https://www.livemint.com/politics/news/where-did-the-bjp-get-its-votes-from-in-2019-1559547933995.html.

61. Guru Prakash Paswan, 'Dalits Have a Special Place in the New Hindutva Matrix. Ram Mandir Is Proof of That', ThePrint, 5 August 2020, https://theprint.in/opinion/dalits-have-a-special-place-in-the-new-hindutva-matrix-ram-mandir-is-proof-of-that/474900/.

62. His name was Kameshwar Chaupal.

63. HT Correspondent, 'How Modi Used Aiyar's "Tea Seller" Barb to Attack Congress', Hindustan Times, 19 January 2014, https://www.hindustantimes.com/india/how-modi-used-aiyar-s-tea-seller-barb-to-attack-congress/story-SwPrLG4v2gHe28P0dx0EzK.html.

64. The Bhakti movement was a reformist movement across India starting from around the sixth century CE to the seventeenth century CE. It sought to reform both Hinduism and Islam and show a path of spirituality beyond religious strife. Nirgun and sagun means the divine without form, and with form.

65. Abhinav Prakash Singh, 'A Common Hindu Identity Has Always Appealed to OBC and Dalit Castes', Hindustan Times, 18 July 2019, https://www.hindustantimes.com/columns/a-common-hindu-identity-has-always-appealed-to-obc-and-dalit-castes/story-n8CXPw1CKTx0V27Zk8VTSJ.html.

66. Ravi Singh Sisodiya, 'Dropping Terror Cases Needs Centre's Nod: HC', the Times of India, 13 December 2013, https://timesofindia.indiatimes.com/india/dropping-terror-cases-needs-centres-nod-hc/articleshow/27265707.cms.

67. PTI, 'Minorities Must Have First Claim on Resources: PM', the Economic Times, 9 December 2006, https://economictimes.indiatimes.com/news/politics-and-nation/minorities-must-have-first-claim-on-resources-pm/articleshow/754218.cms.

68. Shiv Vishvanathan, 'How Modi Defeated Liberals like Me', *The Hindu*, 22 May 2014, https://www.thehindu.com/opinion/lead/how-modi-defeated-liberals-like-me/article6034057.ece.

69. Pooja Sitaram Jaiswar (ed.), 'India's Per Capita Income Doubles since 2014-15, Uneven Wage Distribution Remains a Challenge', Mint, 5 March 2023, https://www.livemint.com/news/india/india-s-per-capita-income-doubles-since-2014-15-uneven-wage-distribution-remains-a-challenge-11678023250808.html.

70. S.P.S. Pannu, 'UPA's 10-Year Report Card: Scams, Policy Paralysis Crashes India's Economy', *India Today*, 28 January 2014, https://www.indiatoday.in/india/north/story/india-manmohan-singh-upa-scams-policy-paralysis-gdp-growth-rate-economy-178631-2014-01-27.

71. The reference to midnight's children comes from the speech Nehru gave when India became independent, which began with the words, 'At the stroke of the midnight hour, when the world sleeps, India will awake to life and freedom.' The British-Indian author Salman Rushdie wrote a book published in 1981 which fictionalized the changes that occurred in India after Independence called *Midnight's Children* and the name stuck.

72. 'India: Another Tryst with Destiny', the *Guardian*, 18 May 2014, https://www.theguardian.com/global/2014/may/18/india-narendra-modi-election-destiny.

73. PTI, 'Target the Youth and First-Time Voters: Narendra Modi to Party Workers in BJP 2014 Campaign Meet', *India Today*, 18 August 2013, https://www.indiatoday.in/india/north/story/narendra-modi-bjp-meet-bjp-national-election-campaign-meet-2014-polls-strategy-174144-2013-08-17.

74. Sanjay Kumar, 'The Youth Vote Made a Difference for the Victory of the BJP', *Research Journal Social Sciences*, Vol. 22, No. 2, 2014, p. 45–51.

75. M. Poddar and S. Chakrabarti, 'Indoor Air Pollution and Women's Health in India: An Exploratory Analysis', Springer Link, 21 May 2015, https://link.springer.com/article/10.1007/s10668-015-9670-x.

76. In Uttar Pradesh, Uttarakhand, Manipur and Goa.

77. Rahul Verma and Ankita Barthwal, 'Why More Women Voted for the BJP in 2022 Elections: Analysis', *India Today*, 14 March 2022,

https://www.indiatoday.in/elections/story/why-more-women-voted-bjp-2022-elections-analysis-1924821-2022-03-13.

78. 'India's Urban Awakening: Building Inclusive Cities, Sustaining Economic Growth', McKinsey Global Institute, April 2010, https://www.mckinsey.com/mgi/our-research/all-research.

79. Ashok Malik, 'What Does India Think? The India That Made Modi', European Council on Foreign Relations, https://ecfr.eu/special/what_does_india_think/analysis/the_india_that_made_modi.

80. Modi has 86.3 million followers at last count.

81. Naina Bharadwaj, 'India's UPI Interface to Become Accessible to More Users', India Briefing, 17 July 2023, https://www.india-briefing.com/news/global-acceptance-of-indias-digital-payment-systems-europe-latest-to-join-26183.html/#:~:text=NIPL%20(NPCI%20International%20Payments%20Limited,to%20use%20India's%20payment%20systems.

82. Ruchika Chitravanshi, 'PM Narendra Modi Launches Health ID, Digital Record for Citizens', *Business Standard*, 28 September 2021, https://www.business-standard.com/article/economy-policy/pm-narendra-modi-launches-health-id-digital-record-for-citizens-121092800016_1.html.

83. Vidhi Doshi, 'Modi Finally Speaks Out against Lynchings of "Beef Eaters"', *Washington Post*, 29 June 2017, https://www.washingtonpost.com/world/modi-finally-speaks-out-against-lynchings-of-beef-eaters/2017/06/29/f171e042-5ccf-11e7-aa69-3964a7d55207_story.html.

84. 'Cow Smuggling Through Indo-Bangladesh Border', Press Information Bureau, Government of India, Ministry of Home Affairs, 10 March 2021, https://pib.gov.in/Pressreleaseshare.aspx?PRID=1703788.

85. Doris Ellin Urrutia, 'India's Anti-Satellite Missile Test Is a Big Deal. Here's Why', *Space*, 10 August 2022, https://www.space.com/india-anti-satellite-test-significance.html.

86. Pradip R. Sagar, 'How India Is Gearing Up for Its Own Hypersonic Ballistic Missile', *India Today*, 26 July 2022, https://www.indiatoday.in/india-today-insight/story/how-india-is-gearing-up-for-its-own-hypersonic-ballistic-missile-1980239-2022-07-26.

87. ANI, '"You're Not Fooling Anybody . . ." Jaishankar Responds to US F-16 Package for Pakistan', *Hindustan Times*, 26 September

2022, https://www.hindustantimes.com/world-news/youre-not-fooling-anybody-jaishankar-responds-to-us-f-16-package-for-pakistan-101664183691205.html.

88. According to international relations scholars Kanti Bajpai, Saira Basit and V. Krishnappa, Nehruvianism, neoliberalism and hyperrealism are major schools, and Marxism, Hindutva and Gandhianism are minor schools of Indian grand strategy making.

89. Vikas Pandey, 'Modi US Visit: Why Washington Is Rolling Out the Red Carpet for Indian PM', BBC News, 21 June 2023, https://www.bbc.com/news/world-asia-india-65947363.

90. Joseph John, 'Chhattisgarh to Buy Cow Urine, Says Chief Minister Bhupesh Baghel', the *Times of India,* 5 May 2022, https://timesofindia.indiatimes.com/city/raipur/chhattisgarh-to-buy-cow-urine-says-chief-minister-bhupesh-baghel/articleshow/91338961.cms.

91. Rohit Parihar, 'Why Gehlot Is Spending a Fortune on Saving Cows?', *India Today,* 24 January 2022, https://www.indiatoday.in/india-today-insight/story/why-gehlot-is-spending-a-fortune-on-saving-cows-1903887-2022-01-24.

92. 'Watch: Delhi CM, Deputy CM, and Other Ministers Take Part in Diwali Puja Event', the *Economic Times,* 4 November 2021, https://economictimes.indiatimes.com/news/india/watch-delhi-cm-deputy-cm-and-other-ministers-take-part-in-diwali-puja-event/videoshow/87527675.cms.

93. 'Rahul Gandhi Offers Prayers at Ujjain's Mahakal Temple', NDTV, 30 November 2022, https://www.ndtv.com/india-news/rahul-gandhi-offers-prayers-at-ujjains-mahakal-temple-in-madhya-pradesh-3563055.

94. PIB Delhi, 'Khadi Exceeds Turnover of Rs 1 Lakh Crore in 2021-22; Beats All FMCG Companies in India', Ministry of Micro, Small & Medium Enterprises, 30 April 2022, https://pib.gov.in/PressReleasePage.aspx?PRID=1821521.

95. This is a bit like the phrase 'champagne socialists' in the United Kingdom.

96. Mayank Bhardwaj, '"Khan Market Gang": Modi Mocks His Elite Adversaries', Reuters, 31 May 2019, https://www.reuters.com/article/india-politics-khanmarket-idUSKCN1T10KM.

97. Special Correspondent, 'India a Civilizational State Reappearing On World Stage: Jaishankar', *The Hindu*, 16 September 2021, https://www.thehindu.com/news/national/india-a-civilisation-state-reappearing-on-global-stage-jaishankar/article36486698.ece.

98. CNBC-TV18, '"Diplomacy In Mahabharata" In The Words Of EAM S. Jaishankar', *YouTube* video, 2:07, 11 December 2022, https://www.youtube.com/watch?v=V_k_bv5YmnA.

99. Lorraine Ali, 'CNN's "Believer With Reza Aslan" Could Use a Little More Enlightenment Itself', *Los Angeles Times*, 4 March 2017, https://www.latimes.com/entertainment/tv/la-et-st-believer-reza-aslan-review-20170304-story.html.

100. Vamsee Juluri, 'CNN's "Believer" Is Reckless, Racist and Dangerously Anti-Immigrant', *Huffington Post*, 5 March 2017, https://www.huffpost.com/entry/cannibals-and-corpses-cnns-believer-is-reckless-racist_b_58bbc5fee4b02eac8876cfad.

101. PTI, 'US Lawmaker Tulsi Gabbard Criticises CNN over 'Negative' Portrayal of Hinduism', *Hindustan Times*, 8 March 2017, https://www.hindustantimes.com/world-news/us-lawmaker-tulsi-gabbard-criticises-cnn-over-negative-portrayal-of-hinduism/story-b9UWTaHdE5UkSmkwKnYmJJ.html.

102. Sandeep Deo, 'Complaint Filed against Sangh Chief Mohan Bhagwat!', India Speaks Daily, 24 January 2023, https://www.indiaspeaksdaily.com/complaint-filed-against-sangh-chief-mohan-bhagwat/.

103. M. Nageswar Rao, Twitter post, https://twitter.com/MNageswarRaoIPS/status/1617767761371103232?ref_src=twsrc%5Etfw%7Ctwcamp%5Etweetembed%7Ctwterm%5E1617767761371103232%7Ctwgr%5Eba72968f26004e5a6ffd5e1ee786a01c6556050b%7Ctwcon%5Es1_&ref_url=https%3A%2F%2Fthewire.in%2Fpolitics%2Fmohan-bhagwat-lgbtq-hindu-sentiments-complaint.

104. Nandita Singh and Nikhil Rampal, 'India's First and Oldest Gay Rights Activist Is Also on the Extreme Right of RSS', ThePrint, 21 July 2018, https://theprint.in/politics/indias-first-and-oldest-gay-activist-uses-a-brand-of-hindutva-to-fight-377/85919/.

105. Refers to the traditional trader caste.

106. Dheeraj Sharma, 'Stereotypicality in Indian Cinema Is Not a Healthy Trend', *Hindustan Times,* 10 August 2015, https://www. hindustantimes.com/editorials/stereotypicality-in-indian-cinema-is-not-a-healthy-trend/story-y6SG1xuOvBb0cZfWJpUg0H.html.

107. Liz Mathew, 'Unnecessary Comments, like Those on Films, Overshadow Our Hard Work: PM Modi', the *Indian Express,* 19 January 2023, https://indianexpress.com/article/india/refrain-from-making-unnecessary-comments-against-films-pm-modi-to-party-workers-8388649/.

108. 'Exclusive Massive Record: Shah Rukh Khan Starrer Pathaan Crosses 100 Million Dollars Worldwide, Among Biggest Film Worldwide In 2023 Including Hollywood Films!', Box Office Worldwide, 5 February 2023, https://boxofficeworldwide.com/box-office/exclusive-massive-record-shah-rukh-khan-starrer-pathaan-crosses-100-million-dollars-worldwideamong-biggest-film-worldwide-in-2023-including-hollywood-films/.

109. Nandita Singh and Nikhil Rampal, 'India's First and Oldest Gay Rights Activist Is Also on the Extreme Right of RSS', ThePrint.

Conclusion: The Age of Ram

1. Khushwant Singh, 'What Happened When Khushwant Singh Met RSS Leader M.S. Golwalkar', Scroll.in, 13 August 2016, https://scroll.in/article/813891/what-happened-when-khushwant-singh-met-rss-leader-ms-golwalkar.

2. Ibid.

3. Ibid.

4. Ibid.

5. Jonathan Evans and Neha Sahgal, 'Key Findings about Religion in India', Pew Research Centre, 29 June 2021, https://www.pewresearch.org/fact-tank/2021/06/29/key-findings-about-religion-in-india/.

6. Ibid.

7. Express News Service, 'Mohan Bhagwat: There Is No Caste Superiority, Illusion Has to Be Set Aside', the *Indian Express,* 7

February 2023, https://indianexpress.com/article/political-pulse/rss-chief-mohan-bhagwat-caste-8426707/.

8. Khushwant Singh, 'What Happened When Khushwant Singh Met RSS Leader M.S. Golwalkar', Scroll.in.

9. 'India and England—Swami Vivekananda', VivekaVani, https://vivekavani.com/india-england-swami-vivekananda/.

10. 'Reply to the Address of Welcome at Madura', VivekaVani, https://vivekavani.com/address-madura-vivekananda/.

11. 'Reply to the Calcutta Address—Swami Vivekananda', VivekaVani, https://vivekavani.com/calcutta-address-swami-vivekananda/.

12. Swami Medhananda, '"The Science of Religion": Vivekananda's Critique of Scientism and His Defense of the Scientific Credentials of Religion', *Swami Vivekananda's Vedantic Cosmopolitanism*, (Oxford: Oxford University Press, 2022), https://academic.oup.com/book/38781/chapter-abstract/337597975?redirectedFrom=fulltext.

13. Vedanta, Tantra, etc. are various sub-streams of Hinduism.

14. 'The Complete Works of Swami Vivekananda/Volume 3/Lectures from Colombo to Almora/Reply to the Address of Welcome at Shivaganga and Manamadura', Wikisource, https://en.wikisource.org/wiki/The_Complete_Works_of_Swami_Vivekananda/Volume_3/Lectures_from_Colombo_to_Almora/Reply_to_the_Address_of_Welcome_at_Shivaganga_and_Manamadura.

15. 'Diwali Saga: 15 Lakh Diyas Lighten Up Ayodhya, Marks New Record In Guinness Book', *Outlook,* 24 October 2022, https://www.outlookindia.com/national/diwali-saga-15-lakh-diyas-lighten-up-ayodhya-marks-new-record-in-guinness-book-photos-232191.

16. In the Hindu epic, the Ramayana, the name of Ram's father is Dashrath.

Index

war with Ahom kingdom, 32
Aurangzeb road, renaming of, 237
Aurobindo, Sri, 81
Axis Powers, 105
Ayodhya, 181
Ayodhya movement, 183, 186,
    192, 197
Azad, Maulana, 19

Babri Masjid, 181, 214
    demand for the Ram temple at
        the site of, 181
    demolition of, 193
        Hindu-Muslim riots due
            to, 193
Babur, Emperor, 32, 181, 264n16
backward castes, reservations in
    government jobs, 188
Bahujan Samaj Party (BSP), 20, 186
Bai, Ahilya, 32
Baji Rao II, Peshwa, 45
Bajpai, Girija Shankar, 139
Bajrang Dal, 197–198
Balagangadhara, S. N., xvii
balance of power, Hindu idea of, 83
Balco, 222
Bangladesh, 138
    creation of, 172
bankruptcy law, 217
Bardai, Chand, 263n11
Barrackpore, Bengal, 3
Basu, Chandranath, 12–13, 258n12
    assessment of the Eastern and
        Western civilizations, 13
    *Hindutva: Hindur Prakita
        Itihas* (1892), 12, 258n12

Basu, Rajnarain (Raj Narayan
    Bose), 8
Bayly, Martin, 83
Believer (CNN show), 239
Benaras Hindu University, 84
Bengal, 102
    Brahmo Samaj and neo-
        Vedantins in, 77
    exposure of Hindutva in, 12
    famine of, 6
    Hindus of, 8
    partition of, 16, 74
Bengal Light Cavalry Regiments, 3
34th Bengal Native Infantry
    regiments, 3
Bengal Regulation III of 1818,
    267n2
Bengal Renaissance, 4, 260n6
Besant, Annie, 77
bhadralok, 133
Bhagavadgita, 268n8
Bhagwat, Mohan, ix, 30, 148, 211,
    240, 246
Bhakti movement, 226, 252,
    296n64
Bharatiya Jana Sangh, 142,
    146–147, 154, 221
    as national party of India, 143
    Upadhyaya's contribution to,
        146
Bharatiya Janata Party (BJP), vii,
    21, 159, 179, 220, 244–245,
    248
    Ayodhya as a core political
        cause of, 187
    Dalit voters for, 225

mandala, doctrine of, 83
Mandalay, Myanmar, 55, 266n52
Mandal, Babu Bindheshwari
    Prasad, 188
Mandal Commission (1980), 188
Mandal, Jogendranath, 135
'mandal-*versus*-kamandal', 188
Mandate of the Muslims of India, 92
Mangeshkar, Lata, 189
Mann ki Baat (radio show), 219
Man Singh I (Raja of Amer), 31
Manu-smriti (*Laws of Manu*),
    268n8
Maoist violence, 229
Mao Zedong, 129, 140
Maratha administration, 45
Maratha Empire, 87
Maritain, Jacques, 147
masculinity, idea of, 65
Masjid Janmasthan, 181
mass civil disobedience, 102
maulvis (cleric-teachers in Islamic
    madrassas), 227
Mavelikkara, Treaty of, 34
Mazzini, Giuseppe, xii, xvi
Mecca and Medina, 70
Mehta, Nalin, 224
member of Parliament (MP), 211
militant Sikh nationalism, rise of,
    180
military co-operation, with the
    British Government, 106
military training schools, 90
Mill, James, 85
minority rights, restoring of, 135
Minto, Lord, 270n52

Minto–Morley Reforms (1909),
    74, 78, 270n52
'Minute on Indian Education'
    (1835), 4
Mir Baqi, General, 181
Mitra, Nabagopal, 8
'mixed economy' plan, 133
Mlechchas (foreigners), destroyer
    of, 66
Modern Food Industries, 222
modern Hinduism, 9, 268n8
Modi, Narendra, vii, 34, 36, 48,
    111, 130, 175, 180, 184, 188,
    207, 209, 229
    approach on the war in
        Ukraine and on Russia,
        236
    as chief minister of Gujarat,
        216
    construction of the Ram
        temple, 210
    construction of toilets and
        the elimination of open
        defecation, 218
    decriminalization of old
        colonial law against
        homosexuality, 240
    economic reforms, 216
    electoral success of BJP under,
        227
    electoral victories for the BJP
        led by, xiv
    Gujarat model, 208
    Gujarat riots (2002), 208
    'India Shining' campaign, 202,
        223

Scan QR code to access the
Penguin Random House India website